Yale Publications in American Studies, 20
Published under the direction of the
American Studies Program

The Evangelical Mind and the
New School Presbyterian Experience

A Case Study of Thought and
Theology in Nineteenth-Century
America

George M. Marsden

New Haven and London, Yale University Press,
1970

To Lucie

Contents

Preface ix

Introduction 1

1 The Rise of New School Evangelicalism 7

2 Theology of Revivalism and Reform 31

3 The Presbyterian Schism 59

4 The Abolition of Black Slavery 88

5 The Waning of United Evangelicalism in the New
  School, 1838–1852 104

6 The Triumph of Denominationalism, 1852–1861 128

7 New Challenges in Science and Philosophy 142

8 The Mediating Theology of Henry B. Smith 157

9 The Kingdom of Christ and the American Nation 182

10 The Civil War: The Flag and the Cross 199

11 Presbyterian Reunion: A Question of Orthodoxy 212

Conclusion: The Evangelical Mind and Mid-Nineteenth-
  Century America 230

Epilogue: The New School Presbyterian Tradition
  in the Twentieth Century—Fundamentalist or Liberal? 245

Appendix 1: Historiography of the Causes of the Division
    of 1837–1838: Doctrine or Slavery?   250

Appendix 2: The Auburn Declaration   252

Selected Bibliography of Primary Sources   256

Index   265

Preface

For many years American historiography was marked by a quiet prejudice against evangelical Protestantism in nineteenth-century American life. Historians during the early twentieth century, in the midst of their own emancipation from Protestant intellectual and moral dogmatism, emphasized the tolerant and the progressive in America's national tradition. Evangelicalism, which in the opening decades of this century was usually masked in the robes of militant fundamentalism, appeared retrograde and obscurantist. Its heritage seemed best forgotten. Standard accounts of nineteenth-century America spoke much of Emerson and Thoreau but relegated the dominant religious tradition to minor sections, implicitly suggesting that its significance was perhaps on a par with canal building or the popularity of *Little Women*. When religion was occasionally treated, the general impression left was of a sideshow filled with fanatics, cultists, nativists, spiritualists, freethinkers, and advocates of free love. Protestant intellectual and theological developments, except those taking place in the immediate vicinity of Boston, were virtually ignored. As late as 1957 John C. Greene, writing on the need for new approaches in American intellectual history, observed, "the vast majority of Americans in the mid–nineteenth century belonged to churches which described themselves as evangelical; yet although we have many studies of transcendentalism, we have no general intellectual portrait of evangelical orthodoxy."[1]

In more recent decades the trend has begun to be reversed, and the formidable impact of evangelicalism on nineteenth-century American culture is increasingly being emphasized. Not only has evangelicalism been shown to be a major force in nineteenth-century American religious life, but its substantial contributions to American intellectual life, American nationalism, the impulse for reform, and the "Victorian" moralism of the middle class has also been widely recognized. Perry Miller, for instance, maintains that the "dominant mentality" of America from the Revolution to the Civil War was "evangelical." William G. McLoughlin asserts, "The story of American Evangelicalism is the story of America itself in the years 1800 to 1900."[2]

The present study does not presume to present the total picture of American evangelicalism or its influence on the culture. Rather, it is an attempt to illumine the major aspects of the evangelical outlook by focusing on one central and representative portion— the thought of New School Presbyterians. By almost any measure, the New School movement in the Presbyterian Church in the United States stood near the center of American religious life in the first half of the nineteenth century. As a Presbyterian party allied with New England Congregationalism during the "Second Great Awakening" of the early decades of the century, it played a key role in the remarkably successful united-evangelical efforts to rescue the nation from sin and apostasy. Emphasizing revivalism, moral reform, interdenominational cooperation, and evangelical piety, New School Presbyterianism embodied the characteristics that virtually all observers agree were typical of the mainstream

---

1. John C. Greene, "Objectives and Methods in Intellectual History," *Mississippi Valley Historical Review* 44(June 1957):72.

2. Perry Miller, *The Life of the Mind in America: From the Revolution to the Civil War* (New York, 1965), p. 67. William G. McLoughlin, ed., *The American Evangelicals, 1800–1900* (New York, 1968), p. 1.

of American Protestantism. When, after a bitter dispute, the party was forced by its Old School opponents to become a separate denomination from 1837 to 1869, the movement confronted the problems of institutionalization and formalization during the era when denominationalism was replacing the earlier cooperative spirit as the dominant force in American Protestantism.

The first half of the nineteenth century was in many respects the greatest age of Presbyterianism in America. Despite more spectacular gains of Baptists and Methodists, Presbyterians, together with their Congregational allies, maintained the intellectual and social leadership they had gained during the Colonial and Revolutionary eras. Presbyterianism, reported Philip Schaff, the German-born American church-historian, in 1854, "is without question one of the most numerous, respectable, worthy, intelligent, and influential denominations, and has a particularly strong hold on the solid middle class." "The religious character of North America," he observed further, "is predominantly of the Reformed or Calvinist stamp."[3] Standing, though somewhat uneasily, in the Reformed or Calvinist[4] camp, New School Presbyterianism was heir to the most fruitful tradition in America. Its intellectual history therefore provides an opportunity to observe American Calvinism in its last days of real strength, as it struggled to survive in an atmosphere permeated, on the one hand, by the activism and emotionalism of the revival and, on the other, by the optimistic humanism of the new republic.

Passing as an analysis of the evangelical mind, this study is admittedly somewhat limited by its denominational focus and will at times seem too Presbyterian. Nevertheless, the denominational limitation, like all such limitations, provides opportunity for study

3. Philip Schaff, *America: A Sketch of Its Political, Social, and Religious Character,* ed. Perry Miller (Cambridge, Mass., 1961), pp. 118, 93.

4. The terms "Reformed" and "Calvinist" are used broadly in this study, in much the same way as they were used in the nineteenth century, to designate the general theological tradition that claimed to descend from John Calvin.

in greater depth. I hope this account will be substantially more than denominational history; but it is inescapably that as well. It is written by a Presbyterian who is filled with subtle Presbyterian prejudices, which readers should feel free to uncover and, if they wish, discount. The study has, nevertheless, both a point of view and a purpose. The point of view (though not implying a general approval or disapproval of New School Presbyterianism) involves the beliefs that there are better and worse ways for the Christian Church to conduct its affairs and that for the last one hundred years American Protestantism has usually chosen the worse. Among the present weaknesses of the Church is its peculiar intellectual irrelevance, the roots of which may certainly be found tangled in nineteenth-century thought. Even more important, as far as finding nineteenth-century precedents, is the Church's persistent tendency to embrace American nationalism and American middle-class mores in the name of Christianity. This study's purpose, which is largely implicit, is to identify the sources of such tendencies in the influential middle-class evangelical Protestant establishment of a century ago. I hope that in the process readers who share neither my point of view nor my purpose will find here a relatively balanced account of one aspect of nineteenth-century American life that will shed some light on their own prejudices as well.

This work has been partially revised several times, largely with the dual intention of giving it a wider focus and obscuring its graduate school origins. Zealots for the study of New School Presbyterianism will find considerable additional information in my unpublished dissertation, "The New School Presbyterian Mind," Yale University, 1966.

Fortunately, I have received considerable expert aid since this project was begun. By far my greatest debt is to Sydney E. Ahlstrom, who suggested the work and, despite travels and the burdens of academic responsibilities, provided invaluable guidance as manager and chief critic from beginning to end. I am indebted also to

Charles W. Forman for serving as co-director during the year that this work first emerged as a dissertation at Yale University. Lefferts A. Loetscher of Princeton Theological Seminary kindly provided some advice at a preliminary stage. Paul Woolley of Westminster Theological Seminary, to whom I owe a great deal of thanks for educating, inspiring, and encouraging me in Church History through the last decade, did the same. I am indebted as well to a substantial number of readers, mostly anonymous to me, who at various stages provided much extremely useful criticism. Finally, my very sincere thanks are due to Alfred H. Jones, now of the University of Minnesota, who graciously read the entire original manuscript and suggested many stylistic improvements, for which every reader should be grateful.

G. M. M.

Calvin College
Grand Rapids, Michigan
March, 1970

Introduction

"It was pretty ornery preaching—all about brotherly love, and such-like tiresomeness; but everybody said it was a good sermon, and they all talked it over going home, and had such a powerful lot to say about faith and good works and free grace and preforeordestination, and I don't know what all, that it did seem to me to be one of the roughest Sundays I had run across yet."[1] Huck Finn had attended a Presbyterian church[2] and had not been overly impressed. His hosts, the Grangerfords, whatever else they did, were at least in one way typical of Presbyterians in the mid-nineteenth century. They knew their theology and were willing to talk about it. Sundays were often pretty rough.

Presbyterians were not alone in America in their ability to hold forth on the fine points of classical Reformed theology. In Congregational New England, Sabbaths had always been just as rigorous. There, Horace Bushnell could recall the remarkable theological awareness among the members of the church of his youth: "Free-will, fixed fate, foreknowledge absolute, Trinity, redemption, special grace, eternity—give them anything high enough, and the muscle of their inward man will be climbing sturdily into it; and if they go away having something to think of,

---

1. Mark Twain, *The Adventures of Huckleberry Finn,* Harper's Modern Classics (New York, 1959), p. 112.
2. The best evidence for this is that the Grangerfords subscribed to the *Presbyterian Observer;* ibid., p. 106.

they have had a good day."[3] The situation was similar in upstate
New York, where Presbyterians and Congregationalists had
cooperated in settling and evangelizing the new areas during the
first half of the nineteenth century. At mid-century, theology was
still an engrossing topic. Religious periodicals accounted for over
one-fourth of the total newspaper circulation in New York state.
The conclusion is inescapable that "a considerable proportion
even of laymen read and relished the theological treatises."[4]

The passing of Reformed theology as a major influence in
American life during the nineteenth century was not a spectacular
event, and its mourners have been relatively few. Calvinism, when
it is mentioned, is still often portrayed as a dark cloud that hovered
too long over early America, acting as an unhealthy influence on
the climate of opinion. Nonetheless, the transition from the theologically oriented and well-informed Calvinism characteristic of
much of American Protestantism at the beginning of the nineteenth century to the nontheologically oriented and often poorly
informed conservative Protestantism firmly established in middle-
class America by the end of the same century remains a remarkable
aspect of American intellectual and ecclesiastical history. The
twentieth century attitude, itself a product of this transition, has
placed strong emphasis on nineteenth-century Protestant activities
—their organizations, their revivals, and their reforms. The mind
of American Protestantism in these transitional years deserves at
least equal attention.

The life of the mind, however, cannot be understood apart from
the activities associated with it, and so the theology of nineteenth-

3. Horace Bushnell, "The Age of the Homespun," in *Work and Play: Or,
Literary Varieties* (New York, 1864), pp. 387–88, quoted by Sidney E.
Ahlstrom, "Theology in America: A Historical Survey," in *The Shaping of
American Religion,* ed. James Ward Smith and A. Leland Jamison (Princeton,
N.J., 1961), p. 233.

4. Whitney R. Cross, *The Burned-over District: The Social and Intellectual History of Enthusiastic Religion in Western New York, 1800–1850*
(Ithaca, N.Y., 1950), pp. 104, 109.

century American Protestantism must be viewed in the context of the evangelical crusades that dominated America's religious life. At the forefront of the evangelical movement that swept America during the first four decades of the century were the revivals. The revival was the all-pervasive religious force. "In fact," says Perry Miller, "the dominant theme in America from 1800 to 1860 is the invincible persistence of the revival technique."[5] Intermittently, the pulse of the nation rose and fell with the excitement of the recurrent awakenings. To the evangelical mind the most engrossing fact was that individual souls must be saved if America were to survive spiritually and morally.

The strategy of nineteenth-century American evangelicals was essentially what had proved so highly successful during the Great Awakening of the Colonial era. Through simple Gospel preaching and intensive evangelism, they stressed the heart-felt spiritual experience of the individual and a rigorous moral code. The roots of these emphases could be traced to German Pietism and English Methodism, as well as to an evangelical strain in the Reformed churches themselves. During the eighteenth century the revivalist impulse had appeared throughout the Protestant world challenging the skepticism of the Enlightenment and the increasingly evident impotence of the established churches to nourish men's spiritual hungers. In the early nineteenth century this international evangelical awakening reappeared with renewed fervor, and nowhere was its effectiveness more evident than in America.

The "Second Great Awakening" in America was, however, far more than a series of revivals. It was a comprehensive program designed to Christianize every aspect of American life—spiritually, morally, and intellectually. Sensing that the divided denominations were by themselves inadequate to fulfill these tasks, evangelicals—particularly those of the Reformed heritage—founded a host of voluntary societies to promote missions and benevolent

5. Miller, *Life of the Mind in America*, p. 7.

reforms. As the nation moved west, this same missionary zeal inspired the founding of numerous colleges, thus ensuring Protestant dominance over the mind, as well as the heart and the conscience of the nation.

The impact of the awakening on the culture was immense by nearly every standard.[6] Church memberships increased at phenomenal rates, especially among Methodists, Baptists, Presbyterians, and new sectarian groups. Equally remarkable was the less tangible influence that evangelicals had in shaping the social and moral ideals of the American people. Virtually all contemporary observers agreed with the estimate made by Alexis de Tocqueville in 1833 that "there is no country in the world where the Christian religion retains a greater influence over the souls of men than in America."[7]

Such a religious revolution was bound to have profound effects upon the Protestant intellect. Much of the revivalists' program had a markedly anti-intellectual tone. This was particularly true in the West (now Midwest), where Methodists, Baptists, sectarians, and sensationalists of the Charles G. Finney variety flourished. It was undeniably a tendency among some evangelicals in the East as well. Mockery of the "learned clergy" and attacks upon the "dead dogma" of traditional orthodoxy had become part of the standard fare of the most successful evangelists. Zeal for interdenominational cooperation unrestrained by theological debate reinforced the trend toward reducing the Gospel to the simplest fundamentals.

The consensus of twentieth-century historical opinion seems to be that this evangelical fervor left nineteenth-century America a theological wasteland. Winthrop Hudson claims that the great

6. Cf. Richard Hofstadter, *Anti-Intellectualism in American Life* (New York, 1966), p. 89, who says of the evangelical movement, "Successful it was, by any reasonable criteria."

7. Alexis de Tocqueville, *Democracy in America,* 2 vols. Vintage Books (New York, 1945), 1:314. Timothy L. Smith, *Revivalism and Social Reform: American Protestantism on the Eve of the Civil War* (New York, 1965), pp. 34–44, assembles much evidence confirming de Tocqueville's estimate.

malady of American Protestantism was "the theological erosion which had taken place during the nineteenth century."[8] Sidney Mead concurs, designating theological structures as the "outstanding failure" of religion in America. The intellectual business of the denominations, Mead says, was "laid on the table at the opening of the nineteenth century and largely ignored during the intervening busy years of institutional proliferation and growth."[9] Richard Hofstadter cites the revivalists' "Religion of the Heart" as historical exhibit number one in his study of anti-intellectualism in American life, and and Perry Miller comments that it constituted at least "a form of revolt against the intellect."[10]

Yet the account of nineteenth-century American evangelicalism is vastly oversimplified if only its anti-intellectual tendencies are emphasized, while its own vigorous intellectual life is neglected. The fact is that in those churches with strong theological traditions—particularly the Congregational and the Presbyterian, but also the Episcopal, Lutheran, German Reformed, Dutch Reformed, and some Baptists—the notorious revolt against the intellect was never entirely successful, even within the evangelical camp. Most of these churches were divided, in spirit if not in body, between traditionalists and evangelicals during the early nineteenth century; yet in few cases was either side willing to concede that the other had a monopoly on either theological sophistication or evangelical zeal. Though the champions of the "Religion of the Heart" battered the walls of theological traditionalism, they were not willing to forsake the banner of intellect. Colleges, theological journals, and the religious press were prominent weapons in their

8. Winthrop Hudson, *American Protestantism* (Chicago, 1961), p. 132.

9. Sidney E. Mead, *The Lively Experiment: The Shaping of Christianity in America* (New York, 1963), pp. 15, 169.

10. Hofstadter, *Anti-intellectualism*, p. 95; Miller, *Life of the Mind in America*, p. 30. Both refer specifically to Charles G. Finney as representative of the evangelical impulse. As becomes clear in the present study (see especially Chapter 5, below), the extent to which Finney typified the whole evangelical movement has been somewhat overstated.

arsenal. Their attack on the intellect, though formidable, was half-hearted.

As might be expected, the intellectual crisis precipitated by the second awakening was felt most keenly in the Reformed denominations. Here, two of the great formative influences in American religious life—Calvinism and revivalism—converged. The alliance between them, though presumably holy, was an uneasy one. Since the Great Awakening the two forces had interacted, often creating more heat than light. While popular evangelicalism became increasingly characteristic of American religious practice, Reformed dogma continued to dominate its theological councils. Calvinist theologians had provided academic leadership for the church, as well as for much of the community, for two centuries and showed no intention of abdicating their position. They had successfully withstood, so it seemed, the threats of Enlightenment infidelity and Unitarian heresy and appeared prepared to meet the challenges of the new age. Yet with the triumph of popular revivalism, sometimes antidogmatic and often anti-Calvinist, they faced a far more subtle challenge from within—for the revivalists were evidently dressed as angels of light.

The task of the Reformed theologians, which became the virtual obsession of much of the Protestant intellectual community, was to reconcile the Calvinist heritage with the realities of nineteenth-century American religious and intellectual life.

I

The Rise of New School Evangelicalism

"For God, for country, and for Yale"

In most respects, Timothy Dwight was a thoroughly sensible man. But on July 4, 1798, he was an alarmist. As president of Yale he was probably the most respected man in Connecticut, yet he had become convinced that America was being subverted by an international conspiracy of Illuminati inspired by the infidelity and immorality of the French Revolution. "The sins of these enemies of Christ," Dwight warned an Independence Day audience, " . . . are of numbers and degrees which mock account or description. . . . No personal or national interest of man has been uninvaded. . . . Justice, truth, kindness, piety, and moral obligation universally have been . . . ridiculed and insulted. . . . Chastity and decency have been alike turned out of doors." Faced with such national calamity, Christians must unite and resist. "Shall we, my brethren, become partakers in these sins?" Dwight exhorted. "Shall we introduce them into our government, our schools, our families? Shall our sons become the disciples of Voltaire, and the dragoons of Marat, or our daughters the concubines of the Illuminati?"[1] No doubt, the upright in Connecticut bolted their doors carefully that night.

Dwight's hysteria was not singular in 1798. President John Adams had been afflicted with similar alarmism during the XYZ

---

1. Timothy Dwight, "The Duty of Americans at the Present Crisis," quoted in Charles Roy Keller, *The Second Great Awakening in Connecticut* (New Haven, Conn., 1942), pp. 19–20.

Affair in April, and early in May he had revealed a supposed plot to burn Philadelphia to the ground a few days hence.[2] When later that same month the General Assembly of the Presbyterian Church in the United States of America met in the still unburned city, its commissioners shared the general consternation. Citing "formidable innovations and convulsions in Europe" and the threat of similar upheavals in America, they declared "that the eternal God has a controversy with our nation." The causes of the national calamities were "a general defection from God, and corruption of the public principles and morals." God had favored Americans more highly than any other people, said the Assembly, yet now he was judging the nation for violating his covenant and rejecting his laws. Only moral reformation, acknowledging "God as our moral governor and righteous judge," could restore his favor. "Let the deepest humiliation and the sincerest repentance," urged the Assembly, "mark our sense of national sins."[3]

Despite the nonexistence of the conspiracy of the Illuminati, the fears of Dwight and his Presbyterian counterparts were not entirely unfounded. As the end of the eighteenth century approached, American Christianity faced its most serious crisis. For over thirty years the mind of the nation had been diverted from religion to politics. The war, together with rapid political and social changes that followed, had disrupted religious activity and undermined church organizations. Presbyterians and Congregationalists, constituting the two leading denominations, still enthusiastically endorsed the Revolution but were beginning to flinch as they realized that independence from the corruptions of England had brought infidelity from other sources. Wartime heroes such as Ethan Allen

2. Charles I. Foster, *An Errand of Mercy: The Evangelical United Front, 1790–1837* (Chapel Hill, N.C., 1960), p. 124.

3. *Minutes of the General Assembly of the Presbyterian Church in the United States of America, 1798* (Philadelphia, 1789–), pp. 152–53 (hereafter cited as *Minutes*).

and Tom Paine now advertised religious heresies. Meanwhile, judging from some orthodox estimates, Thomas Jefferson was running strong as chief candidate—against Voltaire and the Pope —for the title of Antichrist. Equally distressing was the grass-roots infidelity and immorality that every clergyman observed and lamented. To make matters worse, the great western migration had begun. Settlers moved faster than church organizations, and the Reformed denominations lacked sufficient trained pastors for the new areas. Without these, there appeared little in the West to restrain the lawlessness, unbelief, and indifference that seemed to be sweeping the nation. The religious order was collapsing.

The evangelical awakening that shaped the mentality of New School Presbyterianism in its formative years during the first four decades of the new century was the organized response to this general religious crisis. The year 1795, when Timothy Dwight became president of Yale, probably best marks the beginning of this crusade as a direct movement. Immediately prior to Dwight's arrival, this Congregational college had apparently reached its religious ebb. "That was the day of the infidelity of the Tom Paine school," recalled Lyman Beecher, who entered as a student in 1793. In the class ahead of him, Beecher claimed, "most . . . were infidels, and called each other Voltaire, Rousseau, D'Alembert, etc. etc."[4] But under Dwight the situation was quickly reversed. Preaching frequently on infidelity, the new president won the respect of the students and inspired a minor reformation. By 1797, students had founded the Moral Society of Yale College—the first of many such organizations Dwight men would sponsor. By 1801, Connecticut had experienced a small awakening, and a revival at the college was in process as well. Already Dwight felt that New England had been secured against the French infidelity, and now he was urging his students to separate themselves entirely from

4. Lyman Beecher, *The Autobiography of Lyman Beecher,* ed. Barbara M. Cross (Cambridge, Mass., 1961), 1:27.

worldly ways and to look to the salvation of the entire nation.[5]

Dwight spoke out at the moment when Yale College was ideally positioned to exert a formidable influence on the rest of the nation. New Englanders in vast numbers, estimated at 800,000 from 1790 to 1820,[6] were beginning to move west, especially into New York state, and later into Ohio, Indiana, Illinois, and Michigan. Most of these emigrants were Connecticut Yankees, and in Connecticut, Yale was indisputably the intellectual and religious center. Yale men who trained for the ministry would inevitably move with the migrations and set the religious patterns in many of these new regions. Under the inspiration of Dwight and his lieutenants, this natural movement became a mission.

The Presbyterian Alliance

Evangelical zeal to rescue the frontiers from infidelity strengthened the long-standing informal alliance between the Congregationalists of Connecticut and the Presbyterians, whose strength lay in the Middle Atlantic states and the South. By the opening of the nineteenth century, Connecticut's churchmen felt far more affinity to Presbyterians than to their prodigal Massachusetts brethren who were well on the road to Unitarianism, and hence to perdition. For several generations Connecticut clergy had moved easily and frequently in and out of Presbyterianism. Even in Connecticut the term *Presbyterian* had become acceptable and common usage for designating Congregational affiliation. Prior to the Revolution, from 1767 to 1776, Congregationalists and Presbyterians had met

5. Timothy Dwight, "A Discourse on Some Events of the Last Century . . ." in *American Christianity: An Historical Interpretation with Representative Documents,* ed. H. Shelton Smith, Robert T. Handy, and Lefferts A. Loetscher (New York, 1960), 1:530–39.

6. William Warren Sweet, *Religion on the American Frontier, 1783–1840,* vol. 3 of *The Congregationalists: A Collection of Source Materials* (Chicago, 1939), p. 13.

together annually with the primary purpose of forestalling the feared appointment of an American bishop. When the disruption of the war subsided, the allies renewed their cooperation. During the 1790s the General Association of Connecticut and the Presbyterian General Assembly regularly exchanged delegates, even allowing the visitors a vote.

The Plan of Union of 1801, the agreement that led eventually to the emergence of New School Presbyterians, grew naturally out of these cordial relations. In the new settlements, particularly in New York, congregations and ministers from the two backgrounds were already cooperating in jointly founding churches. The Plan of Union gave formal sanction to this practice. Congregations could choose their ministers from either denomination and could govern themselves either by congregational rule or by the Presbyterian system of a session of ruling elders. In any case they could send representatives either to the Congregational consociations and associations or to the Presbyterian local presbyteries, regional synods, and annual General Assembly. As the Plan worked out, Presbyterians gained most from the union. Despite the predominantly New England background of the settlers, the stronger, more systematic, and nationwide Presbyterian order seemed to have greater appeal, and any sense of difference between the two groups was nearly absent. When the union was subsequently elaborated and extended, whole consociations of Congregational churches transformed themselves into Presbyterian presbyteries. By the 1820s, in some areas such as central and western New York state, large-scale Congregational organization had virtually disappeared.[7]

The effect was that the Presbyterian Church grew phenomenally, largely through the addition of New Englanders. Between 1807 and 1834 the General Assembly reported an increase in com-

7. The above account and interpretation of the Plan of Union is based largely on Robert Hastings Nichols, "The Plan of Union in New York," *Church History* 5(March 1936):29–51.

municant membership from 18,000 to 248,000.[8] The strength of the Presbyterians was even greater than these figures indicate. Since an account of a conversion experience was prerequisite to church membership, especially in areas with a New England heritage, the "allied population" of the Presbyterians was far larger than the actual membership; the former fairly reliably estimated at about two million in the mid-1830s.[9] As a result, in the evangelical campaigns emanating from New England, the Presbyterians joined their Congregational allies in playing a leading role. The origins of New School Presbyterianism are found, therefore, in the fervor of the international and interdenominational evangelical reformation that was becoming the consuming religious passion of the day.

The Voluntary Principle

In America, the evangelicals who generated this fervor were indelibly impressed with one lesson learned from the eighteenth-century religious and political experience: if the church or any other group were to influence American society, it must depend not on imposed authority, but rather on the voluntary response of the people. This lesson was reinforced by the disestablishment of American churches. In Connecticut, for instance, even though antidisestablishmentarianism remained strong in the Dwight camp, the voluntary principle had been prominent since the Great Awakening and had prepared the way for disestablishment in 1818. Lyman Beecher, Dwight's chief lieutenant, later observed that the end of dependence on state support was *"the best thing that ever happened to the State of Connecticut."* The churches,

8. *Minutes, 1807*, p. 394; ibid., *1834*, p. 187. The first figure is reportedly incomplete and, based on subsequent yearly reports, should be perhaps several thousand higher.

9. Cross, *Burned-over District*, p. 41. The figure is based on an 1836 estimate of Calvin Colton's, a former Presbyterian then turning Episcopalian, whom Cross designates "a reliable witness."

said Beecher, thrown "on their own resources and on God," now increased their influence "by voluntary efforts, societies, missions, and revivals."[10] American evangelicals had long recognized the principle dramatized in Connecticut: if Christians were to win victory in democratic America, their only recourse was to go to the people and lead them to respond voluntarily.

For this purpose, the revival was at first the major weapon. To American evangelicals the Great Awakening of the 1730s and 1740s marked a lost golden age. Their strongest hopes were for a renewal of such outpourings of God's Spirit. Scattered showers of blessings had never entirely disappeared, and these recurred increasingly in Connecticut and then New York state between 1797 and 1801. Manifestations of the new awakening emerged again in 1807–08 and then reappeared with great regularity in four- or five-year cycles until the 1830s.[11] On the distant frontier, in the meantime, the showers were more like thundershowers, being marked with unrestrained emotionalism and violent physical contortions after the camp-meeting style of the famous Cane Ridge, Kentucky, revival of 1800. The relation of these manifestations to the awakening in the East, however, was very slight. Eastern evangelicals, in fact, generally took great pains to dissociate themselves from such extremes, fearing that emotional excesses would give a bad name to all revivals.

Again the experience of the first Great Awakening set the pattern of response. The pro-revival party in New England, growing from the New Light group in the earlier revival, was now the strong New Divinity, or Edwardsean, party. They scrupulously reaffirmed Jonathan Edwards' analysis of religious affections. Strong emotions, Edwards maintained, are inherent in genuine religious experience, but not all strong emotions are either genuine or desirable. Timothy Dwight took exactly this position in 1801

10. Beecher, *Autobiography*, 1:252–53.
11. Keller, *Second Great Awakening*, pp. 36–69; Cross, *Burned-over District*, pp. 9–13.

when promoting revival among Yale students. He pointed out
with pride that the recent local revivals had "absolutely, or at least
very nearly, been free from every extravagance."[12] Similarly, the
Presbyterians, who by 1810 had suffered two secessions by
frontier revivalist groups—the Cumberland Presbyterians and
the Christian movement—adamantly maintained their moderate
stance. The Presbyterian General Assembly of 1808, for example,
declared approvingly that the recent "times of refreshing from the
presence of the Lord" in New York state and New Jersey "progressed with great silence, uncommon solemnity, and free from all
appearance of extravagance."[13]

Coordinated with unabated zeal for revivalism was the evangelicals' organization of missionary societies. The immediate precedent for such organizations was the founding of the London
Missionary Society by British evangelicals in 1794. In 1796, New
Yorkers of several Reformed denominations formed a similar
society, citing directly the British example.[14] Two years later Congregationalists instituted the Missionary Society of Connecticut,
which pledged to work for the salvation of the "Heathen in North
America, and to support and promote Christian knowledge, in
the new settlements, within the United States."[15] During the next
decade New Divinity men organized similar societies in other New
England states, and in 1810 dedicated students at Williams College
and the newly founded Andover Seminary inspired the formation
of the American Board of Commissioners for Foreign Missions.
Timothy Dwight, who was a founder of the Connecticut Missionary Society and one of the original Commissioners of the
Foreign Missions Board, expressed in 1813 the prevailing hopes
for such organizations. Through them, he proclaimed, Americans

12. Dwight, "Discourse," in Smith et al., *American Christianity*, 1:531.
13. *Minutes, 1808*, p. 401.
14. Foster, *United Front*, p. 65.
15. Quoted in Keller, *Second Great Awakening*, p. 75.

would hasten the millennial days of peace, justice, and virtue. *"The private conduct of men* will experience a mighty and wonderful revolution," Dwight predicted. Moral reformation, however, would not be reached unless it accompanied the widespread salvation of men throughout the world.[16]

By the time Dwight expressed these sentiments, the missionary movement had established a form of organization—the voluntary society—which would compete with revivalism as the most prominent feature of the evangelical awakenings. The voluntary character of these independent societies indicates again the evangelicals' increasing recognition that success would depend on persuasion of a free people.

Within the next two decades evangelicals founded literally hundreds of local or national voluntary societies. Almost every form of vice or oppression had a corresponding moral or benevolent society to stamp it out. By the 1830s this "benevolent empire" included not only societies for major reforms, as the American Colonization Society, the American Anti-Slavery Society, the American Temperance Society, and the American Peace Society, but also organizations dedicated to less well-known good causes, as the Seventh Commandment Society, the New York Anti-Tobacco Society, the American Seamen's Friend Society, the Protestant Half Orphan Asylum Society, and the Society for the Encouragement of Faithful Domestic Servants in New York. Whereas nearly any society seemed able to flourish, those campaigning for missions or the direct presentation of the Gospel generated the most enthusiasm and support. In 1826 the six most prosperous agencies were the American Education Society, which supported divinity students; The American Board of Commissioners for Foreign Missions; The American Home Missionary Society; the American Bible Society; the American Sunday-School Union; and the

16. Timothy Dwight, *A Sermon before the American Board of Commissioners for Foreign Missions* . . . (Boston, 1813), pp. 16, 23, and passim.

American Tract Society.[17] The combined budgets of these major evangelical organizations easily rivaled the major expenditures of the federal government,[18] and in some respects their influence seemed as great.

The literature of the movement is filled with plans to saturate the world with evangelical revivals, Bibles, tracts, and educational institutions. The output was phenomenal, and with a formidable network of local agencies supporting the movement in nearly every village, together with control of almost every college in the country, the movement's influence was pervasive.[19] A bizarre example is indicative of the extravagant enthusiasm possible within the evangelical perspective. The plan initiated in 1831 at Oswego, New York, consisted of a surprise attack on the Antichrist to destroy him in his own citadel. By a verse-a-day scheme, France would be converted. Eighty-six laymen, one for each Department of France, would be sent to distribute Testaments, while in America evangelicals of all persuasions would support the work with unanimous daily prayer and verse recitation. The project, sponsored by some respectable evangelical newspapers, was billed as "an unsuspected though powerful assault upon the man of sin."[20]

Such projects were conceivable only within the context of the immense success of the evangelical movement at home. Only a few decades after infidelity had seemed to threaten the very existence of Christianity, the United States appeared to be a Christian nation. De Tocqueville, whose own country apparently had not heard the news from Oswego, noted in 1833 that America was the world's most Christian nation. American evangelicals agreed. Ac-

17. Foster, *United Front,* p. 121; see also ibid., pp. 277–79, where several hundred evangelical societies in America and Great Britain are listed.

18. Ibid., p. 121.

19. See Bernard A. Weisberger, *They Gathered at the River: The Story of the Great Revivalists and Their Impact upon Religion in America* (Chicago, 1966), p. 3.

20. Cross, *Burned-over District,* p. 232.

cording to Presbyterian Calvin Colton in 1832, the work of establishing "the supremacy of Christianity in the respect of mankind" was "done and done for ever." Christians now had only to "start from this point, and, by one united and vigorous onset, march directly to the conquest of the world, in the use of the simple and marked weapons of evangelical truth."[21]

Evangelical Unity and National Morality

The united evangelicals enjoyed this success in the heyday of American nationalism, especially during the relatively peaceful years after the War of 1812. Evangelicals themselves viewed their mission as a patriotic one, and seldom missed a chance for flag-waving in the cause of Christ. "A national object unites national feeling," announced the newly founded American Bible Society in 1816, " . . . and the Catholic efforts of a country, thus harmonized, give her a place in the moral convention of the world; and enable her to act directly upon the universal plans of happiness which are now pervading the nations."[22] The American Home Missionary Society echoed the same sentiments ten years later as it proclaimed in its constitution "we are doing a work of patriotism, no less than that of Christianity." The union of local home-missionary efforts, the national society claimed, was *"indispensable to the moral advancement and the political stability of the United States."* Even foreign missions were a national duty. America's resources impelled her to take the lead in this field, lest the nation suffer God's punishment for neglected duty and "we and our father's house . . . be destroyed."[23]

21. Calvin Colton, *History and Character of American Revivals of Religion*, 2d ed. (London, 1832), pp. 142–43, quoted in Foster, *United Front*, p. 212.
22. Quoted from *The Panoplist and Missionary Magazine* 12(1816):271–73, in Smith et al., *American Christianity*, 1:555.
23. Quoted from *Memoirs of the Rev. Samuel J. Mills* (New York, 1820), p. 28, in Foster, *United Front*, p. 213. Quotations from the American Home Missionary Society are in Foster, *United Front*, pp. 184, 185.

The moral welfare of America was invariably the crucial issue in evangelical nationalism. "The government of God is the only government which will hold society, against depravity within and temptation without," stated Lyman Beecher's periodical, *The Spirit of Pilgrims,* in 1831.[24] "What has religion to do with the State?" asked New Haven's *Christian Spectator.* "In the form of ecclesiastical alliances, nothing; but in its operations as a controlling purifying power in the consciences of the people, we answer, it has every thing to do, it is the last hope of republics; and ... if ever our ruin shall come ... the true evil will lie ... in the moral debasement of the people."[25]

The character of such moralism is illuminated when the specific evils against which evangelicals most sought to legislate are identified. Sabbath-breaking including carrying of mail and the operating of any public transportation on Sunday, usually led the list, followed by drinking and profanity. Nonlegislative pressures brought a decline in dancing, card playing, and theatre attendance as well.[26] Moralism, as much as revivalism, typified the evangelical mentality of the day. As Charles I. Foster observes in his comprehensive study of the British and American movements, the "Evangelical united front" had brought about "the rise of American Victorianism."[27]

Moral action together with missionary and revival campaigns provided the practical basis for evangelical unity throughout the nation, and for a time it even appeared as though the united voluntary societies might provide an alternative to denominationalism in America. Many of the societies' leaders hoped this would be the case. In the American Bible Society, said its founders in 1816, "local feelings, party prejudices, sectarian jealousies, are excluded by its very nature. ... In such a work ... sectarian littleness and

24. Quoted in Miller, *Life of the Mind in America,* p. 36.
25. Quoted in ibid., pp. 71–72.
26. See Keller, *Second Great Awakening,* pp. 148–61.
27. Foster, *United Front,* p. vii.

rivalries can find no avenue of admission."[28] The American Sunday-School Union in 1830 was even more bold. While acknowledging that such societies had not been designed to supersede denominations, the Sunday-school promoters flatly stated that "the Churches of Christ have slumbered for ages over the miseries of the world; and now, while individuals are associating to relieve these miseries, the Churches, with here and there an exception, are slumbering still."[29]

The evangelical union was, however, not quite as broad as its own literature might suggest. Though it represented the dominant religious sentiment of the era, that sentiment was still dominated by at least a vaguely Reformed theological bias. The individuals who made up the interlocking directorship of the "benevolent empire," as well as their constituencies, were predominantly Presbyterians and Congregationalists. Dutch Reformed participated frequently also, as did some Baptists and Low Church Episcopalians. Methodists, however, who then appealed to a less-educated class, cooperated relatively little and by the late 1820s came bitterly to regard the "empire" as a rival.[30] By this time the "Evangelical united front" was successful enough to have enemies, and these were quick to point out its implicit denominational leanings. Nathan Bangs, a vociferous Methodist critic, insisted that the entire scheme was a Presbyterian conspiracy, including only token representation of other denominations as window dressing.[31] Fanny Wright, viewing the united front from a thoroughly liberal stance, dubbed it the "Presbyterian Idol":

> Whether it gain its notoriety
> Under the name of the Tract Society

28. *Panoplist* in Smith et al., *American Christianity,* 1:555.
29. Quoted from *The American Sunday-School Magazine* 7(1830):131, in Foster, *United Front,* p. 127.
30. Ibid., pp. 123, 233 ff.
31. Ibid., p. 236.

Or the Foreign Mission Board
The Idol still must be adored.[32]

Gilbert Barnes, studying the movement a century later, claimed that "the benevolent empire was dominated by 'New-School' Presbyterians."[33] Charles I. Foster concurred, suggesting as well that the Presbyterian General Assembly itself was "rival of the federal government for popular influence and esteem."[34]

New School Presbyterianism emerged as an integral component of this larger evangelical awakening and could hardly be distinguished as a separate movement before it was attacked by the Old School in the 1830s. Until that time its most conspicuous characteristics were that its origins lay in a close tie to New England and Congregationalism, its outlook was broadly evangelical, its tone was moralistic, and its aspirations were nationwide.

Lyman Beecher and God's Chosen Nation

During these formative years the man who unquestionably best embodied this broad New School spirit was Lyman Beecher (1775–1863). Though an unmistakable New Englander and for many years a Congregationalist, Beecher shared the widespread enthusiasm for the Presbyterian alliance. He himself had been a Presbyterian pastor from 1799 to 1810 and returned in the 1830s, when he became a storm center in the New School controversy. Vigorous and optimistic, Beecher's practical Yankee temperament and persuasive ability to marshal information behind arguments suited him ideally for organization and command. A great admirer of Timothy Dwight, he eventually became his mentor's acknowledged heir as commander in chief of the "Second Great Awakening" in the East. His outlook reveals the temper of that

32. Quoted in Gilbert Hobbs Barnes, *The Antislavery Impulse, 1830–1844* (New York, 1964), p. 19.
33. Ibid., p. 18.
34. Foster, *United Front*, p. 218.

evangelical uprising; it also indicates the ideals of the best-known
of the leaders of New School Presbyterianism.

The leading theme in Beecher's thought, as in much of evangelical literature, was the moral welfare of the nation. Beecher
developed this theme around the "Moral Government of God," a
phrase implying that God governed the world by his moral laws.
To Beecher this concept was especially crucial for the success of a
republic, where civil government depended on the will of the
people. Without popular recognition of God as true governor and
without obedience to his laws, liberty would bring judgment and
calamity. The short-lived republics of ancient Greece and modern
France evidenced this principle. "Did a condition of unperverted
liberty," asked Beecher, "uninspired by Christianity, ever bless the
world through any considerable period of duration?"[35]

Beecher's emphasis on the "Moral Government of God" was
essentially a republican restatement of the Puritan theory of the
national convenant. Both taught that national well-being depended on the citizens' acknowledgment of allegiance to the sovereign God. Seventeenth-century Puritans developed their concept from a direct application of the Old Testament covenant to
New England. Beecher did the same for the American republic.
He had discovered, as the Puritans had not, that the Old Testament revealed the essentials of republican government. "Our own
republic, in its constitutions and laws, is of heavenly origin,"
Beecher declared. "It was not borrowed from Greece and Rome,
but from the Bible." Among the evidences of republicanism in
the Old Testament, Beecher described the covenant renewal cere-
monies by which the people of Israel periodically reaffirmed their
allegiance to God and his laws. In Beecher's account this ancient
ritual became remarkably American: "once in seven years, the
tribes met in a great national convention, and solemnly ratified the

35. Lyman Beecher, "The Perils of Atheism to Our Nation," in Lyman
Beecher, *Works,* 3 vols. (Boston, 1852–53), 1:115–16; see also ibid., pp.
110–14.

constitution. They took what might be called the freeman's oath, to observe that constitution." The essentials of the national covenant, nevertheless, remained much the same in Beecher's modern rendering. Central to the Israelites' constitution were "the laws which God condescended to bestow upon them, as a pattern of his wisdom, and an evidence of his benevolence."[36] In Beecher, as in the Old Testament and in Puritan covenant-theory, God rewarded or punished nations, depending on their obedience to his laws. "A moral government," said Beecher, "is *the influence of law upon accountable creatures.* It includes a lawgiver, accountable subjects, and laws intelligibly revealed and maintained by rewards and punishments."[37]

The evangelicals' transformation of the covenant concept into the moral-government scheme is particularly important in that it preserved the Old Testament model for evaluating the conditions of nineteenth-century America. This Old Testament emphasis helps explain why seemingly legalistic moralism played so large a part in evangelical thought. Doubtless, the moralism characteristic of the secular Enlightenment contributed as well; but the Old Testament model helps account for some of the peculiar emphases of evangelical moralism and, indeed, nineteenth-century American Victorianism in general.

The emphasis on Old Testament precedent also illuminates the character of evangelical nationalism. National blessings, such as victory in the Revolution and an abundance of resources, were signs that America was favored by God. These resulted from "Christianity which, in this country, rocked the cradle of our liberties."[38] The new awakenings supported this conclusion. "These revivals, then," said Beecher, "falling in with all these antecedent indications, seem to declare the purpose of God to give a promi-

36. Lyman Beecher, "The Republican Elements of the Old Testament," in *Works,* 1:189, 179, 178.
37. Lyman Beecher, "The Bible, a Code of Laws," in *Works,* 2:155–56.
38. Beecher, "Perils of Atheism," in *Works,* 1:113.

nent place to this nation in the glorious work of renovating the earth."[39] Such blessings entailed obligations as well as sanctions. "The unexampled power and prosperity of our nation does but amplify the causes of our ruin, . . . without the corresponding moral influence of the government of God," Beecher warned.[40]

Evangelicals of Beecher's vintage viewed this system of divine rewards and punishments of nations entirely literally. As in Puritan New England, there was a direct causal relation between lawbreaking and national calamity. Such, for example, was the importance of enforcing observance of the Sabbath. "Europe," Beecher predicted, "never will be qualified for liberty until she keeps her Sabbaths in a better manner; and this happy nation will not long [prosper] after the influence of her Sabbaths has passed away."[41] The effect of such a view of the national destiny was that evangelicals were thoroughly convinced that it was their most solemn duty to mind everyone else's moral business; otherwise, the entire nation would suffer for the sins of a few. Hence, a further impulse to the crusading spirit.

The Mentality of Moralism: "Total Abstinence"

Lyman Beecher was a superb organizer of campaigns to rescue America from immorality; but of all the causes he championed, the most strikingly successful was the temperance crusade. Among major evangelical projects the temperance movement was most distinctly American in origin, lacking at the outset a significant counterpart among British evangelicals or elsewhere. Though other reform efforts, such as the Sabbath campaigns, were pursued with equal vigor, the temperance movement, because of its unique nature, provides the clearest illustration of the uncompromising mentality of American evangelical reform.

39. Lyman Beecher, "The Memory of Our Fathers," in *Works,* 1:327.
40. Beecher, "Perils of Atheism," in *Works,* 1:113.
41. Ibid., p. 124.

How the temperance campaign and eventually the total-abstinence crusade crept into nineteenth-century evangelicalism is difficult to determine. Methodists had adopted total abstinence in the 1780s; but except for the possible influence of example, there is little evidence of direct connection. Lyman Beecher, who had no great love for Methodism, seems to have developed the idea from reading Dr. Benjamin Rush's accounts of the physical dangers of alcohol. At any rate, when Beecher returned to Connecticut in 1810, he professed to be shocked by what was actually a long-established practice of serving liquor at ministerial ordinations and meetings of the Congregational consociations. He recounted with dismay that at the meetings of clergymen, "when they had all done drinking, and had taken pipes and tobacco, in less than fifteen minutes there was such a smoke you couldn't see. And the noise I can not describe it; it was the maximum of hilarity. They told their stories, and were at the height of jocose talk. They were not old-fashioned Puritans."[42] Beecher himself was determined to be a latter-day Puritan and in doing so presaged the misleading identification of Puritan and prohibition.

While the damaging physical effects of alcohol were impressive, said Beecher, "it is the moral ruin which it works in the soul, that gives it the denomination of giant wickedness." Typically, Beecher viewed intemperance in relation to the national destiny. In characteristic overstatement he proclaimed, "Intemperance is the sin of our land . . . and if anything shall defeat the hopes of the world, which hang upon our experiment of civil liberty, it is that river of fire. . . ."[43] Timothy Dwight, who had been enlisted in his protégé's campaign, concurred. "Our health, our reputation, our safety, our reason, our usefulness, our lives, our souls, our families, our friends," he urged, "in solemn and affecting union, urge, entreat, and persuade us to abstain."[44]

42. Beecher, *Autobiography,* 1:179; see also ibid., p. 184n.
43. Lyman Beecher, "Nature and Occasions of Intemperance," in *Works,* 1:349–50.
44. Quoted in Keller, *Second Great Awakening,* p. 147.

Apparently the use and misuse of alcohol was so widely prevalent that the alarm was not totally unwarranted. At first the ambitions of the reformers were moderate; they attacked only the manufacture and use of "ardent spirits," meaning distilled liquors such as rum and whisky, but not wine, beer, and hard cider, which seem to have been daily fare for most American families. Even the moderate use of "ardent spirits," however, was attacked. "Let it, therefore, be engraven upon the heart of every man," said Beecher, "THAT THE DAILY USE OF ARDENT SPIRITS, IN ANY FORM OR IN ANY DEGREE, IS INTEMPERANCE."[45]

Despite the presence of well-organized societies to achieve this goal, the temperance campaigns had only limited success for about a decade, until the mid-1820s. It did, however, have an impact, particularly among religious groups. The Presbyterian General Assembly, for instance, which had traditionally imbibed in much the same ways as their Connecticut brethren, in 1818 recommended that "the officers and members of our church . . . abstain even from the common use of ardent spirits." The assembly noted that this principle had "already been tried with success in several sections of our Church,"[46] referring probably to New York state, where the temperance crusade, like most other unlikely causes, first caught fire.

Temperance became closely tied to revivalism in areas such as New York state.[47] The attack on alcohol had an obvious appeal to evangelists. Drinking was a visible sin so common that they easily could reach the consciences of much of their audience by dramatizing the horrors of its effects and the guilt it entailed. Abstinence provided as well an ideal project to evidence a convert's personal reformation.

By the mid-1820s the temperance movement, nursed by revivalism, had grown strong and began to be transformed into a cam-

45. Beecher, "Nature and Occasions of Intemperance," in *Works*, 1:352.
46. *Minutes, 1818*, pp. 689–90.
47. Cross, *Burned-over District*, p. 211.

paign for total abstinence from *all* alcoholic beverages. New England's New Divinity party, especially at Andover Seminary, played an active role in promoting this phase of the campaign.[48] The shift toward total abstinence was particularly remarkable in that unlike almost every other evangelical reform this principle lacked Biblical example, the Bible and Christ himself providing precedents to the contrary. Only a mentality attuned to finding moral absolutes could lead to this identification of total abstinence as a major tenet of American Christianity. Such was the mentality of the revivalists and reformers. Each of the other reforms in which they engaged involved clear questions of right and wrong, and moderation simply did not fit into their scheme of things. They lived in a world divided between Christ and Anti-christ, the kingdom of God and the kingdom of Satan, the saved and the lost, and where conversions were sudden and radical. There was no middle ground.

A halfway-temperance movement therefore did not succeed nearly as well as the total-abstinence measures that by the late 1820s were becoming dominant. Arthur Tappan of New York City, who together with his brother Lewis financed much of the "benevolent empire," added a monetary incentive to the drive. Presbyterian congregations, overwhelmingly New School, under the American Home Missionary Society would receive twenty-five dollars each for adopting the abstinence principle as a condition of membership.[49] It happened that Arthur Tappan was also a champion of more frequent services of Holy Communion, and by 1830 a cynical critic had pointed out the dangers of that:

> Arthur Tappan, Arthur Tappan
> Suppose it should happen—
> Mind, I'm only *supposing* it should—

48. See Foster, *United Front*, pp. 171–77.
49. Cross, *Burned-over District*, p. 213.

> That some folks in the Union,
> Should take your Communion
> Too often by far for their good.[50]

Not to be outdone, friends of the movement were soon pointing out this danger themselves. In the early 1830s they reached the inevitable conclusion of their absolutist logic. They launched a formidable campaign, sponsored by the predominantly New School Presbyterian paper, the *New York Evangelist,* urging the substitution of grape juice for wine in the communion service![51]

In 1836 the American Temperance Union accepted as its basic platform the principle of "total abstinence from all that can intoxicate."[52] This formula allowed no exceptions. Four years later, the New School Presbyterian General Assembly adopted virtually the identical rule.[53] Teetotalism, though a minor issue distinguishing New School Presbyterians from Old School, was indicative of the New School mentality.

Albert Barnes (1798–1870), who next to Lyman Beecher was the best-known of New School leaders, typifies the evangelical moral-absolutism within the New School party. Barnes, noted as a Biblical commentator, a revivalist, a heretic—in Old School accounts—and an antislavery champion, met his first successes as a temperance crusader. As a young pastor in Morristown, New Jersey, from 1825 to 1830, Barnes practically put the local liquor industry out of business. Combining revivalism and temperance,

---

50. *Priestcraft Unmasked* 1(1830):116, quoted in Foster, *United Front,* p. 176.

51. Cross, *Burned-over District,* p. 216. This move, though eventually very successful, at first faced some opposition even within the New School evangelical camp.

52. Quoted in ibid., p. 215.

53. *Minutes of the General Assembly of the Presbyterian Church in the United States of America, 1840,* New School (New York, 1838–69), p. 15 (hereafter cited as New School *Minutes*).

his efforts (as he later recalled) brought the closing of seventeen of nineteen places where liquor was manufactured in the area, and eighteen of twenty places where it was sold.[54] After moving to a Philadelphia pastorate in 1830, Barnes continued his drive, having in the meantime shifted to the new total-abstinence stance. Like Beecher, Barnes identified reform with patriotism. In this interest he sponsored "dry banquets" for Philadelphia workingmen on the 4th of July each year. Preaching on "the Connexion of Temperance with Republican Freedom" on such a gala occasion in 1835, Barnes outdid even Beecher in his interpretation of the causes of the success of the American Revolution. "Had John Hancock, and Samuel Adams, and Roger Sherman, and Benjamin Franklin been intemperate men," Barnes asked the workingmen, "where today would have been the record of our freedom."[55]

As was common in New School and other evangelical leaders, Barnes did not confine his moral efforts to the antiliquor campaign. He, together with another New School leader and accused heretic, George Duffield (1794–1868), led the campaigns to keep Pennsylvania closed on Sunday. Dancing was another target for frequent attack. Such amusements evidenced "conformity to the world." "It is to be presumed," said Barnes, "that no professing Christian ever dreamed that he was imitating the example of Jesus Christ, or promoting his own salvation, or the salvation of others, or honoring the Christian religion in a theater, or a ballroom, or a splendid party of pleasure."[56] Such a mentality, uncompromisingly dedicated to eradicating the sins of the entire nation, takes on wider significance when, as shall be seen subsequently, it was applied by many of these leaders to the abolition of slavery.

54. Albert Barnes, *Life at Three-Score: A Sermon . . . Nov. 28, 1858* (Philadelphia, 1859), pp. 42–44.
55. Quoted in Edward Bradford Davis, "Albert Barnes—1798–1870: An Exponent of New School Presbyterianism" (Th.D. diss., Princeton Theological Seminary, 1961), p. 344.
56. Albert Barnes, *The Rule of Christianity in Regard to Conformity to the World* (Philadelphia, 1833), p. 45, quoted in ibid., p. 370.

Intellect

Despite the prominent activism, the evangelical movement was not characteristically anti-intellectual. The intellectual front, in fact, received high priority throughout the evangelical crusades. The crisis of infidelity at the turn of the century was believed rooted in the teachings of the French *philosophes* and had gained particular strength in American colleges. The counterattack began also in the academic world, as at Timothy Dwight's Yale where the president's persuasive apologetic was the primary step in transforming the college into an evangelical center. Victory over the skeptical intellect remained a crucial issue.

Lyman Beecher's attitude is again representative. Intellectual reformation, he maintained, was as essential as moral reformation to the welfare of the nation. God's truth was revealed to rational men and therefore must be received intelligently. "It is a law of heaven," said Beecher, "that men shall acquire knowledge on all subjects, in the first instance, by instruction, and careful, persevering mental application."[57] Any threat to the nation was a threat to the intellect as well. Referring to "priestcraft" and the danger of the Roman Catholic Church reinstituting the Dark Ages as its immigrants moved into the American West, Beecher portrayed a "conspiracy against your liberties" which "will dwarf the intellect of the laboring classes. . . ." Intellect and moral purity were equally necessary to preserve the nation from the supposed lawlessness of Roman Catholics and infidels. "The extent of our country renders the efficient supervision of our laws impossible, without a vigorous all-pervading tone of intelligence and moral principle," said Beecher.[58] In the cause of temperance as well, Beecher pointed out the dangers of alcohol to intelligence and hence to civil liberty. "It is admitted," he claimed, "that intelligence and virtue are the pillars of republican institutions, and that the illumination of

57. Lyman Beecher, "Causes of Scepticism," in *Works*, 1:63.
58. Beecher, "Perils of Atheism," in *Works*, 1:138, 110–11.

schools, and the moral power of religious institutions, are indispensable to produce this intelligence and virtue."[59] Beecher, who increasingly looked to the West as the key to American success or failure, eventually felt compelled to care for both the intellect and the morals of that area himself, as he moved in the early 1830s to the presidency of Lane Seminary in Cincinnati.

Evangelicals were convinced that any rational man, properly instructed, could see the superiority of the Christian system. They therefore emphasized the importance of education at all levels. The Sunday-school movement, originally designed to teach the poor to read, had as its rationale the assumption that the primary reading materials would be the Bible and the myriad evangelical tracts. Evangelicals encouraged also the establishment of elementary schools in the new settlements, where the New England predisposition for education remained strong. Colleges were even more crucial, and the evangelical victory in higher education marked one of the movement's most solid and lasting achievements. In 1839, of the presidents of the fifty-four oldest colleges in the nation, fifty-one were clergymen; and of these fifty-one, forty were Presbyterians or Congregationalists.[60] As the nation moved west, evangelicals maintained this ratio, founding new institutions wherever they went. Ministerial education was also essential to the cause. The American Education Society, designed for that purpose, became the most prosperous of the institutions of the "united front," and the rise of the evangelical ventures coincided with the movement to establish theological seminaries in America.

Theology, which provided the groundwork for evangelical thought and the rationale for much of the crusaders' activity, eventually proved, however, a major cause of the movements undoing.

59. Lyman Beecher, "The Evils of Intemperance," in *Works*, 1:386.
60. Foster, *United Front*, p. 241.

2

Theology of Revivalism and Reform: A New School in Presbyterianism

Jonathan Edwards recognized first and most clearly the problems of developing an American theology. For a time he provided most of the solutions. Throughout the century after his death at Princeton in 1758, few American evangelical theologians spoke without at least paying their respects to "President Edwards." Only a small percentage, however, followed Edwards consistently.

When Jonathan Edwards began his career in the 1720s, Protestant Christianity was in the midst of one of its periodic crises. Eighteenth-century New England reflected on a small scale the cleavages that had elsewhere already dissipated the strength of the Reformation traditions. Outside the church was a growing secularization, supported by the rationalistic and humanistic trends associated with the Enlightenment. Increasingly, men viewed themselves as autonomous, capable through science and cold logic of finding the natural laws that ran the universe. God, though reportedly alive, had been retired to the edge of his creation. Humanitarian moral laws, discoverable by reason, were replacing supernatural religion.

Within the church two basic responses to this eighteenth-century crisis could be discerned. On the one hand were those who continued to defend the faith largely on intellectual grounds. This group included not only traditionalists, who held to orthodox theology, but also their liberal opponents, who attempted to keep pace with enlightened intellectual trends. On the other hand was a resurgent Pietism. This movement, begun in Germany, was spreading throughout Christendom, reviving faith through heart-felt emotions. In America the issue was drawn when in the 1730s the Great Awakening challenged the intellectualized complacency of conservatives and liberals alike.

Much of Edwards' theological work grew from his analysis of the basic issue raised by the Great Awakening. What is legitimate in religious experience? Edwards was convinced both by personal experience and his success as an evangelist that heightened emotions were inherent in genuine religious conversion. He sought, therefore, to reconcile the Calvinist intellectual tradition to such intense emotionalism without opening the door for emotional excess. *Experience* is the key to understanding Edwards' thought on this crucial question. Mere intellectual assent, without vital experience, is not true religion. Illustrating this point Edwards often depicted the difference between the rational judgment that honey is sweet and the experience of the taste of honey. So, true religion must involve the *experience* of the sense of a vital relation to God. "The work of the Spirit of God in regeneration," Edwards pointed out, "is often in Scripture compared to the giving of a new sense, giving eyes to see, and ears to hear, . . . and turning from darkness unto light."[1]

Such expressions suggest a radical difference between the regenerate and the unregenerate, and this difference affects the whole of man's experience, both intellectual and emotional. Regeneration brings a change of heart. Edwards describes this revolutionary change in various ways—as a change in one's basic inclinations, will, or affections. The essential dispositions of men are decisively altered by the Holy Spirit. Such personal transformations bring a change in the object of the most fundamental of the affections— love. Whereas the wills of fallen men are controlled by self-love, the Spirit in regeneration awakens men's capacity for true love. This love Edwards designated by the inclusive phrase, "benevo-

1. Jonathan Edwards, *Religious Affections,* ed. John E. Smith (New Haven, Conn., 1959), p. 206.

lence to Being in general."[2] Such love of God and of the harmony of his entire creation pervades the experience of the regenerate man with a profound sense of beauty, and from this experience grows the life of true virtue.

The aspect of Edwards' analysis that aroused the most interest among his evangelical followers in New England was the moral revolution that is basic to regeneration. Edwards had, of course, said a great deal more on other subjects, particularly in his analyses of God's vital sustaining relationship to his creation. These formulations, however, depended on his idealistic philosophical assumptions, which were alien to most eighteenth-century American theologians. Reflecting the spirit of the age, they were much more interested in morality.[3] Their most pressing concern was to understand how sinners could be changed and how that process might best be effected by the human means through which the Spirit worked. Particularly engrossing to them was the question of the nature of the unregenerate sinner. Calvinists traditionally believed that the guilt of Adam's sin had been imputed to men by God and that the corruption resulting from that original sin was transmitted to all Adam's natural descendants, leaving them unable to do good without divine aid. But what did such inability involve? On this question Edwards' most lasting contribution was the distinction he drew between "moral inability" and "natural inability." Men, he said, were by nature potentially able to do good if they willed to. Their problem was that their wills, because of original sin, were inclined to self-love, making them morally unable to will anything good. Men were naturally free to do what they wanted, or willed, said Edwards; but they would want to do good only if

2. Jonathan Edwards, *The Nature of True Virtue,* in *Jonathan Edwards: Representative Selections,* ed. Clarence H. Faust and Thomas H. Johnson (New York, 1935), p. 350.

3. For this theme I am indebted to the perceptive work of Joseph Haroutunian, *Piety Versus Moralism: The Passing of the New England Theology* (New York, 1932).

the Holy Spirit graciously changed their basic dispositions from self-love to true love, or "benevolence to Being in general."[4]

Hopkinsianism

By the early nineteenth century the best-known of Edwards interpreters was Samuel Hopkins (1721–1803), and most of the current modifications of Edwards' thought were identified as "Hopkinsian." Hopkins had been a student and friend of Edwards but was more than a disciple. In important respects, he and his Edwardsean colleagues remained independent thinkers.

The most original contributions of Edwards' followers dealt with moral issues. Most symptomatic of the ethical concerns dominating their theological outlook was their zeal to demonstrate that God himself was moral. Such questions were difficult to avoid for eighteenth-century Calvinists, whom the enlightened of the era repeatedly accused of believing in a grossly immoral deity who arbitrarily condemned helpless sinners to perdition. Edwards' sense of God's infinite perfections in contrast to man's infinite culpability allowed him to justify God's condemnations in traditional terms, that is, that man deserved nothing better. His disciples were not entirely satisfied with such a stark solution, however. Both Hopkins and his associate, Joseph Bellamy (1719–90), dealt extensively with the question of the wisdom of God in permitting sin in the universe. They argued basically that without sin there would be no salvation from sin and hence no joy of salvation. The rejoicing in heaven was increased, after all, by the rescuing of the one lost sheep, and so it could be argued that the permission of sin ultimately brought the greatest possible degree of happiness to the universe. The Calvinist God thus conformed to the best eighteenth-century standards of morality. He was sovereign, indeed, but he was a benevolent governor who ultimately had the happi-

---

4. See Jonathan Edwards, *Freedom of the Will*, ed. Paul Ramsey (New Haven, Conn., 1957), p. 159.

ness of his subjects in mind. His wise government ensured the best of all possible worlds. Bellamy termed this God the "Moral Governor," the phrase that soon became prevalent among Edwardseans and other evangelicals. In this framework the necessity of observing God's moral law was also defended. This law, said Bellamy, "is essential to the being and glory of God's moral government and kingdom, . . . declaring the duty of rational creatures, or moral agents."[5]

Hopkins' own original contribution centered around his analysis of man's moral behavior. Beginning from Edwards' analysis of sin as self-love and virtue as "benevolence to Being in general," Hopkins subtly, and perhaps unconsciously, altered his mentor's concepts. Rather than virtue being the spontaneous response to experiencing the awesome beauty of God's love, Hopkins shifted the emphasis to the traditional summary of the divine law—love of God and other intelligent creatures. "The love required in divine law, in which holiness consists," said Hopkins, "is disinterested benevolence."[6] It "is love to God and our neighbor, including ourselves, and is universal benevolence, or friendly affection to all intelligent beings."[7] Thus the "disinterested benevolence" that became the watchword of Hopkins' system combined the obligations to keep God's law with a "friendly affection" not alien to the humanitarianism of the age.[8] His analysis did, nonetheless, support the impulse for evangelical moral reform, Hopkins himself being one of the earliest of American antislavery advocates and the subsequent "benevolent empire" reflecting in both word and action his ideals of "disinterested benevolence."

Hopkins' analysis of morality required some modification of traditional Reformed doctrine. By defining virtue and sin in terms

5. Quoted in Haroutunian, *Piety,* p. 92. The above interpretation is based on Haroutunian, *Piety,* pp. 30–42, 90–92.

6. Samuel Hopkins, *System of Doctrines,* vol. 1 of *The Works of Samuel Hopkins,* 3 vols. (Boston, 1852), p. 237.

7. Hopkins, *Works,* 3:16, quoted by Haroutunian, *Piety,* p. 84.

8. This interpretation is from Haroutunian, *Piety,* pp. 82–88.

of benevolence and self-love, he necessarily limited the meaning of sin to the disposition or acts of moral agents capable of love. "All sin," he said, "consists in the nature and quality of the exercises which take place in a moral agent, and not in any thing which goes before, or follows after them, and which is not of the same kind."[9] This line of reasoning, defining sin solely in terms of man's inclinations and actions, rather than in terms that include the legal aspect of God's judgment, necessitated revision of the doctrine of the imputation of Adam's sin. In the traditional Reformed view, imputation consisted *both* in the imputation of Adam's guilt—the legal judgment of God—and in the imputation of a morally corrupted nature from which sinful acts inevitably proceed.[10] Hopkins admitted that men were depraved by nature to the extent that "it was made certain . . . that all mankind should sin as Adam had done." But, because he defined holiness and sin in terms of an active relationship instead of a legal state, he had to deny the imputation of Adam's *guilt* to men before they themselves actually sinned. "The children of Adam are not answerable for his sin," he said, "and it is not their sin any further than they approve of it, by sinning as he did."[11]

Although Hopkins modified the traditional Reformed emphasis on the imputation of Adam's guilt, he was careful to retain the doctrines of man's complete moral depravity and complete moral inability to do good. Maintaining Edwards' distinction between

9. Hopkins, *Works*, 1:231; see also ibid., 1:225.

10. Chapter 6 of the Westminster Confession of Faith reflects this two-sided view of imputation: "[Our first parents] being the root of all mankind, the guilt of this sin was imputed, and the same death in sin and corrupted nature conveyed, to all their posterity, descending from them by ordinary generation." From Philip Schaff, ed., *Bibliotheca Symbolica Ecclesiae Universalis. The Creeds of Christendom, with a History and Critical Notes*, 6th ed. 3 vols. (New York, 1905), 3:615. The Confession was framed by the Westminster Assembly of 1648. For a clear résumé of the views of the classic Reformed theologians on imputation, see John Murray, *The Imputation of Adam's Sin* (Grand Rapids, Mich., 1959), pp. 78–85.

11. Hopkins, *Works*, 1:218–30.

natural and moral inability, Hopkins stressed that fallen man is wholly culpable for his moral depravity even though "he has lost his power to do that which is good, and is wholly unable to change and renew his depraved heart." Man is still blamable, he asserted, because "man has not lost any of his natural powers of understanding will, etc., by becoming sinful." All that has been lost is his *inclination* to do good, and this has been lost most completely.[12]

Hopkins' emphasis on the unregenerated man's inability to do any good had important practical implications, especially for personal morality, social reform, and the content of revival preaching. Because the controlling inclination of the unregenerate man is always that of self-love, his attempts at moral reform, or true benevolence, are inevitably fruitless. For the regenerate man the exact opposite is the case. His controlling inclination is love of others, or disinterested benevolence, which is the essence of all true reform. This radical contrast between the moral state of the regenerate and of the unregenerate provided the impulse for all true revival preaching. In Hopkins' view, the unregenerate sinner should be—indeed, must be—told that there was absolutely no hope for him unless there were a radical change in his heart. Since man himself is totally unable to change his own heart, the only agent and cause of this change is the Spirit of God. In this radical and instantaneous change, known as regeneration, "the heart of man is passive." But the effect of this change, known as conversion, is "activity." Conversion is the "voluntary action" of the regenerated heart, which implies belief, repentance, faith, and submission and "which consists in turning from sin to God, or in holy exercise, which is true love to God, and loving our neighbor as ourselves." In short, conversion entails *"universal benevolence."*[13] This distinction between regeneration, in which the heart is pas-

12. Ibid., pp. 232–33.
13. Ibid., pp. 367–75.

sive, and the response of conversion, in which the heart is active, was not new with Hopkins, being implied in the Westminster Confession of Faith.[14] But by stating the distinction in terms of the radical contrast between self-love and disinterested benevolence, he provided a means for the preacher to dramatize the desperateness of the sinner's moral condition, the immediacy of his need of the regenerating work of the Holy Spirit, and the certainty that the converted heart would express itself in a life dedicated to benevolence.

One other modification of the traditional statements of Reformed theology that was usually associated with Hopkinsianism was the "Governmental Theory of the Atonement." This theory was not actually held by Hopkins himself and so was not an integral part of his system, but it indicated the same concern to explain the tenets of Calvinism in rational and moral terms that might appeal to men of the Enlightenment. The theory, which originated with the seventeenth-century Dutch jurist, Hugo Grotius, was introduced into New England by Joseph Bellamy[15] and elaborated by his pupil, Jonathan Edwards, Jr. The younger Edwards felt that the traditional theory that the death of Christ paid the debt for sin[16] was inconsistent with God's free grace in forgiving

14. It is discussed under the title "effectual calling," Chapter 10 of the Westminster Confession of Faith: "This effectual call is of God's free and special grace alone, not from any thing at all foreseen in man, who is altogether passive therein, until, being quickened and renewed by the Holy Spirit, he is thereby enabled to answer this call, and to embrace the grace offered and conveyed in it." From Schaff, *Creeds of Christendom,* 3:624–25.

15. Bellamy also advocated the theory, which became widely popular in New England, known as "general atonement." This was in contrast to the older Calvinist view that the atonement, though sufficient for all men, was *designed* for the elect only. For Bellamy's view, see Frank H. Foster, *A Genetic History of New England Theology* (Chicago, 1907), pp. 113–17.

16. The Westminster Confession of Faith, Chapter 11, says, "Christ, by his obedience and death, did fully discharge the debt of all those that are justified, and did make a proper, real, and full satisfaction to his Father's justice in their behalf." From Schaff, *Creeds of Christendom,* 3:626–27.

sins. To resolve this problem he suggested that the death of Christ for sins was necessary to demonstrate God's "moral government" of the world. Moral laws require a penalty to sustain the authority of the lawgiver, said Edwards, else they would be merely advice. The atoning death of Christ is a substitutionary payment of the penalty due for sin and is required not as a merely legal satisfaction of God's justice but as a display to accomplish the same end as any other punishment of sin—to warn others of the consequences. "By the atonement," says Edwards, "it appears that God is determined that his law shall be supported; that it shall not be despised or transgressed with impunity; and that it is an evil and a bitter thing to sin against God."[17] So the doctrine of the atonement was transformed from a seemingly abstract legal theory into an eminently practical moral lesson. It could be used to warn sinners of the awful consequences of their sin and to preach the urgency of forgiveness through the free grace of Christ.

The Presbyterian Conflict Emerges

The presence of New Englanders had been a source of tension within the Presbyterian Church almost since its organization in 1706. American Presbyterianism was predominantly Scotch-Irish, and the Scotch-Irish were notorious hagglers over doctrinal detail. Open controversy first broke out in 1729 when the church officially adopted the Westminster Confession of Faith as its theological standard. This issue remained important because it was never clearly resolved and so reappeared with every doctrinal dispute. The Scotch-Irish and their conservative heirs insisted that the Adopting Act of 1729 constitutionally bound officers to accept the Westminster Confession with no reservations. The New Englanders

17. Jonathan Edwards, Jr., *Three Sermons,* in Foster, *Genetic History,* pp. 201–02. For a more complete account of the development of this doctrine, see Ralph Oren Harpole, "The Development of the Doctrine of the Atonement in American Theology from Edwards to Bushnell" (Ph.D. diss., Yale University, 1929).

and, later, Broad Churchmen, on the other hand, argued that a related declaration, adopted the same day and allowing minor reservations, was also part of the constitution.[18] Since no major doctrinal issue arose in eighteenth-century Presbyterianism, this aspect of the debate remained at a low key for about a hundred years. Meanwhile, the revivalism of the Great Awakening divided the denomination between Old Side and New Side from 1741 to 1758. Though this dispute somewhat cut across the party lines emerging in 1729, most of the New England group were on the pro-revival New Side and the Scotch-Irish on the Old. When the schism healed in 1758, the New Side spirit was dominant. Though no real theological issue had been involved, this outcome brought temporary popularity to the New Divinity of Jonathan Edwards and his followers. In 1768, however, John Witherspoon and Scotch philosophy were imported to the Presbyterian college at Princeton, and soon both the old issues and the New Divinity disappeared as the church entered an era of Revolutionary concerns. Scotch-Irish immigrations, nevertheless, were at their height during this period and were swelling the ranks of the vigilant.

The theological innovations of Samuel Hopkins were by this time becoming the focus of some apprehension, and the question of Hopkinsianism was brought before the Presbyterian General Assembly as early as 1798. Hezekiah Balch, one of the pioneer preachers in East Tennessee, and the founder of Greenville College, had traveled to New England in 1795 and came back an enthusiastic proponent of the views of Hopkins. Apparently, he used little discretion in proclaiming the new system and was soon accused of teaching doctrines contrary to the Westminster Confession. When his case came before the Assembly, he was found guilty. Balch conceded his error but then returned to East Tennessee where he promptly resumed preaching views that sounded very

18. Cf. Leonard J. Trinterud, *The Forming of an American Tradition: A Re-examination of Colonial Presbyterianism* (Philadelphia, 1949), for a recent Broad Church interpretation of eighteenth-century Presbyterianism.

much like those of Hopkins. Balch's influence probably helped make the Synod of Tennessee the only synod in the South with a New School majority in 1837. For a time after 1798, however, the issue of Hopkinsianism was dropped in the General Assembly,[19] and the question of New England theology seems not to have interfered seriously with the adoption of the Plan of Union

The real alarm over Hopkinsianism in the Presbyterian Church was sounded in 1811 with the publication of *A Contrast between Calvinism and Hopkinsianism* by Ezra Stiles Ely, a Presbyterian minister in New York City. The Hopkinsians, Ely charged, had departed from both Calvin and the Westminster Confession by their claim that men were held guilty only for the actual sins they committed. Traditional Calvinism, Ely pointed out, taught that men were judged guilty of Adam's original sin as well as of their own actual sins. Furthermore, Ely argued, the distinction between moral inability and natural ability was too lax a view of total depravity, and it might deceive sinners into thinking they could contribute something to their own salvation—an implication that Hopkinsians themselves decisively denied. Ely attacked the "Governmental" theory of the atonement as well, on the ground that it subverted the substitutionary aspect of the atonement, by which Christ bore men's sins and imputed to the elect his own righteousness.[20]

Soon a bitter controversy broke out among Presbyterians in New York City and Philadelphia. The dispute reached its peak when, in the fall of 1816, the Synod of Philadelphia adopted a pastoral letter written by Ely advising the presbyteries to resist "the introduction of Arian, Socinian, Arminian, and Hopkinsian heresies, which are some of the means by which the enemy of the

19. On Balch, see Ernest Trice Thompson, *Presbyterians in the South* (Richmond, Va., 1963), 1:352–54, 409; and Elwyn A. Smith, "The Doctrine of Imputation and the Presbyterian Schism of 1837–38," *Journal of the Presbyterian Historical Society* 38(September 1960):144–47.

20. Ezra Stiles Ely, *A Contrast between Calvinism and Hopkinsianism* (New York, 1811), pp. 73–75, 105–07.

soul would, if possible, deceive the very elect."[21] When the Assembly reviewed the records of the Synod of Philadelphia the next year, the Hopkinsians objected to being numbered with such a select company of heretics. A council of moderate men prevailed and the Assembly expressed regret "that zeal on this subject should be manifested in such a manner as to be offensive to other denominations. . . ."[22]

Dr. Samuel Miller of Princeton Seminary was chairman of the committee that drafted this refusal to condemn the Hopkinsian teachings as heresy. His irenic action marked a division in the orthodox party between the moderates of Princeton and the strict confessionalists of Philadelphia. Princeton Seminary had been founded in 1812 as the first theological institution of the Presbyterian Church in America. The theology taught there was clearly the "old Calvinism" of the seventeenth-century Westminster Confession of Faith. Princeton's professors, however, refused to join the archconservative Philadelphians in their strict interpretation of the requirements of subscription to the Confession by officers of the church. "We go on here," said the seminary's first professor, Archibald Alexander, "upon our old moderate plan, teaching the doctrines of Calvinism, but not disposed to consider every man a heretic who differs in some few points with us."[23]

Though the question of subscription to the Confession continued to be argued for some years after the Assembly's moderate declaration of 1817, the Hopkinsian controversy abated somewhat, and only an occasional tremor disturbed the relative calm.[24] It was, after all, the era of good feelings.

21. Quoted in Samuel J. Baird, *A History of the New School* (Philadelphia, 1868), p. 241.

22. *Minutes, 1817*, p. 653.

23. Quoted in John Oliver Nelson, "Archibald Alexander, Winsome Conservative (1772–1851)," *Journal of the Presbyterian Historical Society* 35(1957):23.

24. For more detailed accounts, see Baird, *New School*, pp. 235–55; see also Earl A. Pope, "New England Calvinism and the Disruption of the Presbyterian Church" (Ph.D. diss., Brown University, 1962), pp. 46–71.

The vigilant who equated Hopkinsianism with heresy still felt, however, that they had good reason for concern during these years. As they looked at the Plan of Union areas, they saw an increasing number of ministers who had been trained in institutions with Hopkinsian leanings. Andover Theological Seminary in Massachusetts, which reportedly sent nearly half its graduates into Presbyterianism,[25] was one primary source of their apprehensions. Andover had been founded in 1808 as a defensive alliance between Hopkinsians and "old Calvinists" against the threat of Unitarianism. Though professors there had to subscribe periodically to the Westminster Shorter Catechism, they accepted at the same time Andover's own creed, which allowed the Hopkinsian interpretations of original sin and depravity. Moreover, in practice, the New Englanders were, by conservative Presbyterian standards, lenient in enforcing conformity to doctrinal standards and tolerated all the moderate innovations of the developing New England theology. Andover's teaching on the atonement, for instance, in 1824 caused concern even at Princeton, and the minor debate that followed led to what was apparently the first use of the terms Old School and New School in Presbyterian discussions.[26] By the 1830s Moses Stuart, a great pioneer in American Biblical studies, was successfully challenging the more conservative Edwardsean Leonard Woods as the most influential of Andover's professors, and in the strict Presbyterian estimate Stuart stood with the wing of New England theology that was moving beyond Hopkinsianism.[27]

A similar situation prevailed at the second oldest of the Presbyterians' own seminaries—Auburn in New York state. Auburn Seminary was founded in 1819 by the Plan of Union Synod of

25. Baird, *New School,* p. 333.
26. See Pope, "New England Calvinism," pp. 126–28.
27. See George M. Marsden, "The New School Presbyterian Mind: A Study of Theology in Mid-Nineteenth-Century America" (Ph.D. diss., Yale University, 1966), pp. 95–114, for fuller discussions of Andover and New School theological education.

Geneva as an outgrowth of the Presbyterian-Congregational alliance and represented "the earliest application of the Andover
model to Presbyterian theological education."[28] As at Andover, the
theological position at Auburn reflected an attempt to unite Hopkinsianism with the standards of Westminster. Its professors were
required to subscribe to the Westminster Confession of Faith and
Cathechisms as containing the system of doctrine taught in Holy
Scriptures[29]—an affirmation interpreted broadly enough to allow
Hopkinsianism and other forms of New England theology.

James Richards (1767–1843), Auburn's leading theologian,
was not the sort of man to cause great alarm, even among the
orthodox. A former moderator of the Presbyterian General Assembly and a director of Princeton Seminary until he left New
Jersey in 1819, he was highly respected in all circles. Though
zealous for revivals, he cautioned against excess and in 1826
actively opposed the extravagant "new measures" of evangelist
Charles Finney. Theologically, Richards was a moderate Edwardsean, much like Leonard Woods of Andover and his own
theological teacher, Timothy Dwight. His moderation was likely
typical of the relatively staid New Englanders who made up the
majority of the emerging New School.

Richards, as most of the New School, claimed to follow Edwards
but did not follow him slavishly. On the question of the imputation of sin, for example, Edwards had proposed a theory of divinely
constituted oneness of the race to account for all men sharing in
Adam's guilt. Richards, following Dwight rather than Edwards on
this point, maintained that man's moral depravity is transferred
from Adam to his posterity "through the medium of their birth"
on the principle that "like produces like." Much of Richards'
teaching reflected such attempts of New England theologians to

28. Elwyn A. Smith, *The Presbyterian Ministry in American Culture*
(Philadelphia, 1962), p. 164.
29. John Quincy Adams, *A History of Auburn Seminary, 1818–1918*
(Auburn, N.Y., 1918), pp. 81–82.

reduce Edwards' theories to common sense. When this common sense method sometimes pointed two ways, Auburn's influential leader usually choose the more conservative path. So, for instance, on the question of man's original depravity, Richards rejected the argument of both Hopkins and Dwight that if sin is an act, it is nonsense to say that men are born in sin before they ever act. It made just as much common sense, Richards argued, to say that a man was born a sinner as to say he was born a prince or a beggar.[30]

Though James Richards' influential position at Auburn Seminary did not cause the hyperorthodox Presbyterians great alarm, it did not give them much comfort either. Richards was a New Englander with definite sympathies for the New England theology. Moreover, he shared New Englanders' tolerance of minor doctrinal innovations.[31] At Auburn Seminary he had little choice in this regard. Among his lesser-known colleagues were avowed Hopkinsians who had been objects of the conservatives' attacks. Matthew La Rue Perrine had been severely berated at the height of the Hopkinsian furor in the mid-1810s, and in the mid-1820s Dirck Cornelius Lansing was cited for his views on the atonement and the ability of sinners. An Old School journal at the time noted that "By the Catalogue of students in the Auburn Theological Seminary, it appears that there are in all 65 students attending that institution, which is devoted to the propagation of the Hopkinsian heresy."[32] Such accusations, however, were in the 1820s relatively isolated and not substantial enough to sustain full-scale theological warfare.

"New Haven Theology"

The period of relative peace might have continued indefinitely

---

30. James Richards, *Lectures on Mental Philosophy and Theology, with a Sketch of His Life by Samuel H. Gridley* (New York, 1846), pp. 55–56, 256, 271, 292–95.

31. Ibid., p. 53.

32. Quoted in Adams, *Auburn Seminary*, p. 231.

had not the New England theologians, in the meantime, provided the extreme Old School men with new evidences of apostasy. This time the source of the questionable teachings was the newly organized (1822) divinity school at Yale, where Nathaniel William Taylor (1786–1856) was the leading spokesman for the "New Haven theology." Taylor claimed to be the legitimate heir to the tradition of Calvin and Edwards, but he soon aroused intense opposition even among New England Congregationalists. Leonard Woods, Andover's conservative Hopkinsian professor of theology, and Bennet Tyler, who founded Hartford Seminary in 1834 to counter the influence of Taylor in Connecticut, both carried on long controversies with the New Haven professor.[33] The leaders of the Presbyterian inquisition soon joined the attack. As far as they were concerned, the spread of Taylor's teachings simply confirmed their predictions that leniency toward minor errors would lead to license for major heresies.

Taylor developed his theology in the context of New England revivalism and reform. First as a Yale student, then as pastor of the Center Church on the New Haven Green from 1812 to 1822, and finally as Dwight Professor of Didactic Theology from 1822 until his death in 1858, Taylor spent virtually all his active life close to the religious activities of Yale College. Outstanding among these were the recurrent campaigns for revival and reform led first by Taylor's teacher, Timothy Dwight, and later by his best friend, Lyman Beecher. These three men were the outstanding leaders in the design to use Yale to save both God and country.

Th problem being debated at Yale was the same as had been debated in New England since the days of Jonathan Edwards: how to reconcile the tenets of Calvinism with effective evangelistic methods. If salvation were entirely the work of the Holy Spirit, how could the evangelist exhort his audience to turn from sin

33. Zebulon Crocker, *The Catastrophe of the Presbyterian Church in 1837* (New Haven, Conn., 1838), pp. 113–297, presents a detailed account of these debates and a valuable bibliography, pp. 298–99.

to a new righteousness? If men were totally depraved and unable by themselves to do any good, how could he urge them to accept the offer of the Gospel? Nathaniel Taylor felt the implications of these questions acutely. His concern was increased by the Unitarians who raised precisely these issues in their attacks on all schools of Calvinism. While Lyman Beecher in the 1820s personally went to Boston to revive true religion in the Unitarian stronghold, Taylor remained at home designing a theology that would at once answer the Unitarian threat and provide a rationale for effective evangelism.[34]

In his desire to appeal to a generation raised on Enlightenment rationalism, Taylor frankly accepted reason as on a par with revelation. *"The clear, unperverted deductions of reason,"* he said, *"are as binding in their authority and not less truly to be relied on, than the word of God; and . . . the former can never contradict the latter."*[35] "Reason" meant the dictates of common sense. "The ultimate appeal," he stated, "on the questions of scripture doctrine, must be made to the bar of common sense—'that the decisions of common sense or reason of mankind, are to be depended on as certain truth, in all cases in which it is *competent* to decide, and *free from perversion.'* "[36]

Taylor's trust in common sense was built directly on the Scottish Common Sense philosophy. By about the third decade of the nineteenth century this philosophy had become dominant in American academic circles, particularly among evangelicals. Common Sense philosophy, developed particularly by Thomas Reid and Dugald Stewart during the eighteenth-century Enlightenment in Scotland, was well-suited to the American evangelical mentality. It was simple and seemed to provide a decisive answer to

34. For Taylor's concern for revivals, see Sidney Earl Mead, *Nathaniel William Taylor, 1786–1858* (Chicago, 1942), p. 125 and passim.

35. [Nathaniel W. Taylor], "On the Authority of Reason in Theology," *Quarterly Christian Spectator*, 3d ser., 9(March 1837):151.

36. [Nathaniel W. Taylor], "Application of the Principles of Common Sense to Certain Disputed Doctrines," ibid. 3(September 1831):453.

skepticism. Basically, Common Sense taught a form of Realism, affirming the existence of both reality and morality. The perceptions common to all men were to be relied upon. All men of common sense, it taught in answer to the skepticism of Hume, could reliably recognize truth when they saw it. Not only could they be sure of the existence of the material world, but also of certain self-evident truths, such as the axioms of logic or mathematics, the arguments for the existence of a Creator, a degree of determination of their own wills, and (most importantly for evangelicals) the first principles of morality.[37]

Evangelicals who adopted the Common Sense method accepted its essentially humanistic conclusions in varying degrees. At Princeton, for instance, where the philosophy was first introduced to America by President John Witherspoon in 1768, the method was generally used with caution lest it contradict Biblical doctrine. Taylor, on the other hand, was more confident in the powers of reason and accepted the method wholeheartedly as a sure way to settle philosophical and theological issues.[38] Though a liberal in evangelical circles, Taylor shared with his fellow theologians of virtually all schools an unwavering dogmatism. "I would rather have ten settled opinions, and nine of them wrong," he told his students, "than [have] none of the ten settled."[39] In the evangelical mind there was seldom any middle ground.

One of the major conclusions of the Scottish philosophy was that the "first principles of morals are self-evident intuitions."[40] And much of Taylor's original contribution to American theology

37. James McCosh, The Scottish Philosophy (New York, 1875), pp. 217–24; Herbert W. Schneider, A History of American Philosophy, 2d ed. (New York, 1963), pp. 208–20; Sydney E. Ahlstrom, "The Scottish Philosophy and American Theology," Church History 24(September 1955):263–64.

38. Ahlstrom, "Scottish Philosophy," pp. 263–66. Even at Princeton Seminary the theology of Charles Hodge was infected by the "stains of humanism" of the Scottish method; see ibid., p. 266.

39. Quoted in Mead, Taylor, p. 159.

40. Ahlstrom, "Scottish Philosophy," p. 261.

grew out of the principles of morality that he derived from common sense. The basic conclusion was that man was a free agent.[41]
In the tradition of Hopkins, Taylor was concerned with the meaning of sin and morality. But for him it was common sense that
man could not be held responsible for sinful acts unless they were
acts of free choice with power to the contrary. "There can be no
sin in choosing evil," he argued, "unless there be power to choose
good."[42]

By defining sin and guilt solely in terms of man's voluntary
actions Taylor excluded the possibility of man's being held guilty
for the sin of Adam. He thought the doctrines of imputation
sufficiently absurd to attack them with the most rudimentary of all
common-sense arguments—the appeal to the man on the street.
"If you would satisfy yourself on this point," he suggested wryly,
"propose it to any common man, who has never before heard of
it; explain it at large; and as you proceed to tell him how it has
been attempted to illustrate it, by supposing all mankind to be
living in the time of Adam, and 'somehow or other, to be growing
out of him,' or to become *deserving* of death by mere representation; mark his look of pity, or sneer of contempt, at such statements."[43]

Although Taylor denied the imputation of sin or guilt, he still
held what he called a Calvinist view that "depravity is by nature."
By this phrase he did not mean that men's natures were themselves sinful, but "that *such is their nature, that in all the appropriate circumstances of their being, they will sin and only sin.*"[44]

41. See [Taylor], "Common Sense," pp. 468–74, for application of this
doctrine.

42. Nathaniel W. Taylor, "Man, a Free Agent without the Aids of Divine
Grace," p. 6, in Articles and Tracts on New Haven Theology, coll. by C. A.
Goodrich, Yale University Library, 1841.

43. [Taylor], "Common Sense," p. 460.

44. Nathaniel W. Taylor, *Concio ad Clerum.* "A Sermon Delivered in the
Chapel of Yale College, September 10, 1828" (New Haven, Conn., 1828) in
Smith et al., *American Christianity,* 2:30–31.

This interpretation of depravity as sinful actions, rather than a sinful state of being or nature, eliminated the sinner's plausible excuse that he was not responsible for his sins because God had brought him into the world already in a sinful state. The practical effects of this teaching were to allow the preacher to dramatize the sinner's desperate state and his responsibility perhaps even more effectively than with Hopkins' view. Taylor applied his doctrine in this way in his famous sermon, *Concio ad Clerum* (1828):

> his guilt is all his own, and a just God may leave him to his choice. He is going on to a wretched eternity, the self-made victim of its woes. Amid sabbaths and bibles, the intercessions of saints, the songs of angels, the intreaties of God's ambassadors, the accents of redeeming love, and the blood that speaketh peace, he presses on to death. . . . —See the infatuated immortal!—Fellow sinner. IT IS YOU.[45]

The vital difference between the messages of Taylor and Hopkins was that Taylor told the sinner that he could, and certainly must, *act* to escape his damnable condition. For Hopkins, on the other hand, regeneration was solely the work of the Holy Spirit, and the sinner remained passive until he was enabled to respond in the converting experience. In Taylor's teaching, the distinction between regeneration and conversion was blurred, and regeneration was presented as a free act of man's will. "Regeneration," Taylor stated, is "that act of the will or heart which consists in a preference of God to every other object."[46]

Lest it appear that his doctrine of man's free agency and ability to choose aright had completely eliminated the work of the Holy Spirit in the conversion process, Taylor maintained that the role of the Spirit was an *influence* on the mind in conversion. The Holy

45. Ibid., p. 40.
46. [Nathaniel W. Taylor], "Review of Spring on the Means of Regeneration," *Quarterly Christian Spectator* 3(January 1829):18–19. This article was attributed to Taylor by C. A. Goodrich, in Articles and Tracts on New Haven Theology.

Spirit did not change the heart but only helped to influence the free agent to change. "Whatever that influence may be, the sinner, under its operation, chooses and acts just as voluntarily, as when he yields in any case to the solicitations of a friend."[47]

The rest of Taylor's system was little more than a restatement of the New England teachings on God's moral government and the atonement. In these teachings Taylor followed his predecessors in emphasizing the morality of both God and man. The "great and comprehensive relation of God to men," was "his relation to men as administering a perfect moral government over them as moral and immortal beings, created in his own image."[48] God's purpose as a benevolent moral governor was to promote *moral action* or benevolence in men. So Taylor repudiated all theories that stated God's relationship to men solely in legal terms. The law, he insisted, is a rule of action, not of judgment. In discussing the atonement and justification, for instance, Taylor never tired of ridiculing the orthodox doctrine of the imputation of the merit of Christ's righteousness to sinners as a satisfaction of the justice of God. To him it seemed "infernal malice" to suppose that Christ should be required to bear the legal penalty for the sins of men and that he should die in order to satisfy the justice of God. The atonement had, rather, an important practical effect. "The atonement as such cannot result in *the right* of the lawgiver to pardon the transgressor, but must produce its whole effect in sustaining the authority of the lawgiver."[49] God, the benevolent moral governor, had sent Christ to die for men's sins as a means to urge men to turn freely and actively from their sins and to choose a life of selfless benevolence.

With unbounded confidence in the reliability of the perceptions of common sense, Taylor furnished an intellectual defense against Unitarian and orthodox alike. At the same time he provided the

47. [Taylor], "Common Sense," p. 475.
48. Nathaniel W. Taylor, *Lectures on the Moral Government of God* (New York, 1859), 2:2.
49. Ibid., pp. 155–56; see also ibid., p. 278.

advocates of revival with an important practical weapon. The evangelist could confront sinners with the challenge, "Choose ye this day." This was exactly the result Taylor intended to produce.[50]

Taylor's explanations of Calvinism appealed to young Presbyterians zealous for revivals in their own congregations. Albert Barnes, a graduate of Princeton Theological Seminary, was among the first to arouse new apprehensions in Old School areas. In a revival sermon entitled "The Way of Salvation," preached to his Morristown, New Jersey, congregation in 1829, Barnes proclaimed doctrines that sounded more like Yale than Princeton. "I stand as a messenger of God," he declared, "with the assurance, that all that *will* may be saved; that the atonement was full and free; and that if any perish, it will be because they choose to die, and not because they are straitened in God." For Barnes this view was a practical matter. It could be used in an appeal to sinners "to embrace the offer of life." The challenge was direct: "Go home this day, impenitent sinner, if God spares a rebel like you to get home—go home and reflect, that if you pass through this revival unmoved; if you resist all the appeals that are made to you, from day to day, and week to week, the probability is, that you will be damned, and the certainty is, that *you* only will be to blame if you are."[51]

George Duffield (1794–1868), grandson and namesake of the Presbyterian chaplain to the Continental Congress, and pastor of a Presbyterian church in Carlisle, Pennsylvania, expressed the same concern for the salvation of souls in his preaching. Duffield had wrestled with the problem in regard to his own salvation. "What authority have I to believe that Christ died for *me* as a

50. "To what purpose, do we preach the Gospel to men," he asked, "if we cannot reach the conscience with *its charge of guilt and an obligation to duty?*" Taylor, *Concio ad Clerum.* "A Sermon Delivered in the Chapel of Yale College, September 10, 1828" (New Haven, Conn., 1842), p. 37.

51. Albert Barnes, *The Way of Salvation.* "A Sermon Delivered at Morristown, New Jersey, February 8, 1829," in *The Presbyterian Enterprise,* ed. Maurice W. Armstrong, Lefferts A. Loetscher, and Charles A. Anderson (Philadelphia, 1955), pp. 147–48.

person?" he asked. The answer was in a free offer of salvation that could be appropriated freely by all men. "This appropriating act of faith, I saw, was like the hand stretched forth to take the free gift, and make it mine in possession as it was mine in the offer. . . . So to preach the riches of His grace, and so to press upon sinners the acceptance of Him as their personal Savior . . . I felt . . . to be the way to preach the very essence and marrow of the Gospel."[52]

The appearance of such teachings within the bounds of Presbyterianism added fuel to the radical Old School fires that had been smoldering since the days of the Hopkinsian controversy. The flames broke out in 1830 when Albert Barnes was called to the First Church in Philadelphia, in the heart of Old School territory. Upon his arrival the Old School presbytery promptly charged him with doctrinal error on the basis of his statements in his sermon "The Way of Salvation." Barnes, his Old School accusers claimed, had combined all the errors of the New England theology into this one sermon. He had denied that men were held guilty for Adam's sin; he had rejected the doctrine that the atonement was a substitutionary sacrifice for the elect only; and, most importantly, he had said that the inability of sinners was limited to the will, implying—so the complainants assumed—that the unregenerate had the ability to contribute to their own salvation.

In defense of the sermon, Barnes pointed out that denials of the imputation of Adam's sin had long been accepted among even the conservatives in New England and were tolerated within Presbyterianism. On the question of the atonement he would not say that the benefits of Christ's sufferings were limited to the elect, but he affirmed clearly its substitutionary character—that "Christ died in the *place of sinners.*" These issues were not substantially different from those raised in the Hopkinsian controversies. The crucial question, however, was unregenerate man's ability in relation to the work of the Holy Spirit effecting salvation. Was the Holy

52. Quoted in *Presbyterian Reunion: A Memorial Volume, 1837–1871* (New York, 1870), p. 233.

Spirit merely an influence on man's free will as Taylor suggested, or did the Holy Spirit supply the whole transforming power in regeneration? On this point, Barnes's sermon had been ambiguous, and so were his explanations. In characterizing what he had meant by saying in "The Way of Salvation" that "all that *will* may be saved," he described the totality of depravity more decisively than Taylor might have but used Taylor's term in referring to the work of the Holy Spirit. What his sermon had meant, said Barnes, was that the unregenerate sinner "was wholly inclined to evil, and opposed to good; and that this native propensity was so strong as never to be overcome but by the influence of the Holy Spirit." Such a statement was not in itself a departure from orthodoxy; but neither did it repudiate Taylor.[53]

The charges against Barnes were sustained by both the Presbytery and the Synod of Philadelphia, and the case reached the General Assembly in 1831. When it did, the party warfare between the Old School and New School broke out in full force for the first time. The contrast to the peacefulness of the preceding years was sharp. In 1829 Ashbel Green, editor of the ultraconservative *Christian Advocate,* had described the Assembly as one of the most harmonious in memory. After the Assembly of 1831, he wrote the opposite: "There occurred such disorder and confusion as we have never witnessed in the General Assembly, and which we devoutly pray may never see again."[54] Green's distress was doubtless heightened by the Old School defeat at the 1831 Assembly. Nathan S. S. Beman (1785–1871), a prominent New School evangelist from upstate New York, had been elected moderator in the first test of party strength. Throughout the Assembly, the New School majority prevailed. Most disturbing to the Old School, Albert Barnes had been acquitted with only the admonition that his sermon "contains a number of unguarded and objectionable pas-

53. Pope, "New England Calvinism," pp. 193–220. Pope argues that the identification of Barnes with Taylorism was unwarranted.

54. Quoted in ibid., p. 192.

sages."[55] After the Assembly adjourned, Green took the lead in marshaling the conservative forces. "Unless in the passing year," he wrote in the *Christian Advocate*, "there is a general waking up of the *old school presbyterians,* to a sense of their danger and their duty, their influence in the General Assembly will forever afterward be subordinate and under control."[56] Old School Presbyterians were indeed waking up, and during the next few years they focused their attention on bringing New School "heretics" to trial.

Prominent among the accused was George Duffield, whose experiences were similar to those of Albert Barnes. In 1832 Duffield published an extensive (613 pages) account of his views on *Spiritual Life: or, Regeneration.* In it he presented essentially the New Haven view of the active character of man's depravity and of the consequent impossibility of inherited sinfulness. Man's "depravity consists in the misdirection and inappropriate exercise of his faculties; not in *wrong faculties inherited,*" Duffield asserted. Men have the necessary faculties or ability to do good, but as a consequence of the fall of Adam, it is *"morally certain,* that they will sin, as soon as they are capable of moral agency." But Duffield did not go all the way in adopting Taylor's emphasis. His book was, after all, a treatment of regeneration, and in presenting the new views of man's abilities, he pointedly refused to deny that the Spirit of God is the author of regeneration. Rather, he stressed that the Holy Spirit initiated the change in the character of man's voluntary exercises by a "moral suasion" sufficient to rouse man's capacities into action.[57]

Duffield's explanations, however, did not satisfy the Old School members of the Presbytery of Carlisle. In 1832 they initiated charges against him. But once more the Old School attempts to enforce discipline were frustrated. The majority in the presbytery

---

55. *Minutes, 1831,* p. 180.
56. Quoted in Pope, "New England Calvinism," p. 230.
57. George Duffield, *Spiritual Life: Or, Regeneration* (Carlisle, Penn., 1832), pp. 310, 363, 430, 480, 485.

contented themselves with a warning against the dangerous character of Duffield's "speculations," but allowed the pastor to continue in the ministry.[58]

Other local controversies in presbyteries where there were men of both Schools were sometimes extremely bitter. One such case was the trial of James Wheelock, a New Englander associated with the American Home Missionary Society who went west to serve Presbyterian churches in Indiana. An elder in one of the churches brought charges against him for several doctrinal errors. Wheelock is said to have responded with the counteraccusation that the opposition to him arose because he refused to preach that hell was lined with the souls of infants. His trial before the Indianapolis Presbytery remained on about the same level of dignity. Finally, after his New School supporters had walked out and boycotted several meetings to prevent a quorum, Wheelock escaped with only an admonishment.[59]

The case of Lyman Beecher in Cincinnati, though perhaps more dignified, received nationwide publicity and was hardly more satisfying to Old School men. When Beecher arrived in Cincinnati to become president of Lane Seminary, he had to transfer to the Presbytery of Cincinnati, which was predominantly Old School. When he did, charges were brought against him for holding New Haven theories regarding man's native depravity, ability, and the work of the Holy Spirit in regeneration. No doubt Beecher's close association with Nathaniel Taylor made him suspect. Apparently, too, he had adopted some of Taylor's terminology, especially in defending his views against Unitarianism, for the Old School men claimed that it was "common fame" that he held erroneous doctrines. Beecher, who combined brilliance with lack of concern for theological precision, disclaimed any intention of preaching doctrines contrary to the Confession of Faith. He insisted, rather,

58. Baird, *New School,* pp. 462–67.
59. L. C. Rudolph, *Hoosier Zion: A Study of Presbyterians in Indiana to 1850* (New Haven, Conn., 1963), pp. 124–27.

that his views were essentially those of Jonathan Edwards. The predominantly Old School presbytery agreed and acquitted him in 1835. At their suggestion, however, Beecher agreed to publish a clarification of his views at an early day. Published in 1836 as *Views on Theology,* it was a carefully worded statement of a moderate New England position. Even the highly unsympathetic Old School historian, Samuel Baird, characterized it as "comparatively orthodox."[60]

The acquittal of three Yale graduates by the Presbytery of Illinois provided more certain evidence of the spread of Taylor's views in the Presbyterian Church. The defendants, Edward Beecher, J. M. Sturtevant, and William Kirby, had recently founded Illinois College, which they intended to be the "Yale of the West." In their statement of faith before the presbytery, they acknowledged agreement with the New Haven teachings. But the presbytery, dominated by New School men, decided that "the accused brethren do not teach doctrines, materially or essentially, at variance with the standards of the Presbyterian Church and the Word of God."[61]

By the early 1830s even the moderates among the orthodox were finding sufficient evidence of doctrinal laxity to unite in condemning the errors of New Haven. The stricter element, led by Ashbel Green of Philadelphia and speaking through the *Christian Advocate* and the *Presbyterian,* had been sounding the alarm with regard to *all* brands of distinctive New England theology ever since the Hopkinsian controversy. The moderate Princeton party, on the other hand, while launching a vigorous campaign in the *Princeton Review* against the New Haven views,[62] consistently

60. Baird, *New School,* p. 471. For Beecher's trial, see Beecher, *Autobiography,* 2:346–61, and Arthur Stansbury, *Trial and Acquittal of Lyman Beecher Before the Presbytery of Cincinnati on Charges Preferred by Joshua L. Wilson* (Cincinnati, Ohio, 1835).

61. Baird, *New School,* pp. 472–74.

62. Charles Hodge and Archibald Alexander contributed a total of seven major articles relevant to the New Haven theology in 1830 and 1831.

refused to condemn indiscriminately the "Hopkinsian peculiarities" along with the "Taylorite errors." The distinctive doctrines of both systems were erroneous, said the Princeton professors, but only the New Haven views actually subverted the foundations of the Reformed faith.[63]

The theological term that Princeton and Old School spokesmen almost invariably used to describe the New Haven system was "Pelagian." Indeed, the nineteenth-century debates on original sin, the freedom of man's will, the active character of sin, and the role of man in salvation closely resembled the fifth-century debates between Augustine and the British monk, Pelagius. Old School critics appealed to the condemnations of Pelagius by both the Ancient Church and the Reformers. More importantly, they contended that the New Haven views contradicted the clear teachings of Scripture—particularly those of Paul in the book of Romans. Basically, the Old School's objection was that the New School taught or tolerated an un-Biblical view of man's nature. The New School's confidence in the dignity, freedom, and ability of man, a confidence in many ways characteristic of the mainstream of American thought in the eras of Jackson and Emerson, was resisted by the Old School on the ground that it subverted the essential Scriptural teachings of God's sovereignty and man's depravity.

The intense friction between these two intellectual positions was increased by their intimate connections with the practical concerns of the parties involved. Not only was the future of the Presbyterian Church at stake, but so was the success of the whole revival and moral reform program of the "Evangelical united front." Out of the theological tensions within Presbyterianism grew a fierce controversy that precipitated substantial alterations in the alignment and programs of American Protestantism.

63. Archibald Alexander Hodge, *The Life of Charles Hodge* (New York, 1880), p. 290.

3

The Presbyterian Schism

"No doubt there is a jubilee in hell every year, about the time of the meeting of the General Assembly," wrote Charles Finney in 1835.[1] The controversial evangelist, who left Presbyterianism to become Professor of Theology at Oberlin the same year, departed just as the real fireworks were beginning in the Presbyterian Assembly. During the next three years, the meetings of the General Assembly were scenes of bitter debates and disorders with few parallels in American church history. Presbyterians gained nationwide notoriety for their contentiousness. One New York newspaper went so far as to suggest that if members of the Old School party tried to enter heaven, St. Peter would reject them on the grounds that they would get up a synod and "turn all heaven upside down with your doctrinal disputations."[2] Even President Jackson, a Presbyterian himself, and hence presumably more sympathetic than St. Peter, was concerned. Political opponents "don't bother me half so much as do the dissensions in the Presbyterian Church," he reportedly told Nathan S. S. Beman.[3]

1. Charles G. Finney, *Lectures on Revivals of Religion* (New York, 1835), p. 269.

2. *The New York Transcript,* November 26, 1835, quoted in Pope, "New England Calvinism," pp. 336–37.

3. Robert Ellis Thompson, *A History of the Presbyterian Churches in the United States* (New York, 1895), p. 109n. Jackson attended an Old School church. There appears, however, to have been no correlation between political loyalties and Presbyterian party lines. See Lee Benson, *The Concept of Jacksonian Democracy: New York as a Test Case* (Princeton, N.J., 1961), p. 191.

The course of development of the New School Presbyterian movement was permanently altered by these notorious dissensions. The controversies in the Presbyterian Assembly provided the context in which many of the distinctive aspects of New School thought were defined, and throughout the denomination's history its theologians looked back to their seemingly epic struggle with the Old School for the vindication of their message.

Contentions and Schism in the Presbyterian Assembly

By 1835 the Old School party in the Presbyterian Church was becoming desperate. At every General Assembly since 1831, the year the controversy broke out in full force, the New School party had commanded a majority, and the Old School had suffered repeated defeats and frustrations. In 1834 they had protested in vain to the Assembly against "the prevalence of unsoundness in doctrine and laxity in discipline."[4] When, as usual, their protest had not been heard, they had issued a doctrinal statement called the "Act and Testimony," detailing the theological "errors . . . held and taught by many persons in our church."[5] As the time for the Assembly of 1835 approached, aggressive Old School leaders attempted to muster their full forces, calling a special party convention prior to the Assembly. There, with support sufficient to ensure a majority at the Assembly, they pledged that "though our earthen pitchers may be broken, our lights shall shine and 'the sword of the Lord and of Gideon' shall turn the eye of a gazing world to that point of the field where victory perches on the 'banner of truth.' "[6]

4. "Memorial to the Moderator and Members of the General Assembly of the Presbyterian Church in the United States to Meet in the City of Philadelphia, May 15th, 1834"—known as the "Western Memorial"—quoted in Issac V. Brown, *A Historical Vindication of the Abrogation of the Plan of Union by the Presbyterian Church in the United States of America* (Philadelphia, 1855), p. 89. Brown's book is a valuable compilation of many Old School documents.
5. "Act and Testimony," quoted in Brown, *Vindication*, pp. 149–56.
6. Quoted in E. H. Gillett, *History of the Presbyterian Church in the United States of America* (Philadelphia, 1864), 2:491.

What followed was not exactly a rout of the Midianites. But the Old School did win a temporary victory. They used their majority in the Assembly of 1835 to strengthen denominational machinery to enforce doctrinal conformity, to increase the authority of the church judicatories, and to decrease cooperation with Congregationalists and the organizations of the "Evangelical united front."[7]

At the 1836 Assembly, meeting in Pittsburgh, the Old School party hoped to consolidate these gains. Victory appeared within their grasp as they elected their candidate for Moderator on the opening day. But the arrival of a steamer "crowded with commissioners from Illinois and Missouri" reversed the trend, and the New School, having regained a majority, annulled most of the Old School programs of the previous year.[8] The real test of strength centered on the second trial of Albert Barnes. In 1835 Barnes had published *Notes on the Epistle to the Romans* as part of a series of popular commentaries. In his exposition, charged the Old School, Barnes had repeated the errors of "The Way of Salvation." The accusations against him were virtually identical with those in his first trial, and the outcome was much the same. The Old School Synod of Philadelphia, convinced that Barnes taught that "unregenerate men are able to keep the commandments and convert themselves to God," had suspended Barnes from the ministry. For nearly a year the young pastor had sat in silence in his own congregation, awaiting the hearing of his appeal by the Assembly. During that interim a heated debate developed,[9] culminating in two weeks of intense argument at the trial in the Assembly of 1836. Finally, the appeal was sustained. Barnes was acquitted. The New School held the field.[10]

The Old School leaders expressed consternation that the members of the New School had "shown their determination to shield

7. *Minutes, 1835*, pp. 27–30.
8. Baird, *New School*, pp. 489–503.
9. See Pope, "New England Calvinism," pp. 300–39.
10. *Minutes, 1836*, pp. 251–69.

error under its worst forms."[11] Launching a vigorous counterattack, they organized a "Committee of Correspondence" and issued a "secret circular" calling for radical action. They considered separation imperative. "Fathers, Brethren, Fellow-Christians," wrote the committee, "whatever else may be dark, this is clear, *we* CANNOT CONTINUE *in the same body*."[12] The only remaining question was: Would the Old School secede or could it force the New School party from the church?[13] The party with the majority at the General Assembly of 1837 would name the terms of the division.

The campaign of the Old School to consolidate its forces succeeded. In the final test of strength at the Assembly of 1837, it was the majority party. At a pre-Assembly convention the Old School adopted a "Testimony and Memorial" containing its most extensive indictment of the New School "errors" and recommending to the Assembly the dissolution of every church, presbytery, or synod "not organized on Presbyterian principles," that is, those founded under the terms of the Plan of Union.[14] Early in the Assembly they won their victory, abrogating the Plan of Union of 1801 by a vote of 143 to 110. The Old School hoped this action would eliminate the major source of New School irregularity—Congregational influence and practice. Reconciliation between the two factions now appeared out of the question. A joint committee appointed to consider a voluntary division could agree on almost nothing, and all hope for an amicable resolution of the disputes had past.[15]

11. William Engles, "State of the Church," *The Presbyterian* (June 18, 1836):94, quoted in Pope, "New England Calvinism," p. 347.

12. Quoted in [Absalom Peters], *A Plea for Voluntary Societies* by a Member of the Assembly (New York, 1837), p. 163.

13. Baird, *New School*, p. 513; cf. *A History of the Division of the Presbyterian Church in the United States of America*, by a Committee of the Synod of New York and New Jersey (New York, 1852), p. 143 (hereafter cited as *Division*).

14. "Testimony and Memorial," quoted in Brown, *Vindication*, pp. 216–26.

15. *Minutes, 1837*, pp. 426–44.

The Old School action that followed was immediate, bold, and conclusive. As soon as the joint committee was dissolved, the Old School proposed that the abrogation of the Plan of Union be retroactive, thus eliminating the Synod of Western Reserve in Ohio and the New York Synods of Utica, Geneva, and Genesee— all formed under the Plan.[16] By passing this proposal they excluded 28 presbyteries, 509 ministers, and 60,000 communicants, or nearly one-fifth of the entire membership of the church.[17] This reduced the voting strength of the New School by about half. The remaining members of the party had little alternative but to withdraw and join forces with their excluded brethren.

The excluded portions of the church were left in a state of confusion. New School men had not wholly anticipated the blow that the Assembly struck at the four synods. "Its decisive character, partly because of its unexpected occurrence, they failed at first to understand"; recalled one of their historians, "to use a modern military phase, it quite demoralized them."[18] "The exscinded party," wrote another, "was at first little more than a confused collection of ministers, churches, organizations, swept away together as by some resistless flood."[19] The course they would take was uncertain. In August 1837 the Congregational Association of New York advised that the churches of the exscinded synods abandon Presbyterianism and become entirely Congregational in organization and fellowship.[20] But the members of the New

16. Ibid., pp. 437–44. The same Assembly passed a resolution declaring that the American Home Missionary Society and the American Education Society were "exceedingly injurious to the peace and purity of the Presbyterian Church" and recommending that "they should cease to operate within any of our churches," ibid., p. 442.

17. D. W. Lathrop, ed., *The Case of the General Assembly of the Presbyterian Church in the United States of America before the Supreme Court of the Commonwealth of Pennsylvania* (Philadelphia, 1839), p. 521.

18. Lewis F. Stearns, "Historical Review of the Church (New School Branch)," in *Presbyterian Reunion*, p. 53.

19. Edward D. Morris, *The Presbyterian Church New School, 1837–1869: An Historical Review* (Columbus, Ohio, 1905), p. 74.

20. Ibid., p. 76.

School party, who met the same month at Auburn, New York, were not willing to capitulate so easily to the desire of the Old School to exclude them from Presbyterianism.

The strategy they adopted at the Auburn Convention was to have a decisive influence on nearly every aspect of the history of the New School denomination. Rather than concede anything to the Old School, they aligned themselves on the high ground of their own Presbyterian constitutionality. On this ground they declared the disowning acts of the 1837 Assembly "null and void" and urged the synods declared exscinded to "retain their present organization and connection, without seeking any other." At the same time, they issued a doctrinal statement, known as the "Auburn Declaration," contrasting the charges of error contained in the Old School "Testimony and Memorial" with a list of "true doctrines" believed to meet the constitutional standards of the Church (the Westminster Confession of Faith and Catechisms) and said to be "the prevalent sentiments of the churches of these Synods on the points in question." To complete this strategic claim to their own constitutionality and orthodoxy, the convention recommended "that the Presbyteries send their commissioners to the next General Assembly as usual."[21]

The dramatic climax to the hostilities came when the General Assembly met as scheduled in the Seventh Presbyterian Church of Philadelphia on the morning of May 17, 1838. The Old School party arrived early and occupied all the seats nearest the moderator's chair. When the New School commissioners arrived they found the doors nearest the moderator's chair locked, forcing them to enter from the back and take the empty seats behind the Old School commissioners. As soon as the retiring Old School Moderator assumed the chair to organize the As-

21. *Minutes of the Auburn Convention* (Auburn, N.Y., 1837), quoted in Baird, *New School,* p. 541; and in Armstrong et al., *Presbyterian Enterprise,* p. 167.

sembly, several New School men attempted to present motions adding to the roll the names of the commissioners from the four excluded synods. When the moderator declared these out of order, the Reverend Miles P. Squier, one of the excluded commissioners, arose and demanded his seat in the Assembly. The Moderator, ascertaining that Squier was from the Synod of Geneva, replied abruptly, "We do not know you."

A tumult followed. In the New School section of the church, the Reverend John P. Cleveland, reportedly urged to "go on" by Drs. Lyman Beecher and Nathaniel W. Taylor, was reading a statement declaring that on the advice of legal counsel "a Constitutional Assembly must be organized at this time and place"; while on the Old School side great confusion was accentuated by repeated calls to order. All semblance of decency and order was lost as the confusion became pandemonium and spread to the crowded galleries. Amid this tumult New School commissioners, crowding around their moderator in the aisles or standing on the pews to get a view, were attempting to constitute a legal Assembly. Parliamentary procedure was reduced to near chaos as they elected officers by loud shouts of acclamation augmented by unsolicited calls to order, votes from the gallery, and reversals of the question from all sides. Finally, the New School completed the necessary formalities and voted to adjourn the "Constitutional Assembly" to a more favorable locale.[22]

Two assemblies now met in Philadelphia, each claiming to be "The General Assembly of the Presbyterian Church in the United States of America." The New School body, with approximately 100,000 communicant members, 85 presbyteries, and 1,200

22. This account is based on Lathrop, *Case of the General Assembly;* see especially Molton C. Rogers's "Charge to the Court," pp. 506–29, and the extensive sworn testimony of many of the participants, pp. 84–264. See also Baird, *New School,* pp. 545–54; *Division,* pp. 155–69; and Gillett, *History of the Presbyterian Church,* 2:528–31.

churches and ministers, represented slightly less than half the
Presbyterian Church in the United States of America.[23] Its constituency included virtually all members from the four excluded
synods of upstate New York and the Western Reserve, the Synods
of Michigan and Eastern Tennessee, majorities from the Synods
of New York, Albany, and Illinois, half the Synods of New Jersey
and Indiana, and strong minorities in those of Ohio and Cincinnati. Elsewhere the lines of cleavage cut sharply through individual presbyteries and even congregations.[24]

The Causes of the Division

Historians have seldom viewed these scenes of disorder in the
Presbyterian Assembly dispassionately. In the wave of polemics
that continued long after schism, partisans marshaled abundant
evidence to support their differing explanations. Participants and
interpreters sympathetic to the Old School invariably maintained
that New School theology was so dangerous as to necessitate division. New School interpreters and their sympathizers, on the
other hand, usually denied the significance of these formal theological differences and therefore emphasized the importance of
other related issues. More recent historians, while not necessarily
following party lines, have based their arguments on essentially
the same evidence and have reached the same diverse interpretations. The consensus, however, is weighted heavily toward the
conclusion (supported also by the following analysis) that theology
was the primary issue.[25] Since the division was engineered by the

23. Edwin F. Hatfield, "Statistics of the Church (New School Branch) since
1837," *Presbyterian Reunion,* p. 500. The Old School in 1840 claimed 126,583
members; 96 presbyteries; 1,763 churches; and 1,221 ministers (David Irving,
"Statistics of the Church (Old School Branch) since 1837," *Presbyterian
Reunion,* p. 494).
24. Thompson, *History of the Presbyterian Churches,* p. 121. For detailed
accounts of local divisions, see Gillett, *History of the Presbyterian Church,*
2:532–52.
25. See Appendix 1.

Old School, the declarations of that party that the doctrinal questions were primary should be accepted unless it can be demonstrated and there was some other more basic underlying cause.

The theological issue, however, was integrally bound up with several other important factors contributing to the division. These interrelated issues may be distinguished as follows: (1) the meaning of confessionalism, (2) Presbyterian polity, (3) the relation of the church to the voluntary societies of the "Evangelical united front," (4) methods of revivalism, (5) theology itself, and (6) slavery.[26] By breaking down the points of contention in this way an analysis of the causes of the division may be made, at the same time presenting a systematic portrait of New School Presbyterian evangelicalism. The place of slavery in the schism, because of its wider implications, will be treated in a separate chapter where it can be considered in a broader context.

THE MEANING OF CONFESSIONALISM

Lyman Beecher, who typified the spirit of the New School movement in most respects, held a characteristically evangelical attitude toward the Presbyterian Confession of Faith.[27] Above all a man of action, Beecher had little time for impractical details. When given the opportunity to carry his campaigns to the West, he was confronted with such details if he were to become a Presbyterian, a requirement for the presidency of Lane Seminary. Beecher could accept the Westminster Confession, in general, but had reservations as to some specifics. At the time of his call to Cincinnati, he reportedly quipped to an Old School visitor that his answer to the standard doctrinal question for Presbyterian ordination ("Do you sincerely receive and adopt the Confession of

26. This breakdown of causes is suggested by Morris, *Presbyterian Church New School,* pp. 46–47.

27. See Pope, "New England Calvinism," for the best account of the details of the confessional controversy.

Faith of this Church, as containing the system of doctrine taught in the Holy Scriptures?") would be, "Yes, but I will not say how much more it contains." His guest, a Mississippian, told him that no such Yankee answer would do![28]

The debate over the meaning of the requirements for subscription to the Westminster Confession was the oldest controversy in American Presbyterianism, and the nineteenth-century debates invariably hinged on appeals to the original Adopting Act of 1729. New School interpreters, maintaining the tradition of New England, claimed that Presbyterians had always permitted a broad interpretation of the confessional requirements and that the Old School heresy hunters were changing the terms of subscription by sounding the alarm over "the slight shades of doctrinal differences always known and permitted in the Church." Furthermore, they charged that such rigid confessionalism undermined the Bible as the Church's sole authority. "We love and honor the Confession of Faith," they declared in 1838, "but it is not the Bible, nor a substitute for the Bible."[29]

To strict Old School men, however, the New School claims to Biblicism could too easily be used to shield the most serious errors in doctrine. It was against such that they testified in the "Act and Testimony" of 1834:

> 1. We do bear our solemn testimony against the right claimed by many, of interpreting the doctrines of our standards in a sense different from the general sense of the church for years past. . . .
> 2. We testify against the unchristian subterfuge to which some have recourse, when they avow a general adherence to our standards as a system, while they deny doctrines essential to the system, or hold to doctrines at complete variance with the system.[30]

28. Baird, *New School*, p. 468.
29. New School *Minutes, 1838*, pp. 664, 666.
30. "Act and Testimony," in Brown, *Vindication*, p. 150.

It was one thing, however, for the Old School to demand strict subscription to the Confession and quite another thing to enforce that demand. One problem was that not even all conservatives would require conformity to the details of the Confession. Ever since the Hopkinsian controversy of 1817, the influential Princeton party had refused to condemn those who did not deny teachings central to the system of doctrine. "It is not enough that a doctrine be erroneous, or that it be dangerous in its tendency," said Charles Hodge (1797–1878) in reviewing the controversy, "if it be not subversive of one or more of the constituent elements of the Reformed faith, it is not incompatible with the honest adopting of the Confession."[31]

Even more distressing to the strict Old School party was that in many areas they lacked any control on who entered the Presbyterian ministry. Presbyteries with New School majorities readily ordained New England men, who could then transfer to any other presbytery. Lyman Beecher's experience is again representative. When he finally accepted the call to Lane Seminary, he wished to avoid the rigid examination of the predominantly Old School Presbytery of Cincinnati. He therefore wrote to the notoriously lax Third Presbytery of New York City, which ordained him in absentia and then immediately released him to Cincinnati.[32] In this instance the strong Old School element managed to examine Beecher anyway, on the basis of his published statements. But with men who said less in print, they had little recourse. Frustrated by the current practices in examining individuals, they turned to a more general reform of Presbyterian polity.[33]

31. Charles Hodge, "Retrospect," *Princeton Review*, Index Volume, 1825–1868 (1869):22. Cf. Charles Hodge, "Remarks on Dr. Cox's Communication," *Princeton Review* 4(October 1831):520–21, for an earlier statement of the same view.

32. "Western Memorial," in Brown, *Vindication*, p. 91.

33. For the best accounts of issues of polity, see Baird, *New School*, for an Old School account; and *Division* for New School arguments.

PRESBYTERIAN RULES OF ORDER

"When the truth is in danger," the Old School declared in the "Testimony and Memorial" of 1837, "we hold but the more steadfastly to our distinctive church order, as affording the best method of detecting and vanquishing error."[34] The immediate occasion for the division was a technical question of Presbyterian order. The Old School excluded the four synods on the ground that the Plan of Union "was originally an unconstitutional act."[35] This disruptive course was chosen, however, only because it appeared the most effective legal means to terminate "the toleration of gross errors in doctrine, or disorders in practice, by inferior judicatories."[36]

The Old School party considered abrogation necessary and just primarily because the four Plan of Union synods had no effective means for trying those who condoned irregularities in doctrine and in order. "Try them!" exclaimed the counsel for the Old School before the Supreme Court of Pennsylvania, "for what? . . . They do not acknowledge your jurisdiction; they participate in governing you by sending their lay delegates into your judicatories, but they are not subject to your tribunals."[37] Strict Presbyterian polity and strict Presbyterian doctrine went hand in hand for most Old School men. Polity, nonetheless, was not a primary end in itself. Rather, it was the means to the end of purging the Church of the reputed doctrinal error.

The immediate occasion for the exodus of the New School party from the General Assembly of 1838 was also a matter of ecclesiastical order. They justified their withdrawal on the basis that the disowning actions of the Assembly of 1837 were unconstitutional. For this position the New School had a convincing case. The 1837 Assembly, under Old School control had reversed

34. "Testimony and Memorial," in Brown, *Vindication*, p. 219.
35. *Minutes, 1837*, p. 421.
36. "Testimony and Memorial," *Minutes, 1837*, p. 422.
37. Lathrop, *Case of the General Assembly*, p. 170.

precedents concerning the Plan of Union, which the Assembly itself had accepted for a third of a century. Moreover, it abrogated the Congregational alliance retroactively, a move that made their action appear especially high-handed. These apparently irregular procedures had a peculiar effect on the New School attitudes toward the Presbyterian constitution. Because of the predominantly Congregational background of New School men, they previously had not been greatly concerned to enforce strict Presbyterian order. Now, however, they claimed to be the "Constitutional Assembly," and in their zeal to vindicate their position before the public they were suddenly making efforts to demonstrate their love of Presbyterian constitutionality.[38]

The assumption of such a constitutional stance had a pervasive effect on the entire subsequent history of the New School movement. The members of the new denomination certainly still thought of themselves as champions of the interdenominational evangelical movement. In fact, however, the division of 1837–38 marked the beginning of the end of evangelical unity, as the New School itself and, soon, most of its allies became increasingly occupied with denominational concerns.

THE "EVANGELICAL UNITED FRONT"

Clearly the issues of Presbyterian confessionalism and polity were subordinate to the theological concerns of the Old School men who precipitated the division. These became major factors only as they related to the doctrinal debates. Cooperation with the "Evangelical united front"[39] had less direct implications for the doctrinal issue. Nonetheless, New School zeal for the united evan-

38. New School *Minutes, 1838,* p. 673.
39. For the best account of the Presbyterian debate over this issue, see Earl R. MacCormac, "The Transition from Voluntary Missionary Society to the Church as a Missionary Organization among American Congregationalists, Presbyterians, and Methodists," (Ph.D. diss., Yale University, 1961). For the best general account, see Foster, *United Front.*

gelical efforts unquestionably added to their determination to maintain a tolerant doctrinal stance. Although many, probably most, New School men were relatively orthodox doctrinally, they refused to join the prosecutions against theological innovators. Intolerance of the Old School variety, they were sure, would endanger interdenominational unity. The Old School in the meantime was becoming increasingly convinced that the operations of the independent agencies within the bounds of Presbyterianism were a major source of divergent opinion and doctrinal laxity.

The question most directly raised by the presence of the "united front" was, however, not that of theology itself but rather that of the nature of the Church. In nearly every American denomination this became a serious point of debate. Anti-Church tendencies were already strong in American Protestantism, and in the early nineteenth century they were fostered by the more general American distrust of both tradition and authoritarianism. Evangelical activism with its demands that practical considerations should outweigh theoretical issues contributed further to the decline in emphasis on the role of the organized church. "On general principles, . . . as well as from all past experience," argued Absalom Peters (1793–1869), a fiery New School champion of interdenominational societies, in a characteristic statement, "we are constrained to believe that the voluntary, associated action of evangelical christians, as far as it is practicable, is much better suited to the object of the world's conversion, than any form of church organization for this purpose, ever has been or can be."[40]

In the intra-Presbyterian debates the issue focused on the role of the Church in relation to the independent societies for missions and ministerial education, particularly the American Home Missionary Society, the American Board of Commissioners for Foreign Missions, and the American Education Society. Men of Old School sentiments were accused by their evangelical opponents of being

40. [A. Peters], *Plea for Voluntary Societies*, pp. 29–30.

"High Church Presbyterians," because they favored denominational control of such activities. "The rallying principle of these brethren," said one New School critic, "is *ecclesiastical order!* They have enlisted under a banner that is *exclusive* and *sectarian.*"[41]

The High Church position of the Old School paralleled similar traditionalist movements in most major American (and British) denominations of this era. Confessional Lutherans, High Church Episcopalians, the representatives of the Mercersburg movement in the German Reformed Church, and the founders of the True Dutch Reformed Church—all assumed comparable conservative positions in response to the activism of the "Evangelical united front." Similar movements could be found among Baptists, Methodists, and Roman Catholics as well. The traditionalist emphases of these movements varied according to the denomination involved. But among the Old School Presbyterians, at least, High Church views were defined first of all in terms of strict confessionalism.[42]

Charles Hodge, whose Princeton party had at last, in 1837, joined the Old School purge, summarized the denominationalists' argument. Responding to Absalom Peters' plea for voluntary societies, Hodge conceded that for certain activities, such as those sponsored by the Bible and Tract Societies and the Sunday School Union, interdenominational cooperation was quite proper. Other activities, however, only the Church could properly perform. These included education of the ministry and supervision of their work, either as pastors or missionaries. Such supervision was necessary to preserve the Church from theological error, and only the Church itself could perform it properly. Hodge knew that this line of reasoning would be opposed by New School Presbyterians who considered the "united front" Protestantism's brightest hope. "People

41. Nathan S. S. Beman, *Review and Vindication* (New York, 1831), quoted in Earl R. MacCormac, "Missions and the Presbyterian Schism of 1837," *Church History* 32(March 1963):39.

42. Cf. Smith et. al., *American Christianity,* 2:66–74.

may cry out against all this as high churchism," he observed, but
"it is Presbyterianism."[43]

The question of cooperation with voluntary societies was an
explosive issue in the Presbyterian Assembly in the years preceding
the division. Though not in itself the primary cause of the schism,
it carried with it major practical considerations.[44] Large sums of
money were involved; and many Presbyterian ministers depended
on the societies for financial support. Of the organizations concerned, the American Home Missionary Society (A.H.M.S.) which
supported nearly one-half the Presbyterian ministers west of the
Alleghenies, affected the work of the Church most directly. Most
of the employees of the A.H.M.S. in these western areas identified
with the New School.[45] Part of the Old School strategy was to
cut off this source of supply for the New School party. At the
Assembly of 1837 they succeeded. The Assembly admonished both
the A.H.M.S. and the American Education Society to cease operations within its churches. Then, to complete the victory, it established its own Board of Foreign Missions as well.[46] In practical
terms these actions were nearly as momentous a blow to the New
School party as the acts of excision. According to the New School
protest, "more than four hundred ambassadors of Christ, within
our bounds, depend on one of these societies (the A.H.M.S.) for
their support. Many more than this number of churches depend
on the same society for the stated ordinances of the gospel."[47]
Such figures would account for over a third of the ministers and

43. [Charles Hodge], "Review of *A Plea for Voluntary Societies* . . .," in
Biblical Repertory and Princeton Review 9(1837):112–14, in Smith et al.,
American Christianity, 2:90–92.

44. These are the conclusions of Earl R. MacCormac, "Missions and the
Presbyterian Schism," p. 43.

45. See, for example, the case study of the controversy in the Indianapolis
Presbytery in Rudolph, *Hoosier Zion,* pp. 122–36.

46. *Minutes, 1837,* pp. 419, 452.

47. "Protest" (June 5, 1837, signed by Absalom Peters and others), in
Minutes, 1837, p. 489.

churches that subsequently affiliated with the New School denomination.

The actions of the Old School Assembly of 1837 in abandoning the independent societies also had disastrous consequences for the work of the "Evangelical united front" in America. Zebulon Crocker, a Congregational witness to the fateful proceedings, expressed the sense of catastrophe, "In addition to the dismemberment of its own body, it struck a blow at benevolent institutions, long cherished and highly valued by multitudes, who had made them the channel of communicating blessings to their fellowmen."[48] Charles I. Foster, the modern historian of the "Evangelical united front," evaluated the effect in even more striking terms. Concluding his study with an account of the Presbyterian schism, he states cryptically, "The united front had ended."[49]

THE PERILS OF REVIVALISM

The positions of the two schools regarding the "evangelical empire" were closely tied to their attitudes toward the revivals— the heart of the evangelical awakening.[50] Throughout the controversy both sides were acutely aware that the real question was the salvation of souls. Out of this concern grew the doctrinal debate. Members of the Old School saw souls imperiled by false teaching. New School partisans, on the other hand, were willing to indulge in doctrinal innovation if men's eternal salvation could be effected more readily. The theologies of Hopkins and Taylor were both developed with this primary concern in mind. The content of New School revival preaching was, therefore, the issue most intimately related to the doctrinal issues in the division. Added to this was a practical concern. Increasingly, evangelists in New School areas

48. Crocker, *The Catastrophe,* p. 2.
49. Foster, *United Front,* p. 273.
50. For the best accounts of the "new measures" for revival in New School areas, see Cross, *Burned-over District;* and William G. McLoughlin, Jr., *Modern Revivalism* (New York, 1959).

were adopting new methods of exciting their audiences to conversion, and these methods, said the Old School, compounded their theological errors.

"The errors of the New Divinity may, to many, seem of no practical importance," wrote Old School historian Samuel Baird, "but the results following are, the ruin of souls, and the desolation of the churches." Such complaints represented the heart of the Old School objection to the New School's tolerance of new theological views. To Old School men, the New School's theology seemed inevitably associated with the notorious "new measures" of revival. "What had been the result upon the Church?" asked Baird,

> Unconverted persons, who were of a susceptible disposition and tender conscience, have been wrought up to an intense state of excitement. This, according to a well-known law of the human mind, which refuses, permanently, to sustain excessive emotion, of any kind, has suddenly given place to apathy. The subject of it is *"broken down,"* and a transition is realized, which is supposed to be a change of heart. Others, more self-confident, have accepted the terms of salvation, presented to them; by electing Jesus as King, and determining, henceforward to be on his side. They have "made themselves new hearts." Thus, the impenitent are deceived. The Church is filled with false professors.

"Such," Baird concluded, "were the fruits, widely realized in Western New York, from the New Haven theology."[51]

Western New York was the center of the agitation over revivals. There, sensational evangelism had developed primarily in the Presbyterian Church, although it soon crossed denominational lines.[52] Charles G. Finney was most responsible for the introduction of the "new measures" into the Presbyterian Church in New York state. Licensed by the Oneida Presbytery in 1824, Finney began conducting revivals that were sensational both in their methods and their success. His vulgar language, theatrical gestures, and the

51. Baird, *New School,* pp. 233–34.
52. Cross, *Burned-over District,* p. 196.

general lack of dignity shocked men of conservative tastes. "Dignity indeed!" cried Finney, "Just the language of the devil!"[53] He preached in the idiom of the people, putting pressure on the sinner in language he could not fail to understand. "There is not a fiend in hell, nor out of hell, so bad as you are," he shouted.[54] Finney increased the pressure by public prayer-meetings, where the unconverted gathered to plead for salvation. The conservative men, shocked even at allowing women to speak in such assemblies, were scandalized when the evangelist added the "anxious bench," on which seekers gathered in the front of the congregation to be exhorted, often by name, to repentance.[55]

At first, New England revival leaders, including Lyman Beecher himself, opposed the "new measures," fearing repetition of the excesses associated with the first Great Awakening and the more recent revivals on the Kentucky frontier. But at the suggestion of Nathan S. S. Beman, a friend of Finney and a renowned New School pastor in Troy, New York, the leaders of each side met at New Lebanon, New York, in 1827. Though the results of this conference were indecisive, Finney himself was more restrained in subsequent years.[56]

Despite earlier reservations, however, Lyman Beecher again best represented the consensus of the New School party. Writing in 1829 to Asahel Nettleton, a conservative Congregationalist evangelist who resisted the "new measures," Beecher argued:

> There is such an amount of truth and power in the preaching of Mr. Finney, and so great an amount of good hopefully done, that if he can be so far restrained as that he shall do more good than evil, then it would be dangerous to oppose him, lest at

53. Quoted in Baird, *New School,* p. 226.

54. Charles G. Finney, *Lectures on Revivals of Religion,* p. 133, quoted in Cross, *Burned-over District,* p. 181.

55. Cross, *Burned-over District,* pp. 173–83; Baird, *New School,* pp. 226–33.

56. Robert Hastings Nichols, *Presbyterianism in New York State,* edited and completed by James Hastings Nichols (Philadelphia, 1963), p. 99.

length we might be found to fight against God; for though some
revivals may be so badly managed as to be worse than none, there
may, to a certain extent, be great imperfections in them, and yet
they be, on the whole, blessings to the Church.[57]

Old School leaders would not agree that erroneous measures
should continue in order that the evidences of grace might abound.
While they might admit that some genuine conversions were
wrought through these means of revivalism, they considered the
methods too dangerous to be tolerated. A large part of their objection arose from their observation that these revivals were very often
associated with errors in theology. Particularly, they said, the new
evangelistic preaching placed an unwarrantable emphasis on the
sinner's ability and responsibility to choose either good or evil. They
objected to the "new measures" on the same grounds. The "new
measures" were designed to increase the pressure on the individual
to make a self-conscious and immediate choice to accept Christ.
This emphasis on the sinner's active choice, the Old School asserted,
implicitly denied the role of the Holy Spirit as the exclusive agent
of regeneration. In 1833 Samuel Miller of Princeton Theological
Seminary stated this connection between the "new measures" and
the New Divinity clearly:

> When this exciting system of calling to "anxious seats,"—calling
> out into the aisles to be "prayed for," &c., is connected, as, to
> my certain knowledge, it often has been, with erroneous doctrines;
> —for example, with the declaration that nothing is *easier,* than
> conversion:—that the power of the Holy Spirit is not necessary
> to enable impenitent sinners to repent and believe;—that if they
> only resolve to be for God—resolve to be Christians—*that* itself
> is regeneration—the work is already done:—I say, where the sys-

57. Lyman Beecher in a letter to Asahel Nettleton, May 28, 1828, in Lyman
Beecher, *Autobiography, Correspondence, etc., of Lyman Beecher,* ed. Charles
Beecher (New York, 1865), 2:106.

tem of "anxious seats," &c., is connected with such doctrinal statements as these, it appears to be adapted to destroy souls whole-
sale![58]

Actually, considerable common ground existed between the two
Schools on the questions of revivals. Old School men were not
opposed to revivals as such. At the Assembly of 1837, for example,
they explicity affirmed that the presence of counterfeit revivals only
increased their ardor for genuine revivals of religion.[59] On the
other side, the members of the New School were not advocates of
all the "new measures," nor did they condone all the new doctrines
associated with the revivals. The doctrinal declaration of the
Auburn Convention acknowledged that in connection with the
excitement of extensive revivals there were some "indiscretions,"
"errors and irregularities," and that "in the attempt to avoid a
ruinous practical antinomianism, human obligation is sometimes
urged in a manner that favors Arminian errors," although these
"errors and irregularities have never been sanctioned by these
synods or presbyteries."[60] James Richards, the chairman of that
convention, privately admitted that in the excitements of the revivals conducted by Finney and his associates "things were said
and done which had better have been avoided." He even acknowledged candidly that there was some ground for the "apprehensions
that some were departing from the faith once delivered to the
saints."[61]

The one doctrine associated particularly with the revivals in upstate New York that both Schools agreed in condemning was
perfectionism. The revivalists, imbued with strong elements of

58. Samuel Miller, *Letters to Presbyterians* (Philadelphia, 1833), quoted in
Foster, *United Front*, pp. 262–63.
59. "Circular Letter," *Minutes, 1837*, p. 508.
60. "The Auburn Declaration," in Armstrong et al., *Presbyterian Enterprise*,
p. 167.
61. James Richards in a letter to the Reverend J. C. Stiles, November 13,
1838, in Richards, *Lectures*, p. 55.

moralism themselves, sought from their converts tangible signs of a change of heart in a life filled with good works. With the evangelists' emphasis on man's ability and responsibility to do good, they found much in common with the position of their Methodist colleagues, who held that man, under divine influence, could and should strive to grow toward moral perfection. Soon Presbyterian itinerants were taking the next step to the more extreme perfectionist view that man actually could reach such a perfect state in this life.[62] Charles Finney himself was apparently contemplating moderate perfectionism when he left Presbyterianism. Other Presbyterian evangelists were less discreet and met firm opposition from Old School and New School alike.

The most notorious of such revivalists was Luther Myrick, an imitator of Finney, who preached over the central part of the state from 1830 to 1834. In 1833, the Oneida Presbytery, a presbytery in the Plan of Union Synod of Geneva, suspended him for his perfectionist views. The Presbyteries of Cayuga and Onondaga, of the same synod, issued a circular warning against him. Among the errors alleged against Myrick were that he taught "that all such professors as have any remaining sin are not born of God, but are going to hell."[63] James Boyle, another Oneida Presbytery evan-

62. Chapter 13 of the Westminster Confession of Faith says on this subject: "This sanctification is throughout the whole man, yet imperfect in this life: there abideth still some remnants of corruption in every part, whence ariseth a continual and irreconcilable war, the flesh lusting against the spirit, and the spirit against the flesh. . . . In which war, although the remaining corruption for a time may much prevail, yet through the continual supply of strength from the sanctifying Spirit of Christ, the regenerate part doth overcome: and so the saints grow in grace, perfecting holiness in the fear of God." From Schaff, *Creeds of Christendom,* 3:629–30.

63. James Wood, "Facts and Observations Concerning the Organization and State of the Churches in the Three Synods of Western New York, and the Synod of Western Reserve" (Saratoga Springs, N.Y., 1837), quoted in Brown, *Vindication,* p. 59. Wood's pamphlet is a strongly biased Old School report, and the above quotation may fall in the category of observations, rather than that of facts. Other information on Myrick is found in Nichols, *Presbyterianism,* pp. 102–03, and in Cross, *Burned-over District,* pp. 191–93.

gelist holding perfectionist views, was suspended in 1835, then deposed and excommunicated.[64] Boyle and Myrick were both morally suspect for their associations with a wing of extreme perfectionists who were apparently moving in a very practical way toward advocating free love as an expression of their perfect spirituality.[65]

Clearly, perfectionist doctrines were not welcome in the Presbyterian Church, even within the most solidly New School areas. James Richards, who lived in Auburn, within the Synod of Geneva, denied outright that "the doctrine of sinless perfection, and other absurd notions" had taken root in the synods of New York state.[66] Even James Wood, a critical observer and propagandist for the Old School, could find in 1837 only scattered evidence of perfectionist beliefs among Presbyterians in these areas. Nearly all the perfectionism that he uncovered was confined to laymen, and even the ministers who held New Haven views were opposed to it.[67]

Despite the measure of agreement between the members of the Old and New Schools in condemning the extremes of doctrine and practice manifested in the revivals, the area of disagreement remained great. Neither the practice of revivalism itself, nor the occasional excesses that it involved, were the issues that divided the two Schools. The real issue was the proper content of the appeal that the evangelist or pastor could make to the members of his congregation. Could he tell the sinner who was deeply concerned about the state of his soul, "Choose Christ this day"? Or must he risk discouraging the sinner by telling him that it is God alone who chooses those whom he will save and that without the gracious

64. Nichols, *Presbyterianism*, p. 103.

65. See Cross, *Burned-over District*, pp. 238–49, for an account of these activities culminating in the sexual communism of John Humphrey Noyes's Oneida community. The exact nature of the connection of Boyle and Myrick with this movement is not entirely clear.

66. James Richards in a letter to the Rev. J. C. Stiles, November 13, 1838, in Richards, *Lectures*, p. 55.

67. Wood, "Facts and Observations," in Brown, *Vindication*, pp. 57–60.

regenerating work of the Holy Spirit the sinner can do nothing
toward his salvation? Here, the seeming abstract theological question took on an intensely practical significance.

NEW SCHOOL THEOLOGY AND THE DIVISION

"We should be unfaithful to the trust reposed in us," the Old
School Assembly of 1837 declared, "were we not to cry aloud and
proclaim a solemn warning against opinions so corrupt and delu-
sive." For them, detection of theological error within the church
was far from a theoretical question.[68] It involved the most important issue they knew—men's eternal destiny. They were persuaded
"that such errors cannot fail, in their ultimate effect, to subvert the
foundation of Christian hope, and destroy the souls of men."
Granted, there were many other considerations; but to the Old
School the presence of "unscriptural, radical, and highly dangerous" doctrines far outweighed all others.[69]

Throughout the controversy, the strict Old School men insisted
that the New School party was riddled with heresy. In the Old
School "Testimony and Memorial" of 1837 they listed sixteen specific errors allegedly taught in the New School, and they claimed to
have "conclusive proof" that these were "widely disseminated in
the Presbyterian Church."[70] These accusations, framed in the heat
of bitter controversy and produced to justify unprecedented ecclesiastical procedure, were undoubtedly somewhat overstated. Nevertheless, they reflected a considerable element of truth as well.
Clearly, some in the New School group were sympathetic to theological views essentially like those of Nathaniel Taylor. On the
question of *tolerance* of such error, the Old School was quite correct, and from their point of view the division could be justified on

68. For the best accounts of the details of the doctrinal controversies, see
Pope, "New England Calvinism"; and Baird, *New School*.
69. "Circular Letter," *Minutes, 1837*, p. 504.
70. "Testimony and Memorial," in Brown, *Vindication*, pp. 217–18. These
errors are listed in "The Auburn Declaration," Appendix 2, below.

these grounds alone. Two considerations, however, must be kept in mind in assessing the realities of the doctrinal issue in the division. The first is that the Old School never did establish that the alleged errors were "widely prevalent" in the New School areas. The available evidence indicates rather that many in the New School party had not ventured beyond moderate Edwardsean or Hopkinsian positions, and others had never departed from strict Presbyterian orthodoxy. The second consideration is that the New School exponents of the more controversial views almost always avoided any outright expression of the most questionable implications that the Old School drew out of their statements.

Accurate estimates of the prevalence of the disputed views within the New School areas are extremely difficult to find. The two parties in 1837 disagreed on the definition of heresy, and each had an interest in obscuring the actual numbers. Probably, however, the most judicious estimates came from the moderate Princeton party, which prior to 1837 attacked the "Pelagianism" of New Haven but refused to identify all New England theology as heresy. Holding such middle ground, they had little reason to distort the facts. In their judgment relatively few Presbyterians held the New Haven views. Samuel Miller estimated in 1833 that "nineteen-twentieths of our ministry and eldership are not liable, in any considerable degree to the charge in question." In 1836 Charles Hodge concurred, stating that the New Haven party was "very inconsiderable as to numbers."[71] These estimates stand up well under scrutiny. Analysis of the education of New School pastors indicates that the overwhelming majority were trained in the moderate New England views, rather than in those of New Haven.[72] Nevertheless, in a day of fine theological distinctions, even one in twenty

71. Samuel Miller, *A Letter of the Rev. Samuel Miller . . . on the Present Crisis in . . . Religious and Theological Concerns* (Hartford, 1833), p. 5. [Charles Hodge], "The General Assembly of 1836," *Princeton Review* 8(July 1836):458.

72. See Marsden, "The New School Presbyterian Mind," pp. 94–97, for some supporting statistics.

who departed from the prevailing standards indicated a considerable trend.

The New School, of course, denied any real danger in such a trend, pointing out that the Old School exaggerated the implications of the disputed teachings. At their Auburn Assembly in 1837 the excluded group insisted that the doctrinal "errors" sometimes associated with revivals were exceptions to their general doctrinal soundness and that such "indiscretions" were consistently opposed by New School synods and presbyteries. To support this claim they adopted a doctrinal statement contrasting a list of sixteen "true doctrines" with the sixteen "errors" alleged against them by the Old School. The Auburn Declaration, they claimed, represented the "prevalent sentiments" in New School areas.[73] It defined for the New School also the limits of doctrinal innovation, becoming after 1837 virtually the unofficial creed of the denomination.

As is true of most successful creeds, the Auburn Declaration represented a compromise. It allowed moderate New England teachings that would not necessarily contradict the essentials of the Westminster Confession, while it clearly excluded the most objectionable errors alleged by the Old School.

The crucial issue, as always, was the nature of unregenerate men. The Old School claimed that New School evangelists were informing impenitent sinners that they were "in full possession of all the ability necessary to a full compliance with all the commands of God." Such teaching, they charged, made regeneration "the act of the sinner himself" and reduced the work of the Holy Spirit (as Taylor had suggested) to "a persuasive exhibition of the truth, analogous to the influence which one man exerts over the mind of another." Each of the accused New School men in the trials before the schism denied such an implication of his teachings, and on this point the delegates to the Auburn Assembly were unequivocal. While maintaining that "sinners have all the faculties

73. "The Auburn Declaration," in Amrstrong et al., *Presbyterian Enterprise,* p. 167.

necessary to a perfect moral agency" and so were justly held accountable for their sins, the delegates affirmed that "such is [sinners'] love of sin and opposition to God and his law, that, independently of the renewing influence or almighty energy of the Holy Spirit, they never will comply with the commands of God." Regeneration, they declared, was not produced by an act of the sinner himself, but rather was an "instantaneous" and "radical change of heart, produced by the special operations of the Holy Spirit."

Even on the less explosive doctrines of original sin and the imputation of Adam's guilt, the Auburn Assembly took a relatively conservative position. "Original sin," their declaration said, "is a natural bias to evil, resulting from the first apostacy, leading invariably and certainly to actual transgression." The common-sense argument that if sin is an act, it is not transferable was still implicit; but contrary to much of New England theology, the doctrine of imputation was not totally abandoned. Though "the sin of Adam is not imputed to his posterity in the sense of a literal transfer of personal qualities, acts, and demerit," because of that sin "the race are treated as if they had sinned."[74] The Auburn Declaration's moderation on this point may be contrasted to the position of Albert Barnes, who asserted in his disputed Romans commentary that the penalties to the race resulting from Adam's sin refer only "to the fact that men sin *in their own persons, sin themselves*—as indeed, how *can* they *sin* in any other way?"[75]

Even the members of the strict Old School party were impressed by the moderation of the Auburn Declaration. Robert J. Breckinridge, one of the chief promoters of the division, admitted this grudgingly in a speech before the Old School Assembly of 1842. "This extraordinary party," said Breckinridge, "could not lay aside

74. Ibid., pp. 167–71. See Appendix 2, below, for a complete list of "errors" and "true doctrines" from the Declaration.

75. Albert Barnes, *Notes Explanatory and Practical, on the Epistle to the Romans* (New York, 1846), pp. 116–17.

its moral characteristics; and after doing so much to destroy the church and corrupt its faith, they drew up and recorded a confession not only at direct variance with their own published declarations, but more orthodox than many who dreaded and opposed them ever held.[76]

No doubt the New School was somewhat overzealous in depicting its doctrinal purity. In the midst of such bitter debate the widely divergent claims of the two sides must be balanced against each other. The New School denomination, nevertheless, did seem determined both to prove and to maintain its claims to Presbyterian constitutionality. "We hazard nothing by the assertion," they declared at their first General Assembly, "that the orthodoxy and energy of our churches, sessions, and presbyteries . . . are not exceeded any where in the bounds of the visible church."[77] Indeed, there was some plausible basis for this extravagant assertion. Following old Puritan practices, the nineteenth-century Presbyterian evangelicals imposed rigid requirements for church membership. Applicants had to present clear testimony to a personal experience of a "saving change of heart"[78] and were at the same time required to subscribe to a church covenant in which they pledged moral purity and mutual vigilance. Furthermore, they had to accept an abbreviated Confession of Faith containing the main headings of the Reformed system of doctrine. A New School committee appointed by the 1838 Assembly to investigate these abbreviated confessions reported that, contrary to Old School accusations, only two churches in Plan of Union areas had altered their creeds so as to be at variance with the Westminster Confession. These two were ordered to conform to the rest.[79]

Such moves toward doctrinal vigilance marked the beginning

76. Quoted by George Duffield, "Doctrines of the New School Presbyterian Church," *Bibliotheca Sacra* 20(July 1863):634.

77. New School *Minutes, 1838,* p. 672.

78. Ibid., *1839,* p. 33.

79. Ibid., p. 18.

of a trend that was changing the spirit of the New School movement. Increasingly its concerns would be denominational. The aggressive phalanx that had marched in the front ranks of American evangelical Protestantism, now thrown on the defensive, was forced to became distinctly Presbyterian. Instead of asserting its rights, it had to defend its constitutionality and prove its orthodoxy. Much of its progressive momentum was lost as its adherents continually looked back to their momentous struggle with the Old School for much of their defense and vindication. Doctrinal investigation continued, but with the continuing claims to orthodoxy, radical theological change was discouraged. Theological innovation was never a primary goal of the American evangelical movement. New doctrines were important only as they served practical ends, and under denominational pressures, moderation, not liberalism, marked their theological stance.

The trend toward moderation was paralleled in the development of the practical concerns of the evangelical movement as well. Effective evangelical social reform was not possible if the reforming zeal was channeled entirely outside the walls of existing denominational structures. Yet in the case of the potentially most significant evangelical social reform—antislavery—the denominations proved to be structured only for moderation, not for radical reform.

4

The Abolition of Black Slavery

Uncompromising abolitionism became the maverick of the benevolent reforms in American churches. Just as the terrible institution of black slavery was the bastard son in the American republic, so the movement for its abolition was only uneasily adopted into the nation's religious life. Wherever the intractable abolitionists' campaigns appeared, Christian brotherhood and unity nearly disappeared. Division and violence trailed the movement from beginning to end. Though some American evangelicals contributed much to awakening the conscience of the North, the outcome of their efforts was at best a tragic victory.

In his provocative analysis of American slavery, Stanley Elkins suggests that one of the causes of the failure of Americans to resolve the sectional crisis peacefully was a breakdown of effective national institutions, including the churches. Evangelical reformers, Elkins further suggests, because of their characteristic unwillingness to compromise morally, failed in their efforts to carry out their programs through national religious institutions.[1] The absolutistic moralism of the independent antislavery agencies left little room for support from Northern moderates, and only drove the South into its extreme defensive stance. In the national denominations a strong abolitionist stand invariably brought only a division between North and South.

1. Stanley M. Elkins, *Slavery: A Problem in American Institutional and Intellectual Life* (Chicago, 1959).

Another factor may be added to explain the failure of the institutional churches to make a truly significant contribution to the peaceful resolution of the slavery problem. American Protestant denominations are, in general, too democratic for effective social action. The republican ideals of the rights of the individual and the right of dissent were by the early nineteenth century too deeply engrained to be excluded from American religious life. As a result, with only a few exceptions, American denominations have been unable to legislate effectively among their own members for reforms of any wide social implications. Often they have participated in important reform movements, but seldom have they been ahead of popular political reforms. They can hardly expect to be. The republican ideology demands that the denominations follow, rather than lead, their constituencies. If the constituency is significantly divided, as is nearly bound to be the case on crucial social issues, effective denominational reform is impossible. Dissenters from the majority opinion, viewing the church as a free agency, which they have every right to leave, in the face of institutional pressure will simply leave. Preaching and propaganda may, of course, alter social mores; but the American denominations as institutions lack any power to effect social revolution. This institutional impotence is classically illustrated in the antislavery campaigns where Christians did attempt to lead a major social revolution during an era when they were remarkably successful in many minor campaigns.

In the Presbyterian Church, which appeared to have both the machinery and the leadership for effective action, all these inherent weaknesses in the evangelical abolition efforts are particularly conspicuous. Presbyterians spoke against slavery early and often. In 1787, when Revolutionary idealism was still strong, the Synod of New York and Philadelphia (forerunner of the General Assembly) declared its high approval of "the general principles in favour of universal liberty that prevail in America, and the interest which many of the states have taken in promoting the abolition of slavery." The position of the Synod was, however, moderate. Acknowledging the dangers of freeing the Negro population, it urged masters to educate their slaves in preparation for eventual emancipation. Though the Synod encouraged all Presbyterians to work "to procure eventually the final abolition of slavery in America," it cautioned that these efforts should be "the most prudent . . . , consistent with the interests of the state of civil society."[2]

This initial declaration, republished by the General Assembly in 1793, set the essential pattern for the official Presbyterian stand on slavery until the eve of the Civil War. The Church would in various ways reaffirm its commitment to abolition, but in deference to its Southern constituency would refuse to give their sentiments any other force than advice.[3] The alternative, often proposed, was to order discipline and possible excommunication of slaveholding members. At the first suggestion of this course, in 1795, the Assembly declined, advising rather that members with differing views on slavery "should live in charity and peace, according to the doctrine and practice of the Apostles."[4]

The General Assembly made its strongest and most comprehensive statement in 1818. Slavery, the Assembly declared, was a sin of the first order, being "a gross violation of the most precious and sacred rights of nature," "utterly inconsistent with the law of God," "totally irreconcilable with the spirit and principles of the Gospel of Christ," and a source of "all the hardships and injuries which inhumanity and avarice may suggest." The Assembly urged that it was "manifestly the duty of all Christians . . . as speedily as possible to efface this blot on our holy religion, and to obtain the complete abolition of slavery throughout Christendom, and if possible throughout the world."[5]

2. *Digest of the General Assembly of the Presbyterian Church in the United States of America* . . . (Philadelphia, 1820), pp. 338–39 (hereafter cited as *Digest*).

3. This is essentially the same interpretation as that of Andrew E. Murray, *Presbyterians and the Negro—A History* (Philadelphia, 1966).

4. *Digest*, p. 340. Similar proposals brought the same response in 1815.

5. Ibid., pp. 341–43.

This 1818 declaration, adopted unanimously, was in subsequent years widely cited as evidence of the denomination's historic dedication to abolition.[6] The impression is, however, somewhat misleading. The unanimity was possible only because the declaration was a compromise over a hotly contested issue. The Assembly, since 1815, had been plagued by the case of an uncompromising Virginia abolitionist, the Reverend James Bourne. Bourne twice had been deposed by the Lexington, Virginia, Presbytery primarily for his inflammatory demands for discipline against some of his fellow ministers who owned slaves. The Assembly in 1815 had refused such demands, and although in 1817 it ordered a retrial concerning Bourne's first deposition, it sustained the Lexington Presbytery's action in 1818, just before adopting its famous resolution. The declaration itself contained the marks of this compromise. While with evident sincerity urging eventual abolition, the Assembly at the same time denounced those who indulged in "harsh censures, and uncharitable reflection on their brethren" who were slaveholders working for gradual emancipation. Most of its Southern constituents, the Assembly affirmed, favored such a gradual course. Reflecting the prevalent sentiments of the North also, the unanimous Assembly asked no more. A good case could be made to show that the slaves were not prepared for immediate freedom, and so the prudent commissioners advised against "emancipating them in such a manner as they will be likely to destroy themselves and others." Discipline against slaveholders, a significant portion of the constituency, was considered uncharitable. The only punitive measure urged was against those who sold a fellow Presbyterian against his will.[7]

The moderate course charted by the General Assembly was in

6. See, for example, Albert Barnes, *The Church and Slavery* (Philadelphia, 1857), p. 57; and Smith et al., *American Christianity* 2:179. This mistaken impression was generally accepted until recently exploded by Murray, *Presbyterians and the Negro*, pp. 20–28, based on the work of John W. Christie. The following interpretation is based on Murray's.

7. *Digest*, pp. 341–47.

full accord with the prevailing evangelical sentiments of the day. These sentiments were evidenced in the policy of the "benevolent empire's" American Colonization Society, founded in 1817. The Colonization Society was already gaining wide support both from the North and the Upper South by combining the interests of the slaves with a plausible solution to the anticipated problems of a free Negro population. The Presbyterian General Assembly, the first ecclesiastical body officially to endorse the colonization movement, expressed these balanced concerns in recommending the Society. "In the distinctive and indelible marks of their colour, and the prejudices of the people," said the Assembly, "an insuperable obstacle has been placed to the execution of any plan for elevating their character, and placing them on a footing with their brethren of the same common family."[8] Throughout the relatively peaceful 1820s the evangelicals' colonization scheme received solid support from all segments in the Presbyterian Church. Among the subsequent Old School group, which as yet had not rejected "united front" organizations, Archibald Alexander and Samuel Miller of Princeton and Robert J. Breckenridge of Kentucky, the chief engineer of the division, were staunch champions of colonization. The nascent New School could look back as far as 1776, when the benevolent-minded Samuel Hopkins first suggested colonization. In the 1820s virtually all members of the emerging party were devoted to the colonization project.

Colonization was a popular reform because it did not seem to hurt anyone. By about 1830, however, evidence was growing that it was not doing anyone much good either. Though the Society prospered, its funds could not sustain a rate of exportation that could compete with the Negro birth rate. Moreover, the word was passing among the blacks themselves that the Liberian colony was not the Promise Land. The futility of the campaign was becoming widely suspected.

8. Ibid., p. 347, from the 1819 minutes. The Colonization Society was recommended in the 1818 statement as well.

The result was that in the early 1830s the antislavery movement took a turn, much like the nearly simultaneous change in the temperance campaign, and shifted to a less compromising abolitionist position. When immediate steps toward abolition were thus seriously proposed, the nearly insuperable difficulties inherent in the cause came to the surface, and the relative harmony of the evangelical camp was turned into dissonance.

Slavery and the Presbyterian Schism

The sharp change in the tempo of the antislavery crusade coincided closely with the rise of hostilities between Old and New School Presbyterians. Because of this coincidence, together with the heat of the Presbyterian debates over slavery, a few interpreters have suggested that slavery was the real underlying cause of the 1837 division (see Appendix 1). However, although slavery indeed played a major role in shaping the course of the division, the suggestion that it was the primary cause is untenable for two reasons. First, the New School party itself was by no means united in support of immediate abolition. Secondly, the Northern Old School leaders who effected the division had only a slight concern over the antislavery position found among New School adherents.

The division within the New School over the radical antislavery movement reveals the tensions that beset this evangelical reform. Though William Lloyd Garrison, Boston's self-styled liberator of the South, took most of the credit for introducing the new phase of the movement, the most effective leaders were very closely tied to the existing evangelical "empire," and hence to Presbyterianism.[9] As was true of most of the "isms" of the day, abolitionism drew much of its strength from Western New York; and as was true of most New School supported "isms," abolitionism grew out of the revivals associated with Charles G. Finney. The apostle

9. This is the interpretation of Gilbert Barnes, *Antislavery Impulse,* on which the following account of Weld's activities and the Lane Seminary dispute is largely based.

of the abolition movement was Theodore Dwight Weld (1803–95), a convert of Finney's New York state campaigns. In alliance with Arthur Tappan, who provided substantial financial support, Weld consolidated much of the force of evangelicalism behind the abolitionist cause.

The most immediate major division within the New School Presbyterian camp came in the famous contest between Weld and Lyman Beecher at Lane Seminary. Weld, a student approaching thirty, actually had been more influential than Beecher in establishing the seminary. Beginning a search for an evangelical academic center in the West in 1831, Weld had discovered Lane Seminary, which until then had only a charter and a site for a campus. Weld then sold the idea to Arthur Tappan, who in turn secured Lyman Beecher to give the new institution prestige. Beecher at the time was thought to be a firm friend of abolition. By 1833, when he arrived in Cincinnati, however, the radical abolitionists were in the process of perpetrating a complete break with colonization, which they now considered a compromise with heinous sin. Beecher, always for evangelical cooperation, was loath to repudiate the brethren who still favored colonization and insisted that the two movements work side by side. During February 1834 Weld sponsored at the seminary two weeks of revival-like debates, at which he converted much of the student body to his uncompromising abolitionist position. The enthusiastic converts formed their own antislavery society and worked fervently to improve the condition of free Negroes in Cincinnati. Popular prejudice against any form of immediate abolition was immense, and quickly the students gained local notoriety. The school's board of trustees, meeting the next summer, reacted predictably. They banned the antislavery society and moved to censor student meetings. Beecher was off in the East at the time of the decision, but when he returned in the fall he stood substantially with the board's decision. Fifty-one students left, mostly to go to Oberlin, where abolitionist Asa Mahan became president. This time Arthur Tappan secured prestige for this latest abolitionist institution by prevailing on Charles Finney to become Professor of Theology. Beecher, the patriarch of reform, reacted somewhat bitterly. Still dedicated to both abolition and colonization, he deplored "the few he-goat men, who think they do God service by butting every thing in the line of their march." He even went so far as to revive an old prejudice against Finney, suggesting that the radicals were the "offspring of the Oneida denunciatory revivals."[10]

Weld was the chief of the "he-goat men." By 1834 he had become the most successful agent of the new American Anti-Slavery Society. During the next several years he traveled endlessly through the North preaching the Society's doctrine of "immediate abolition, gradually accomplished," assuring his hearers that slavery was a sin that deserved eradication and nothing else. Wherever he went, even in the western New York heartland of the revival, riots followed, but converts were won.

Among New School Presbyterians, despite Beecher's defection to moderation, the abolitionists had some important friends, including Albert Barnes in Philadelphia and Nathan S. S. Beman in New York. Many others, it was clear, could be gained through education to the new approach. With this intent Weld went to the General Assembly of 1835 to lobby for abolition. Two years earlier the Assembly had reiterated its frequent urgings of support for the Colonization Society, and in 1834, so far as Weld knew, only two commissioners had favored emancipation as an immediate duty. Through his efforts at the 1835 meeting Weld claimed to have raised the number of commissioners "decidedly with us on the subject of slavery" to forty-seven, "nearly *one fourth part of the* Assembly!"[11] A committee was appointed to consider the

10. Lyman Beecher in a letter to William Beecher, *Autobiography,* 2:260.
11. Quoted in Thompson, *Presbyterians in the South,* 1:384. The following account of slavery and the Assembly of 1836–37 is based largely on Thompson, 1:384–412, which is the most complete treatment of the subject.

whole slavery question and to report back to the next Assembly. Southern delegates were becoming uneasy.

At the Assembly of 1836 a division of the Church over slavery was feared. Before the Assembly, the strength of the abolitionists had been claimed to be as high as 150 commissioners; but the solidarity of the New School had been overestimated. Lyman Beecher appeared and once again urged unity between abolition and colonization. More significantly, at least one-third of the majority New School party was unwilling to support any strong stand for abolition. The committee appointed the previous year reported that slavery was recognized by the Bible and that Assembly action on abolition would constitute an unwarranted ecclesiastical interference with state laws. Furthermore, such action would be likely to divide the church. A recommendation "that the whole subject be indefinitely postponed" was carried 154 to 87. The lack of New School unity is indicated by the fact that abolitionists could find only 87 votes on the day after the New School had acquitted Albert Barnes by a vote of 134 to 96.[12]

Nevertheless, the strength of abolitionism appeared in 1836 to be growing steadily, and in the year until the next Assembly the fears of Presbyterians in the South concerning the New School grew to alarm. The complicating factor in evaluating this development is the difficulty in determining whether the sudden enthusiasm of Southerners for the proposed divisive measures of the Old School was due to abolitionism or to a genuine doctrinal concern. Probably it was something of both with the fear of New School abolitionism predominant. In the year between the 1836 and the 1837 Assembly three of the four New School synods that were subsequently expelled passed resolutions demanding that slaveholders be disciplined, and several Southern presbyteries adopted declarations to the contrary. But Southern presbyteries were pass-

---

12. *Minutes, 1836*, pp. 247, 271, 272–73, 268. Nearly all the eighty-seven votes against slavery were cast by men who voted to acquit Barnes.

ing resolutions condemning the New School's doctrinal stance as well.[13] Apparently the strenuous efforts of the militant Old School to demonstrate that the second acquittal of Barnes proved the hopeless apostasy of the New School were having some effect. Southerners who previously had not much direct contact with New School theology were, with the addition of the antislavery threat, becoming champions of strict orthodoxy.

There was a connection, as Old School leaders were quick to point out, between New School theology and abolitionism. Both emphasized the rights of man and his moral obligations. Both seemed to the orthodox to place rationalistic theories concerning man's nature above Biblical precedents. As James Thornwell, the most eloquent of conservative Southern Presbyterian spokesmen, observed, the New School theological heresies had grown out of the same humanistic doctrines of liberty that had inspired the Declaration of Independence.[14] Indeed New School friends of abolition frequently appealed directly to such American republican sentiments. In the defeated abolitionist minority-report on slavery at the 1836 Assembly, for instance, they had urged a declaration of "unwavering and undiminished attachment to those principles of liberty, which are so clearly expressed in the Declaration of Independence . . . that *all men* are by nature free and equal. . . . "[15] A Southern delegate to the next Assembly alleged, in response to such uncritical acceptance of secular standards, that the New School was "perseveringly introducing a new gospel, and with it a new system of moral relations, new grounds of moral obligation, and a new scale of human rights."[16]

By the opening of the General Assembly of 1837, the South had been won solidly into the Old School camp. At the Old School

13. Thompson, *Presbyterians in the South,* 1:388–89.
14. C. Bruce Staiger, "Abolition and the Presbyterian Schism, 1837–38," *Mississippi Valley Historical Review* 36(December 1949):393–94.
15. *Minutes, 1836,* p. 248.
16. Quoted in Staiger, "Abolition," p. 394.

pre-Assembly convention, called to plan strategy for the division, there was considerable concern to prevent any introduction of the antislavery issue that might divide the Old School between North and South. Robert Breckinridge, chief spokesman for the radical Old School and an active moderate antislavery man himself, insisted that the motive for silence was to keep the real issues clear. The 1818 antislavery declaration, said Breckinridge, was a sufficient statement of the church's position. "We cannot eat those words," he told the convention. "But I hope here to settle a great controversy, and not to be embarrassed by the introduction of the problem of slavery. We are a Convention met about doctrine and order—the very quintessence of Presbyterianism."[17] At the Assembly itself, the South remained loyal to the Old School, and the question of slavery was not raised.

Though the slavery issue was not central to the division, the consolidation of the South into the Old School was of major significance. The importance of the Southerners' shift can be seen by comparing the voting pattern at the Assembly of 1837 with that of 1836. In 1836 on the crucial vote to sustain the appeal of Albert Barnes the Southern delegates were sharply divided, 36 voting with the Old School and 26 with the New School. Yet, the next year the Southerners had shifted to overwhelming support of the Old School, favoring the abrogation of the Plan of Union 50 to 9. Without this Southern change, the Assembly of 1837 would have been divided almost exactly evenly. In the vote on the abrogation of the Plan of Union, the Northern delegates supported the New School 101 to 93.[18] If 42 per cent of the Southern

17. "Proceedings of the Convention," *The Presbyterian,* May 20, 1837, p. 77, quoted in Pope, "New England Calvinism," p. 364.

18. For the difficult job of analyzing the voting behavior of the delegates to the two Assemblies, I am indebted to the work of Gary Broekhuisen presented at Calvin College, Grand Rapids, Mich., as a Senior Seminar paper, "The Role of Slavery in the Presbyterian Schism of 1837." Broekhuisen's work indicates that the figures here cited were representative of the voting patterns on the crucial issues at these Assemblies.

delegates had voted with the New School in 1837, as they did in 1836, their vote on the abrogation would have been approximately 34 to 24, thus bringing the total vote to 127 for the Old School and 126 for the New School. Decisive action would hardly have been possible under such circumstances. Thus the Southern vote was indeed the decisive factor in guaranteeing that the Old School could name the time and the terms of the division.

Slavery was, therefore, an important factor in determining the nature of the division, but it was not the primary cause of the division itself. For the Old School Northerners, who engineered the division, slavery was never the primary concern. They showed every intention of freeing themselves from the New School prior to the time that the abolition question was seriously raised and in all probability would have done so eventually even had they remained in the minority.[19]

A question remains as to whether the Old School in the North had betrayed the cause of abolitionism simply as a means of winning Southern support. Clearly, by 1837 the Old School and the South had reached a remarkable understanding in silencing debate on the antislavery issue. Moreover, in subsequent years the Old School denomination declined to go beyond the 1818 pronouncement and continued to recommend contributions to the Colonization Society. Nevertheless, these refusals to take a strong stand do not appear to have been primarily a deal with the Southerners in return for their support of the New School expulsion. Regardless of the Southern alliance, the prevailing attitude in the Old School probably would have been sincere support for gradual emancipation and colonization, together with conscientious refusal to endorse a more radical position. Deeply rooted in the Old School tradition, growing out of Scottish dissent, was the principle that the organized church should not be used to

19. Cf. Elwyn A. Smith, "The Role of the South in the Presbyterian Schism of 1837–38," *Church History* 29(March 1960):60.

legislate on moral issues where the Bible had not spoken explicitly. This attitude was embodied in the Westminster Confession of Faith: "God alone is the Lord of the conscience, and hath left it free from the doctrines and commandments of men which are in any thing contrary to his word, or beside it, in matters of faith or worship."[20] This was the basis of the position taken by Charles Hodge in 1836 at the height of the crisis over the abolition question. According to Hodge, the church should not go beyond Scripture in its declarations. The Scripture do not explicitly condemn slaveholding as a sin. Therefore, he said, "slaveholding is not necessarily sinful," and the church should not pretend to make laws to bind the conscience.[21]

To be sure, Hodge and his Old School supporters emphasized this doctrine just at the moment when it did the most good to gain Southern backing for the Old School cause. But their position was not simply a matter of good politics. It was also a question of principle—a principle that the New School did not share. This is confirmed by the close parallel to the respective positions taken toward the much less explosive issue of total abstinence. The New School Assembly of 1840 adopted a resolution endorsing "the only true principle of temperance—total abstinence from everything that will intoxicate."[22] Hodge and the majority of the Old School opposed such a denominational stand for exactly the same reason that they opposed condemning all slavery as sin—the church should not speak where Scripture is silent.[23]

The antislavery debates reflected the basic differences between the two Schools in facing the great moral issues of the day. The New School stood closer to the spirit of the age with its sense of injustice and outrage at the enslavement of one race by another,

20. Chapter 20, section 2. From Schaff, *Creeds of Christendom*, 3:644.
21. Charles Hodge, "Slavery," *Princeton Review* 7 (April 1836):277.
22. New School *Minutes 1840*, p. 15.
23. "The General Assembly of 1843," *Princeton Review* 15 (July 1843), p. 468.

and its optimism toward the possibilities for social reform. The moral emphases in its theology inclined its adherents to uncompromising support of the humanitarian campaigns. The Old School felt that the New School's repudiation of church tradition had led to extremism in pursuing these otherwise excellent causes. "The restless spirit of *radicalism*," said the Old School Assembly of 1837, "has, in succession, driven to extreme fanaticism the great causes of revivals of religion, of temperance, and of the rights of man."[24]

The New School failed to live up to its alleged radicalism. In subsequent years the New School denomination was only slightly more successful than the Old School in bringing any considerable institutional weight behind the antislavery movement. A few thousand Southerners remained with the New School after 1837–38, and some of these were slaveholders. Their presence was sufficient to stifle any decisive denominational action against slavery for twenty years. During most of that time the New School did little more than attempt to apply the principles of the 1818 declaration, condemning the institution of slavery but not disciplining members who held slaves. For two decades the rights of a tiny minority prevailed.

The ineffectiveness of the New School antislavery reform indicates not only the inherent weaknesses of denominationally sponsored social reforms, but also one of the intellectual dilemmas that plagued the evangelical antislavery movement. Though the evangelical reformers were committed to the general principle that human rights were self-evident truths of common sense, they were at the same time bound to a strong loyalty to divine revelation. Albert Barnes, who became the leading antislavery spokesman in the New School during the 1840s and the 1850s, pointed out the crucial importance of Biblical precedents to the evangelical mind. "The Bible," he said, "is the acknowledged standard of

24. *Minutes, 1837*, p. 507.

morals in this nation. . . and there is not a department of government that would not admit that if the Bible has settled a question,
it is final." The problem, however, was to demonstrate that the
Bible condemned slavery. Barnes had to concede that Christ and
the Apostles had not excluded slaveholders from the church. On
the other hand, he could show that they had not explicitly approved of slavery either. This cleared the ground for his primary
argument—that the Bible revealed general moral principles incompatible with slavery. Citing Francis Wayland, president of
Brown University and the leading evangelical moral philosopher
of the era, Barnes argued that the New Testament reveals in its
doctrine of the brotherhood of believers "that all men are by
nature equal in regards to their rights." Such equality included the
natural rights that slavery denies, like those of marriage, family,
and property. Quoting Wayland, Barnes declared that "the Savior
and his apostles deal with this universal sin" by "promulgating
such truths concerning the nature and destiny of man . . . as should
render the slavery of a human being a manifest moral absurdity;
that is, a notion diametrically opposed to our elementary moral
suggestion." By such an appeal, Scripture and the dictates of Common Sense philosophy seemed to be in full accord. "If a professed
revelation *did* countenance slavery as a desirable institution," said
Barnes, ". . . it would be impossible to convince the mass of mankind that it is from God."[25]

By such appeals to the presumed harmony of divine revelation
and the self-evident truths of common sense, the dilemma created
by the apparent Biblical silence could be resolved. The argument,
however, was convincing only to those already committed to
abolition. Southerners could never be convinced that God had revealed the doom of their peculiar institution. Moreover, not until

25. Albert Barnes, *Inquiry into the Scriptural Views of Slavery* (Philadelphia,
1846), pp. 21, 312, 341. See also ibid., pp. 347–55; and Barnes, *The Church
and Slavery,* pp. 183–84.

the 1850s would the New School take an unequivocal stand for abolition. When it did, the Southern membership simply withdrew. Throughout the era slavery remained one of the most frustrating of the many problems that beset the evangelical cause.[26]

26. Additional information on the New School and slavery after 1838 is found in Chapters 5 and 9, below. A more complete account is to be found in Murray, *Presbyterians and the Negro,* pp. 112–18.

5

The Waning of United Evangelicalism in the New School, 1838-1852

The Evangelical Climate of Opinion

"It is the revealed purpose of God to evangelize the world by the instrumentality of his church," wrote Absalom Peters in 1837, "and both prophecies and providential signs indicate that the time is at hand for the accomplishment of this glorious event." The New School's champion of voluntary societies depicted the mission of the united church in unmistakably apocalyptic terms.

> The *twelve hundred and sixty* prophetic years are drawing to a close; and the day of vengeance is in his heart, because the year of his redeemed is come. The overturnings, which are to bring down the mountains and exalt the valleys, have commenced. The sun is darkened and the moon is blood; and the stars of heaven fall. All the forms of governmental opposition to the gospel are tottering. Pagan, Mahometan and Papal governments are in their dotage; and it is remarkable that, just at this time, christianity, with the vigor of a renewed youth, and armed with all the facilities of modern science, arts, wealth and enterprise, is organizing her legions for the last onset and for certain victory.[1]

1. [Absalom Peters], *Plea for Voluntary Societies,* p. 2. These signs were all considered precursors of the millennial reign of Christ. The duration of the pagan, Mahometan, and papal governments was believed to be revealed as 1,260 years. The Mahometan and papal governments supposedly rose in the seventh century A.D. and were expected to fall in the nineteenth. See Chapter 9, below, for a discussion of the widespread millennial views in American Protestantism of this era.

The array of Christian soldiers who were to usher in the millennium were armed with all the weapons that American culture could provide. All the resources, the arts, the sciences, and the government of the new nation were to be marshaled in support of the crusade to carry the banner of Protestant Christianity to every tribe and nation. The sense of unity and the confidence of the Protestant and reforming civilization are difficult to comprehend for those who have lost the vision. Evangelical Christianity had triumphed over the Enlightenment, or at least it had appropriated all its tools. No aspect of constructive human achievement was excluded from the unified Christian vision. The age of the millennium would bring the reign of Christ and his Church over every aspect of man's spiritual, cultural, and intellectual endeavors.

Absalom Peters, the outstanding New School defender of united efforts for evangelical action, assumed the leadership in ensuring that cultural and intellectual concerns would remain an integral part of the evangelical program. In 1838, in the midst of the Presbyterian crisis, Peters took over the editorship of the *American Biblical Repository,* a major theological and literary journal. Peters proclaimed in his opening editorial that the journal would henceforth provide a new basis for evangelical unity. Christian scholars from all evangelical denominations could unite "in the diligent study of Scriptures apart from the influence of what may be peculiar in their several creeds and confessions." Dialogue in Biblical studies and in other areas of intellectual concern need not endanger "the fundamental doctrines on which it is supposed all Christians are substantially agreed." Nor should theological disputes impede evangelical action. "The present," Peters observed, "is an age not of light and knowledge, but of benevolent actions."[2]

2. Absalom Peters, "Introductory Observations," *American Biblical Repository,* 2d ser., 1 (January 1839):8, 15 (although the exact title varies, it will hereafter be cited as *ABR*).

While evangelical concern for benevolent action was more conspicuous than positive cultural achievements, the character of the *American Biblical Repository* indicates that contemporary intellectual endeavor would not be neglected. Protestant clergymen still maintained leadership in nearly every area of learning, and contributors from the "Evangelical united front" filled the hundreds of pages of each issue of the journal with fact and expert opinion on every phase of nineteenth-century culture. Byron, Shelley, Wordsworth, Melville, Hawthorne, Emerson, Bancroft, Prescott, de Tocqueville, Hegel, Coleridge, and Schleiermacher were among the many they reviewed and studied. Until 1850, when it ceased publication, the *American Biblical Repository* provided the most important outlet for New School scholarly and scientific expression.

In these early years it was uncertain what direction the New School would take. Initially, however, the leaders of the denomination still identified their cause with united evangelical Protestantism. Thus, the interdenominational quarterly furnishes the best gauge to the climate of opinion in which New School theologians searched for an identity and raison d'être for the doctrinal positions that their Church claimed.

Theological discussion consumed much of the review, but not as a detached and esoteric discipline. Rather, it remained queen of the sciences. As such, it represented both an integral part and the leading feature of this comprehensive literary enterprise. New School theologians who shared Absalom Peters' vision of a unified Christian culture assumed that a truly Scriptural theology would provide its basis.

Much of the doctrinal discussion dealt with topics that, in an age of greater compartmentalization, would fall in the realm of the psychology of religion. The most engrossing of such topics seem to have been the questions concerning the relation of the activities of man's own faculties to the work of the Spirit of God in his heart. This subject—the relation of free agency to grace—

had been the essential point at issue in the debates with the Old School, and the continuing discussion of it in the *Biblical Repository* is a further indication that considerable differences remained within the Congregationalist–New School alliance itself. A good portion of this discussion was simply a repetition of the opposing New England views on the subject. Samuel Cox, formerly of Auburn Seminary and later pastor of a New School Presbyterian church in Brooklyn, made an early contribution to this discussion in 1839, reiterating the New Haven view (and his own) that an individual plays an active role in his own regeneration.[3] Leonard Woods of Andover took the opposing side and from 1840 to 1844 provided the quarterly with an almost interminable series of articles answering a previous anonymous defense of free agency.

The same argument took a slightly different form in a debate over Jonathan Edwards' doctrine of the will. Here it centered around the publications of a New School man, Professor Henry Philip Tappan of New York City. Tappan, a teacher at the University of the City of New York (now New York University) until 1837 and later (1852) the first president of the University of Michigan, published in 1839–41 a series of works attempting to refute the basic thesis of Edwards' argument on the freedom of the will. Edwards had argued that the essential character of the motives that caused a man's willful actions was determined either by his sinful nature or by the regenerating grace of God. Tappan attempted to refute this argument by an appeal to the principles of Common Sense philosophy, maintaining that common consciousness told men that their wills were self-determining. The notices of Tappan's works in the *American Biblical Repository* were somewhat equivocal, commending his independence but questioning his conclusions and siding rather with Edwards. An extensive defense of Tappan, however, was written for the quarterly by a New School man, George B. Cheever, an Andover graduate, an irre-

3. Samuel Cox, "The Phrases 'Born of God,' and 'Born Again' in the New Testament," *ABR*, 2d ser., 2 (July 1839):182–91.

sponsible reformer, and pastor of the Allen Street Presbyterian church in New York City. Appealing directly to the authority of the Scottish philosopher Dugald Stewart, Cheever maintained with Tappan that Edwards' thesis was incompatible with a consistent Common Sense philosophy. Edwards' system on the will, he said, "is contrary to the common consciousness and experience of mankind; and we also think that it is contrary to the common language of Scripture."[4]

The appeal to common sense as a means of interpreting human experience and Scripture was a standard weapon in the theological debates of this era. But already a few dissenters in New School circles were looking to the Kantian tradition in German philosophy for more adequate means of expressing the Biblical message. "Literary intelligence" from Germany was a regular feature of the *American Biblical Repository*. New School theologians, however, disagreed widely on the merits of German thought. The advent of Transcendentalism in America had created a strong prejudice against anything German among many evangelicals. The few who dared praise German thought had to be careful to dissociate themselves from the "hyper-spirituality" that bordered on pantheism;[5] and even then they were subject to sharp criticisms.

Within the New School denomination the pioneer of German philosophical methods was Laurens P. Hickok (1790–1888),

4. Henry Philip Tappan, *A Review of Edwards' "Inquiry into the Freedom of the Will"* (New York, 1839); *An Appeal to Consciousness* (New York, 1840); *The Doctrine of the Will, Applied to Moral Agency and Responsibility* (New York, 1841); George B. Cheever, "Prof. Tappan on the Will," *ABR*, 2d ser., 7(April 1842):422; see also ibid., pp. 420, 430–33.

5. Taylor Lewis, *The Believing Spirit* (New York, 1841), quoted in a review in *ABR*, 2d ser., 7(April 1842):421–22. Cf. Laurens P. Hickok, *The Idea of Humanity in Its Progress to Its Consummation*, "An Address Delivered before the Philomathian Society in Middlebury College, July 29, 1847" (New York, 1847), p. 20. Speaking of philosophical Idealism, Hickok says, "Its only God is the inner law of thought. . . . Its ultimate termination is in logical necessity and a transcendental pantheism. This last has been carried to its ultimate analysis and highest generalization in Germany."

James Richards' successor as Professor of Christian Theology at Auburn Seminary. Hickok, "the first American theologian and professor to become a systematic expositor of German idealism,"[6] based his system on a sharp dichotomy between the spiritual and the sensual in man, a strong emphasis on the superiority of the spiritual, and a confidence in the ultimate triumph of the Idea of the law of the spiritual in human history. "The interests of humanity will be perfected," he predicted, "in that which gives the consummation to humanity itself—the spiritual controlling the sensual." It is the spiritual character of man that constitutes the "image of God in man" as he was created, and the effect of the regenerating work of the Holy Spirit is to restore the governing law of the spiritual over the sensual. As was typical of New School systems, Hickok's philosophy had a distinctly moralistic emphasis suited to practical reforms. "The very essence of virtue," he said, pressing home an attack on the "sewers of literary pollution," is "a manly struggle against inordinate appetite, and a valorous beating down of the flesh to serve the behest of the spirit."[7]

Hickok's emphasis on the work of the Holy Spirit and on men's moral responsibilities had much to appeal to the New School mentality. But the general prejudice against German thought was difficult to overcome. As a reviewer in the *American Biblical Repository* put it in 1849, Hickok's work was admirable except that it was pervaded by "a certain air of Germanism or transcendentalism."[8]

The involved philosophical and psychological discussions of New School theologians were not divorced from their most important practical concern—to preach the Gospel effectively. In the last analysis they would agree that new philosophies were use-

6. Schneider, *History of American Philosophy*, p. 379.
7. Hickok, *Idea of Humanity*, pp. 15–23.
8. Review of Laurens P. Hickok, *Rational Psychology: Or, the Subjective Idea and the Objective Law of All Intelligence* (Auburn, N.Y., 1849), *ABR*, 3d ser., 5(April 1849):374–75.

ful only in so far as they aided a better understanding of either the Bible[9] or of the men who heard the Gospel message.

Biblical studies held first place in New School literature. Edward Robinson (1794–1863), the New School's leading Biblical scholar, pursued extensive geographical and archeological researches in Palestine that were surpassed by no one in his day.[10] Likewise, Albert Barnes' *Notes* on the books of the Bible were republished in numerous editions,[11] becoming one of the most popular Biblical commentaries of the century. Analyses of Scriptural passages and essays on Biblical preaching were among the most common features of the *American Biblical Repository*. Though New School men attempted to cut away the underbrush of old doctrinal formulas, they did so in order to uncover the pure teachings of Scripture. As Richard Hofstadter observes, in references to Albert Barnes and the New School movement, "The objective was to return to the pure conditions of primitive Christianity, to which Scripture alone could give the key."[12]

Their other primary concern was effective communication of the Biblical message. Writing for the *American Biblical Repository* in 1846 on "The Relation of Theology to Preaching," Albert Barnes elaborated on this theme. His analysis represents the theological ideals of the New School denomination and reflects a major component of mid-nineteenth-century evangelical thought. The ultimate test for each system of theology, he maintained,

9. Laurens P. Hickok, writing on "Christian Theology as a Science," says, for example, that "the field in which the facts are to be sought, is the inspired word of God." *ABR*, 3d ser., 1(July 1845):462; see also ibid., p. 483.

10. Robinson contributed a large number of articles on Biblical researches to the *American Biblical Repository*. In 1843 he founded his own journal, the *Bibliotheca Sacra,* devoted solely to Biblical study. The next year the journal passed into the hands of the Andover faculty and commenced a long career as a more general theological journal.

11. Albert Barnes's *Notes . . .,* published originally under various titles from 1833 to 1868, are still in print over a century later (Baker Book House, Grand Rapids, Mich.).

12. Hofstadter, *Anti-intellectualism,* p. 83.

should be the question—can it be preached? "We place ourselves in the pulpit," he said "and look around on society, and ask what may be preached so as to answer the ends of preaching—so that men will perceive it to be true, and so that they will be converted to God."

There were three kinds of theology, according to Barnes, that *could not* be preached. The first was the form of religion that repels the darker and the sterner features of Christianity and is founded on the beautiful and grand in the works of nature or on the scenes of redemption. "It finds pleasure in the contemplation of the starry heavens; of hills, and streams, and lakes, of the landscape and of the ocean; and is willing in these things to admire and praise the existence and perfections of the Creator." Such a religion, said Barnes, may be of some artistic value. But it was different from ancient paganism and could not be preached. No doubt Barnes would have commended Ralph Waldo Emerson for leaving the ministry.

The second type of theology which, according to Barnes, could not be preached was that which made preaching secondary to the forms of worship and transformed the preacher into a priest who claims the power of the church. Even Protestant churches were in danger of such a tendency. "Its home, its embodiment, its most finished form, is in the church of Rome; its spirit is abroad in nearly all other churches, and it is striving, every where, for the ascendency." Barnes opposed "High Churchmanship" in all its forms.

The third type of unpreachable theology was clearly that of the Old School Presbyterians. It was the theology of tradition and the old Reformed confessions. "It contains dogmas so abhorrent to the obvious teachings of the Bible; so repellent to the common sense of mankind; so at variance with what are found to be just principles of philosophy, so fitted to retard a work of grace; and so utterly contradictory to what man is constrained to preach when his heart is full, and when he has the most enlarged and elevated views of the work of the Savior, that he *cannot* preach them."

In stating the characteristics of a theology that *could* be preached, Barnes outlined the essential principles of New School theology. The first and most important was that it must be derived from a proper interpretation of the Bible. The preacher's job, he maintained, is above all the interpretation of *a book*. His sermons, therefore, must be "based on obvious and honest principles of interpretation." Contemporary preaching, according to Barnes, overemphasized elaborate exegetical arguments, mystical meanings, and the use of proof texts. Such methods of Biblical interpretation were neither clear nor convincing. Even Jonathan Edwards, he charged, had erred in this respect. Edwards' force was in his rational argument and seldom in his appeal to Scripture. The Bible should, rather, always be clearly central to preaching. Its interpretation should be in plain terms that anyone could comprehend. "The point will at last be reached," Barnes said, " . . . that the Bible is to be interpreted as other books are, and that men cannot hide themselves in the midst of an occult meaning when they rely on proofs that shock the common sense of the world."

Common sense was, in fact, his second criterion for a preachable theology. "That theology which can be preached must be such as shall commend itself to the common sense of mankind." Ministers should therefore be practical men, well acquainted with men and with the world.

The final requirement for an effective theology was that it reflect thorough knowledge of the progress of the age. "The theology that is to be preached," Barnes advised, "should sustain a proper relation to the spirit of the age." Preachers must think and speak in the terms of their own times, apply Christian principles to every great issue of the age; indeed, they must be in advance of their age.[13]

13. Albert Barnes, "The Relation of Theology to Preaching," *ABR*, 3d ser., 2(October 1846):572–602.

The New School Dilemma

In speaking of "The Relation of Theology to Preaching," Albert Barnes depicted the ideals for New School theology. But New School theologians and preachers were faced with a dilemma. They sought a distinct theological identity for their denomination without repudiating their heritage. They had rejected the traditionalism of the Old School; yet they still claimed the Presbyterian and the Biblical tradition. They searched for a theology at once simple, Biblical, and relevant to the spirit of the age. Yet none of the theological alternatives in nineteenth-century America was entirely satisfactory. They rejected the extremes of Roman Catholicism and Transcendentalism outright. The distinctive doctrines of Unitarians and Baptists held no appeal because New School men judged them clearly un-Biblical. All these subjects were standard polemics in the *American Biblical Repository.* But New School men also rejected more plausible alternatives for the theology of a church cut away from its moorings.

One such rejected alternative was the theology of the Disciples of Christ, or the Christian movement. This movement had grown out of the Presbyterian revivals on the Kentucky frontier in the early years of the century and bore many resemblances to the later New School movement. Volume I of Absalom Peters' New Series of the *American Biblical Repository,* however, began a series of articles denouncing the teachings of Alexander Campbell (1788–1866), the leader of the Disciples movement. A former Presbyterian himself, Campbell now proposed to unite Christendom on the principles of the sole authority of Scripture and a return to the practices of the Ancient Church. But New School men, who themselves had attacked the confessionalism of the Old School on much the same principles, would have nothing to do with Campbell's views. Campbell, said the reviewer in the *American Biblical Repository,* had omitted portions of Scripture in his new translation of the New Testament; taught the heresies of Unitarianism; and advocated the necessity of baptism by immersion for salvation. In short, Campbell's doctrines were "entirely subversive to the Word of God."[14]

Campbell defended his principles of Christian unity by denouncing Absalom Peters for having "most wantonly and cruelly slandered" him and threatening legal prosecution for damages.[15] Peters responded by making an apparently sincere effort to calm the enraged Disciple of Christ and publishing Campbell's reply to the original articles with appropriate editorial remarks.[16] But Campbellism was clearly one direction in which the New School was not moving.

Yet interdenominational unity was an alternative that many New School leaders hoped would be a primary goal of their movement. One of Absalom Peters' first acts after he purchased the old *Biblical Repository* in 1838 was the initial publication of Samuel Schmucker's now famous "Fraternal Appeal to the American Churches." Schmucker, Professor of Theology at the Lutheran Theological Seminary in Gettysburg, Pennsylvania, was an opponent of High Church Lutheran confessionalism. In his "Fraternal Appeal" he maintained that the sectarian and divided state of Christendom could no longer be viewed with indifference by those who knew the love of Christ. He suggested that the American churches could be united on inclusive Broad Church principles and proposed an "Apostolic, Protestant Confession" containing the Apostles' Creed and a statement of twelve basic doctrines as a basis for unity.[17] Peters himself urged that Schmucker's proposals

14. R. W. Landis, "Campbellism," *ABR,* 2d ser., 1(April 1839):327.

15. "Campbell on Campbellism," ibid., 2d ser., 3(April 1840):469–70. Campbell requested that his name be stricken from the list of subscribers to the *American Biblical Repository* in the same letter.

16. Ibid., pp. 469ff.

17. Samuel Schmucker, "Fraternal Appeal to the American Churches, Together with a Plan for Catholic Union on Apostolic Principles," *ABR,* 1st ser., 11(January 1838):880; and ibid., 11(April 1838):408–14.

"should be seriously and prayerfully pondered by all who pray for the coming of the kingdom of Christ to earth."[18]

The New School quest for unity was, however, limited by its own Broad Church principles. By demanding that Christians be united on the basis of the fundamental Biblical doctrines, the advocates of unity automatically excluded the members of the High Church and confessionalist parties in most of the major American denominations. New School men instinctively took the side of the Low Churchmen in the intradenominational debates of the era. For example, James W. McLane, a New School minister from New York City, in reviewing a High Church Episcopal sermon, charged that it "concerns itself chiefly with the externals of religion, and inclines strongly toward superstition and popery."[19] George B. Cheever, in surveying High Church trends, asserted that "the religion of imitation is Churchianity; the religion of experience is Christianity"[20] and suggested that in an age of conflict and evangelism only a religion of experience was satisfactory. Calvin E. Stowe (1802–86), professor at Lane Seminary (and husband of Harriet Beecher), concurred: "All the religion of high church prelacy, whether papal or Puseyite, is a religion of the imagination only."[21] It was standard practice for New School Presbyterians to identify all High Church views with Romanism. Such an accusation in the era of the "Protestant Crusade" against Roman Catholics amounted to a scathing denunciation.[22]

18. *ABR*, 2d ser., 3(January 1840):255.

19. James W. McLane, "Review of Haight's 'Guide' and M'Ilvaine's 'Solemn Responsibility of Ministers,' " *ABR*, 2d ser., 11(January 1844):1–2.

20. George B. Cheever, "The Religion of Experience and That of Imitation," *ABR*, 2d ser., 11(January 1844):93.

21. Calvin E. Stowe, "The Principles of Presbyterianism: Reasons for Upholding Them," *ABR*, 2d ser., 12(October 1844):289.

22. See Ray A. Billington, *The Protestant Crusade* (New York, 1938); and John R. Bodo, *The Protestant Clergy and Public Issues, 1812–1848* (Princeton, N.J., 1954), pp. 61–84, for accounts of the anti-Catholic hysteria of this era. New School men such as George B. Cheever and Lyman Beecher were active

The New School quest for unity was further limited by loyalty
to the Presbyterian tradition. New School Presbyterians and Methodists, for example, had relatively little contact. In 1837 the delegates to the Auburn Convention affirmed their Presbyterian constitutionality, and the great majority of them were unwilling to
seek ecclesiastical and theological alternatives that would force
them to forsake that heritage. Calvin Stowe, for instance, defended
both the theology and the polity of Presbyterianism (broadly defined to include Congregational Associations) as the most Scriptural and the best suited to the age. The principles of Presbyterianism, he said, "should be insisted upon and propagated at the present
time, and in this country."[23]

Cut off from the Old School, yet claiming the doctrinal tradition
of Presbyterianism, the New School Presbyterians were left in an
ambiguous position. The most likely alternative for cooperation
that remained open for them was Congregationalism.[24] Even if
the Presbyterian denomination were not assimilated into the New
England Church, it might have been expected that the development of New School theology would follow Congregationalist

---

in the crusade. The *American Biblical Repository* contained many anti-Catholic
essays, but these indicate considerable restraint in characterizing the evils of
Rome.

23. Stowe, "Principles of Presbyterianism," pp. 258–59; see also ibid., p. 286.

24. Among the smaller Presbyterian denominations in America, the New
School had the most affinities to the Cumberland Presbyterian Church,
founded during the era of revivals on the Kentucky frontier in 1810. The
Cumberland movement, which was a revolt against the strict confessionalism
and high standards of ministerial education in the Presbyterian Church in the
United States, has many similarities to the later New School movement. The
Cumberland Church had considerable success in the old Southwest and was
about half the size of the New School. The two denominations began ex-
changing fraternal delegates in 1849, but, apparently because of sectional
rivalries, no more solid basis of cooperation was ever reached. See Lewis G.
Vander Velde, *The Presbyterian Churches and the Federal Union, 1861–1869*
(Cambridge, Mass., 1932), pp. 9–10. See also *A New Digest of the Acts and
Deliverances of the General Assembly of the Presbyterian Church in the
United States of America* (Philadelphia, 1861), p. 448.

patterns. But in the early years of the New School's history even this most plausible alternative for cooperative thought and action was eliminated.

From Cooperation to Denominationalism

In many respects the New School Presbyterians' search for theological identity paralleled their search for ecclesiastical identity after the schism of 1837. Their theological position was intimately involved with, and almost a function of, their ecclesiastical situation. The parallels between their theological development and their development as a denomination are not difficult to find.

The ecclesiastical character of the New School changed rapidly during the first decade and a half of its independent existence. At the end of his account of the "Evangelical united front" Charles I. Foster presents a concise summary of the early years of the New School denomination:

> The united front had ended. Schism changed the character of the New School movement in a flash; its members gathered promptly at Auburn, N.Y., to take up the duties and responsibilities of a denomination. No longer carrying the vision of a united Evangelical Christendom marching to world conquest, the New School became another sect. The forms and habits of co-operation lingered a few years, but the spirit of the united front was dead.[25]

The change was not quite so sudden or complete as Foster portrays it. Considerable zeal for interdenominational cooperation survived throughout New School history. New School men, for instance, assumed the American leadership in supporting the international Evangelical Alliance both before and after the Civil War.[26] Nevertheless, by the end of its first fifteen years, the New

---

25. Foster, *United Front,* p. 273.

26. When the Alliance was organized in London in 1846, Samuel Cox, William Patton, and Lyman Beecher were among its most active American promoters. After the Civil War, Henry B. Smith was chairman of the American committee of the Alliance. Cf. Nichols, *Presbyterianism,* pp. 146, 153.

School Church was unmistakably finding its identity in denominationalism.

The change from cooperation to denominationalism was never altogether a matter of choice for the New School men. In the early years the cooperative spirit still dominated their councils. Their associations with the agencies of the "Evangelical united front" continued. The Plan of Union was still in effect and the New School Assembly maintained cordial fraternal relations with the Congregationalists. The Presbyterians of the New School even went so far as to reorganize their own system of government in the direction of the model of the Congregational Associations. In reaction to the high-handed methods of Old School Presbyterianism they gave the synods, instead of the General Assembly, the final appellate jurisdiction in the denomination. After 1840 the General Assembly was to meet only triennially, instead of annually, and was left little function other than as an advisory association.[27]

Soon, however, it became evident that the cooperative tide was turning and that the New School was in danger of being left high and dry. One of the early portents of the change was the reestablishment by New England Congregationalists of their own scholarly theological journals. In 1843 the *New Englander* was inaugurated in New Haven, Connecticut, and the next year the faculty of Andover began publication of their own quarterly, the *Bibliotheca Sacra and Theological Review*.

At about the same time prominent New School men of New England background began to return to Congregationalism. In 1844, for example, Absalom Peters left all his activities in New York to assume a Congregationalist pastorate in Williamstown, Massachusetts. The same year Edward Beecher left his post as president of Illinois College to take a New England pulpit. George B. Cheever moved from his Presbyterian charge to the Church of

27. New School *Minutes, 1840*, pp. 16–17.

the Puritans in New York City, organized in 1845 to provide a
better platform for his antislavery and reforming views.[28] Calvin
Stowe accepted a post at Bowdoin in 1850, and two years later
went to teach Sacred Literature at Andover. And in 1850 Lyman
Beecher retired from Lane Seminary to spend the last years of his
life with his Congregationalist son, Henry Ward, in Brooklyn,
New York.

Ardent antislavery men such as George Cheever became dissatisfied when the New School appeared to be moving too slowly
on the greatest issue of the day. However much slavery may have
been a factor in the Presbyterian schism, after the division the
New School Assembly refused to take an unequivocal stand. At
every Assembly slavery was the primary subject for debate. At
some almost nothing else was discussed. At none was decisive action taken. In deference to its small minority of Southern members, the Assembly voted in 1839 to leave the matter to the discretion of the local synods. In 1843 the commissioners again
refused to make any pronouncement. In 1846 they condemned
the institution of slavery but not the individuals who supported it.
This lack of definite action left no one completely satisfied. Among
radical antislavery men, it bred only disillusionment.[29]

Furthermore, New Englanders seemed no longer to view New
School Presbyterianism as the best means for carrying .the Christian banner across the continent. During the decade of the 1840s
effective cooperation between Congregationalists and Presbyterians
steadily diminished. The Plan of Union fell into disuse, and the
relations between Presbyterians and the various independent agencies for interdenominational action became increasingly strained.

Soon it also became apparent that New School theological

28. Timothy L. Smith, *Revivalism and Social Reform in Mid-Nineteenth-Century America* (New York, 1957), p. 209. Cheever's antislavery
views are studied in George I. Rockwood, *Cheever, Lincoln and Causes of the
Civil War* (Worcester, Mass., 1936).

29. Smith, *Revivalism*, pp. 196–98; Gillett, *History of the Presbyterian
Church*, 2:555; Barnes, *The Church and Slavery*, pp. 72–78.

development would not follow the lines set by its interdenominational and Congregationalist allies. By the mid-1840s New School
men showed signs that they too could play the role of defenders of
the pure Presbyterian faith. Critics within the Church began to
express dissatisfaction with the lowest-common-denominator theology of the interdenominational agencies, on the one hand, and
with the extreme theological positions tolerated in Congregationalism, on the other.

An excellent example of early New School dissatisfaction with
the theology propagated by the independent "benevolent empire"
is the case of the Synod of New York and New Jersey versus the
American Tract Society. In the years when the synods were the
highest courts of appeal, the Synod of New York and New Jersey
(including New York City) was probably the most influential
judicatory in the Church. In 1845 a special committee of that
synod investigated the publications of the American Tract Society
and brought back a highly unfavorable report. Concentrating
upon republications of certain works of Jonathan Edwards and
the Puritan author John Flavel's *Method of Grace,* the New
School committee found that the Tract Society, in an attempt to
bring these writings up to date, had substantially altered their contents. In part, the committee objected to the publisher's failure to
indicate that alterations had been made. Their primary objection
was far more serious and far more revealing of at least one aspect of
the changing New School temper. The committee reported that in
these altered books "the doctrines of God's absolute sovereignity
in saving men, in predestination, election, perseverance—of the
nature and the extent of the atonement, of man's ability, and of
infant baptism, are, in many instances materially modified, and in
others wholly excluded."[30]

The evidence that the committee presented sounded like an

30. *Proceedings of the Synod of New York and New Jersey at Their Late
Session, in Reference to the Publications of the American Tract Society* (New
York, 1845), p. 7.

echo from an Old School Assembly. Citing the changes in the Tract Society's edition of Flavel's *Method of Grace,* the representative of the committee listed the doctrines that had been altered. On original sin, he stated, "where the author says of man, 'that he is wholly polluted, and plunged into original and actual pollutions of nature and practice,' they omit the words *'original and actual.'* " On imputation, "they omit, 'If Adam's sin becomes ours by imputation, then so doth Christ's righteousness also become ours by imputation.' " On ability, "they omit . . . 'Nature hath neither ability nor will, power or desire to come to Christ.' " On grace and free will, "they omit what Flavel says of the role of Christ's righteousness, that it is 'all made by *free-grace,* and not free will.' " And on regeneration and conversion, "if Flavel says, . . . 'till God draw, the soul *cannot come* to Christ,' they make him say, 'the soul comes not to Christ,' and . . . where Flavel says, 'no man *can* come till God drew him' they say, 'no man will come,' &c."[31]

These were the very same doctrines that the Old School had debated with the New. But the statement of the committee made it perfectly clear that at least some New School men considered these teachings of no little consequence:

> The Committee view these doctrines of vital importance to the system of truth to which they belong. Those, therefore, who have embraced that system, cannot be indifferent to these doctrines, much less can they give countenance or support to an attempt to remove them from the religious literature of the country—to blot out from the books of the Puritan fathers the proclamations of their Puritan faith. The voice of God within them forbids it. Fearful consequences may follow from it.[32]

31. Ibid., pp. 24–25.
32. Ibid., p. 7. The synod received a pledge from the Tract Society to adjust its policies, and they therefore postponed any definite action on the report. The synod subsequently established its own publishing committee, which was a forerunner of the New School denominational publishing-committee established in the next decade.

More signs of growing New School vigilance appeared in regard to doctrines tolerated within Congregationalism. Hardly a
decade had passed in the Congregationalist–New School alliance
before some of the New School leaders were expressing almost
the same apprehensions about the trends in Congregationalism as
had the Old School before the schism.

During 1848 and 1849 George Duffield contributed a long
series of articles to the *Biblical Repository* reviewing Charles
Finney's perfectionism—one of the most controversial developments in recent Congregationalist theology. Duffield remained
one of the favorite targets for Old School polemics. Nevertheless,
in these articles even he proved unwilling to adopt the standards
of tolerance found in some areas of Congregationalism. Duffield
began by emphasizing his long-standing affection for Finney. He
had always given the evangelist the benefit of the doubt and had
tolerated his erratic views because of his reputation for piety, his
skill as a popular preacher, and his success in the conversion of
men. Now, however, Duffield had changed his mind. With the
publication of Finney's *Lectures on Systematic Theology,* he wrote,
"it is a matter of regret, that we have been constrained to appre-
hend that there is more reason for censure than we had suspected."[33] It was time to dissociate his own views from those of
Finney. Because of the perfectionist teachings and methods, he
observed, "the very name of revivals and spiritual religion, as well
as the religious profession of multitudes, have been rendered a
taunt and a reproach."[34]

Duffield's principal objection to Finney's teachings was that the
revivalist had imposed his own peculiar philosophical system on
Scripture. Finney's emphasis on the freedom of the will had led him
to the view that man is capable of "continual abiding consecration,

33. George Duffield, "Review of Finney's *Theology,*" *ABR,* 3d ser., 4(April
1848):212.
34. Ibid., 5(January 1849):129.

or obedience to God."[35] Duffield challenged this doctrine of the possibility of "sinless perfection" on the ground that it denied the Biblical teaching of the depravity of man. The main issue, he argued, was that Finney implicitly denied that there is "any tendency, bias, inclination, or disposition, call it what you please, whether impulse or complex, negative or positive, which operates, with determining influence, as a cause or reason why men, uniformly and invariably, in all the appropriate circumstances of their nature, choose to do evil."[36] Furthermore, he said, Finney's views implied that men were under law rather than under grace.

> The views he slanders are those of the Westminster Confession of Faith, which teaches that "believers be not under the law as a covenant of works to be justified or condemned," and they are in accordance with the apostle Paul's, for he says of himself, "I through the law, am dead to the law, that I might live unto God. I do not frustrate the grace of God, for if righteousness come by the law then Christ is dead in vain."[37]

The New School critic was amazed and alarmed at how far his former colleague had "departed from the faith he once held in common with the Presbyterian Church."[38]

The New School trend toward exclusivism soon took institutional form. The most important change came in the General Assembly. In 1846, at its second triennial meeting, extensive debates on the slavery issues forced adjournment until the next year to complete unfinished business. At the adjourned meeting in 1847 the delegates concluded that the advisory capacity of the Assembly and its infrequent meetings were insufficient for the needs of a major Presbyterian denomination. In 1849, therefore, the constitutional rules were restored to their condition prior to

35. Ibid., 4(October 1848):715, quoted from Charles G. Finney, *Lectures on Systematic Theology.*
36. *ABR,* 3d ser., 5(January 1849):96.
37. Ibid., 4(July 1848):441.
38. Ibid., p. 417.

1840, reinstituting the annual meetings of the Assembly and re-
turning its judicial authority.[39]

The reorganization of the form of government was part of a more
general reappraisal of the constitutional position of the Church.
In 1849 a committee on "Alterations in the Constitution" recommended, instead of alterations, a more thorough loyalty to the
Confession of Faith. "As it is of great importance to preserve this
conformity to those ancient standards," the committee explained,
it was issuing an authorized edition of the Westminster documents
based on a collation of the most ancient British editions and cor-
recting numerous typographical errors in the later American
texts.[40] Confessionalism had survived in the New School, and
where it was languishing the Assembly now took steps to see that
it would be revived. One of the resolutions passed by the Assembly of 1849 recommended the restoration of the "good old
practice of our fathers" of teaching the Westminster Shorter
Catechism to the young. "The institution of Sabbath Schools," the
Assembly declared, "does not exonerate ministers and parents
from the duty of teaching the Shorter Catechism to the children of
the church."[41] The spirit of the nineteenth century was to be
channeled along Presbyterian lines.

The next year the commissioners to the Assembly took another
step toward asserting their denominational identity. Ever since
their reluctant exodus from the Old School Assembly in 1838,
they had been making periodic overtures for reunion or fraternal
recognition. In 1846, when the two Assemblies were meeting in
Philadelphia at the same time, they had proposed mutual recognition by joining together in the celebration of the Lord's Sup-
per. The Old School had politely declined. Now, in 1850, the

39. New School *Minutes, 1849*, p. 183.
40. Ibid., p. 198.
41. Ibid., p. 181. The Westminster Shorter Catechism is indeed a
formidable document to teach anyone, being a lengthy question-and-answer
exposition of much of the Confession, the Ten Commandments, and the
Lord's Prayer.

New School Assembly declared "that we cannot, as a body, at the present time, take any further action in this matter."[42]

Of far more practical importance were the changes in the denomination's attitude toward the conduct of home missions. In the 1830s the New School advocated cooperation in the Plan of Union and with the American Home Missionary Society as the best means for promoting church extension. Now the Congregationalists were founding their own churches rather than cooperating in the Plan of Union. In 1846 Congregationalists of the Midwest, meeting at Michigan City, Michigan, declared their opposition to the Plan of Union.[43] Thereafter, relations between Presbyterians and Congregationalists in the American Home Missionary Society became increasingly strained. In 1847 the New School Assembly appointed a "Standing Committee on Home Missions," thus beginning a gradual process toward denominational control of home missions. By 1850 the spirit of cooperation was waning rapidly. The Assembly adopted a resolution declaring "that, in the last command of Christ to his disciples, we recognize a command obligatory to our branch of the church" and recommending that new churches be established by the denomination, rather than entirely through the agency of the Society. In 1852 the spirit of denominational missions was institutionalized, as the Assembly, still giving grudging approval to the work of the American Home Missionary Society, instructed each presbytery to elect a "Standing Committee on Church Extension" to direct the founding of new churches.[44] Five months later the Albany Convention of Congregationalists formally terminated the Plan of Union. The old missionary alliance of New England and the New School was shattered.

Evangelical Protestant cooperation in publications ended as

42. New School *Minutes, 1850*, p. 322.
43. Nichols, *Presbyterianism*, p. 149.
44. For the above actions, see New School *Minutes, 1847*, p. 152; ibid., *1850*, p. 315; and ibid., *1852*, p. 171.

well. The Assembly of 1852, rather than continuing to depend exclusively on the publications of the American Tract Society, appointed its own denominational publication committee. At the same time, it purchased a weekly religious newspaper, the *New York Evangelist*. Finally, to fill the gap left by the demise of the *American Biblical Repository* in 1850, the Assembly accepted the new *Presbyterian Quarterly Review*[45] as its official denominational theological journal.[46]

In the first issue of the *Presbyterian Quarterly Review* its editor, Benjamin J. Wallace (1810–62), surveyed the ecclesiastical position of the New School Church after the first fifteen years. "It may be regarded as a 'fixed fact,' " he asserted, *"that our church is to be and remain a distinct, independent, and permanent ecclesiastical denomination."* Till now it had not been clear that the New School would survive as a distinct organization. "It was predicted," he said, "that without the cohesive attraction of their more orthodox brethren, their union would be a rope of sand. . . . Each successive General Assembly was pronounced the last that could be held." But now there was no question of restoring the New School's old affiliations. With regard to the Old School, Wallace observed, "we know of no one in our communion so void of self-respect as to advocate a renewal of overtures of union, which have been coldly repulsed." Cooperation with the Congregationalists in missions was now little more than an empty formality. "We yield to our orthodox Congregational brethren the right to organize, when people prefer it, Congregational churches any where, or to any extent," the editor conceded, "but insist on our right to do the same, under our own preferences."

The theological complexion of the Church had a similar Pres-

----

45. Published in Philadelphia. Benjamin J. Wallace was editor; Albert Barnes, Thomas Brainerd, E. W. Gilbert, and Joel Parker were associate editors. They were assisted by professors of the New School Theological Seminaries, Union, Auburn and Lane.

46. New School *Minutes, 1852*, pp. 174–76.

byterian hue. Independence, Wallace claimed, had made the Church more Presbyterian, not less so. "It was not likely that men who had suffered so much for principle would hold lightly by either truth or the order of the church; and hence after fifteen years, in the body with which we are connected, no man has moved to alter a tittle of the Confession of Faith, or an essential principle of Presbyterian government." Extremists had drifted away from the Church during these fifteen difficult years, and now the Church was homogeneous and "in opinion, Presbyterian, and Calvinistic." It was also thoroughly Biblical in its basis, thoroughly dedicated to "the only infallible standard, the word of God." The great appeal to Scripture as the banner for evangelical unity had now become a denominational slogan. " 'Our church standards as symbols for union, but the Bible for authority,' is the motto of our denomination," the editor proclaimed. The new *Presbyterian Quarterly Review* was itself a symbol of exclusive denominational identity. "We have been unjust to ourselves," wrote Wallace.

> We have left it to others to do our thinking and writing for us, to inundate our churches with periodicals, either indifferent to our interest, or inimical to our doctrines and institutions. Roman Catholics, Episcopalians, Methodists, Baptists, Congregationalists, and the Presbyterians separated from us, have their Quarterlies, which invigorate and develop the intellectual power of their members, and advocate their doctrines. Has our denomination less genius, learning, pecuniary resources, literary cultivation and taste?[47]

The legions of Christianity that Absalom Peters had so recently predicted would usher in the millennium "armed with all the facilities of modern science, arts, wealth and enterprise" had now emerged from the deadlocks of the decade of the 1840s reorganized as competing denominational corporations, each claiming that it would be first in the Kingdom of God in America.

47. "Our Church and Our Review," *Presbyterian Quarterly Review* 1 (June 1852):1–7 (hereafter cited as *PQR*).

6

The Triumph of
Denominationalism 1852–1861

Defining a Denominational Theology

COMPETITIVE PRACTICES

"They have milked our Congregational cows, but they have made nothing but Presbyterian butter and cheese," testified a delegate to the Congregationalists' Albany Convention in support of its abrogation of the Plan of Union.[1] The Congregationalists justified termination of the Plan by stating that it had always been unequal in its provisions, favoring Presbyterians. In the interests of peace on the home-missions fields, they stated, Congregational churches should no longer be formed in connection with presbyteries.[2]

The New School reacted to this new declaration of competitive practices with righteous indignation and a sense of betrayal. "This from New England!" declared the *Presbyterian Quarterly Review.* "These are the men who were to stand by us, shoulder to shoulder. Et tu Brute!"[3] The Congregationalist action forced even the most optimistic of the New School men to reconsider their hopes for Protestant unity. "All that we can suggest now," wrote the con-

---

1. *Proceedings of the General Convention of Congregational Ministers and Delegates in the United States, Held at Albany, New York, 1852* (New York, 1852), p. 71 (hereafter cited as *Proceedings*), quoted in Nichols, *Presbyterianism,* p. 150.

2. *Proceedings,* pp. 19–20, quoted in "The Albany Convention and the New Englander," *PQR* 1(March 1853):637.

3. "The Albany Convention and the New Englander," p. 641.

tributor to the *Review*, "is the query whether our plans hitherto for union have not been superficial."[4]

Cautions against excessive denominationalism continued within the New School; but the course actually pursued in the next decade amounted to a virtual promotional contest with the Congregationalists. When, in 1852, the Albany Convention voted a $50,000 fund for the building of new churches, the General Assembly of the next year authorized $100,000 for the same purpose.[5] When the Albany Convention affirmed the superiority of the Congregational system, the New School Presbyterian Synod of Albany, meeting the next year, responded directly by announcing a similar sectarian preference. "Among all the divisions in the household of the faith," the Synod declared in a display of something less than humility, "our decided preference is for our own."[6]

In New York state, where contact between the two denominations was most extensive, relations were especially poor. In 1855 the fraternal delegate to the General Assembly from the General (Congregational) Association of New York appended to his customary "Christians salutations" a rebuke for the Assembly's inaction on the subject of slavery. The New School Assembly had debated this subject extensively at almost every session since 1838 and had already condemned the evils of the system several times. It had not, however, attempted to enforce any rules banning slaveholding among its Southern members. In 1855 debate was particularly intense as the Assembly approached the point of taking the first positive steps toward such enforcement—a policy that two years later led to a Southern exodus.[7] In the midst of their own

4. Ibid., p. 653. Articles in *PQR* were usually unsigned.

5. New School *Minutes, 1853*, p. 376; Nichols, *Presbyterianism*, p. 150.

6. *Minutes of the Fifth Anniversary of the Synod of Albany, Convened in Schaghticoke, Sept. 20th, 1853* (Albany, N.Y., 1853), p. 26.

7. A small minority of Southern churches, representing six synods, twenty-one presbyteries, and about fifteen thousand communicants, withdrew in 1857 to form the United Synod of the Presbyterian Church. For the New School Assembly's declarations on slavery, see *New Digest*, pp. 275–95.

debates on the subject, the commissioners to the Assembly of 1855 hardly welcomed unsolicited advice from the Congregationalists. The Assembly declared that the resolutions from the General Association of New York were addressed to them in "a discourteous and objectionable manner" and requested "that future communications of the Association to us be couched in courteous language." The year 1855 was the last that the Assembly exchanged fraternal delegates with the General Association of New York.[8]

With such a spirit prevailing between New School Presbyterians and Congregationalists, continued cooperation between the two in the American Home Missionary Society was hardly the order of the day. At the Assembly of 1855 the New School appointed its own permanent Committee on Church Extension to handle virtually all home-missionary work.[9] Finally, in 1861, all official connections between the Assembly and the American Home Missionary Society were severed.[10]

The breakdown of rapport with the Congregationalists had definite theological overtones. In reviewing the actions of the Albany Convention of 1852, the first objection listed in the *Presbyterian Quarterly Review* was: *"The Albany Convention took Oberlinism under its protection."* As evidence for this accusation the reviewer cited a noncommittal resolution on the subject of Oberlin perfectionism (i.e., of the Charles Finney variety) issued by the Albany Convention, and a statement in the Congregationalist magazine the *New Englander* that "it is time this terror of Oberlin were frankly and honestly discarded East and West." Contrasting these statements with an outright condemnation of the doctrines of Oberlin adopted by the New School Synod of Michigan, the reviewer concluded that the Congregationalists had

8. Ibid., pp. 449–51.
9. New School *Minutes, 1855*, pp. 20–22.
10. Ibid., *1861*, pp. 466–69; cf. ibid., *1860*, p. 260. The New School did, however, continue to work through the American Board of Commissioners for Foreign Missions.

let the denominational spirit override doctrinal considerations. "The Spirit of sect rides the air," he proclaimed. "As in the high party times of the Presbyterian church from 1833 to 1838, almost any man was orthodox who would vote right, so now Congregationalism is very lenient to her own children."[11] The New School had assumed the role of the latest in a long line of Presbyterian critics of Congregationalism's lack of doctrinal vigilance.

The new spirit of denominationalism had another very practical effect on theology in the New School Church. The direct influence of the New England seminaries on the New School declined sharply. Only 35 of the 272 men who graduated from Andover Seminary in the years from 1853 to 1861 took charges in any of the American Presbyterian churches before the reunion of 1869, and many of these remained Presbyterians for only a brief time.[12] Presbyterian graduates of the New Haven Seminary were even more unusual. Only 3 of the 97 men who studied at Yale's Divinity School during these nine years took Presbyterian pastorates, and only one held a Presbyterian charge for more than three years.[13] The New School was being forced to become more Presbyterian in character and personnel. It was clear that, if it were to have a distinctive doctrinal message to offer to mid-nineteenth-century America, it must be developed in its own seminaries and bear a definite Presbyterian trademark.

11. "The Albany Convention and the New Englander," pp. 632–36.

12. *General Catalogue of the Theological Seminary, Andover, Mass., 1808–1908* (Boston, [n.d.]). In the 1850s the theology of Andover was dominated by Edwards Amasa Park (1808–1900), whose teachings were suspect in Old School Presbyterian circles. His famous address, "The Theology of the Intellect and That of the Feelings" (Boston, 1850), for example, brought sharp criticism from Charles Hodge in the *Princeton Review:* 22(October 1850):642–74 ("Professor Park's Sermon"); and 23(April 1851):306–47 ("Professor Park and the *Princeton Review*"). Park's theology is described sympathetically in detail in Foster, *Genetic History*, pp. 471–540.

13. *A General Catalogue of the Divinity School of Yale College, 1822–1872* (New Haven, Conn., 1873). These were lean years at Yale, as the small number of students indicates. The theology of Nathaniel Taylor (d. 1858) continued to be taught during this period.

Perhaps the best indication that the New School was becoming more Presbyterian and more conservative in its theology, instead of less so, is the character of the debates with the Old School, which flourished during this era. Ever since the division, the adversaries from the Old School had been shooting their fiery polemics at the New School pilgrims as they wandered in search of the way to the heavenly city. Now the School, having passed safely through the gate of denominationalism and relieved of the burden of active ecumenism, could stop and return the fire. During the decade of the 1850s the renewed conflict between the two Schools reached its peak. In the previous decade the major contributions to the literature of the debate had come from the Old School side, notably two polemic volumes: *Old and New Theology,* by James Wood,[14] and *Differences between the Old and New School Presbyterians,* by Lewis Cheeseman.[15] But in 1852 the New School began to respond in true sectarian spirit. In that year a committee of the Synod of New York and New Jersey provided the most complete defense of the New School position in *A History of the Division of the Presbyterian Church.* The next year Nathaniel L. Rice, an Old School minister from Kentucky, who had been one of the most active promoters of the division, responded with a careful doctrinal study, *The Old and New Schools.* From 1854 to 1856 the *Presbyterian Quarterly Review* reviewed the works of Wood and Rice in a series of four major articles, "Old and New Theology," expounding in detail the disputed doctrinal points. In 1855 Isaac Brown, an Old School minister, published his *Vindication of the Abrogation of the Plan of Union;* and an "Old Disciple" offered *The Alleged Doctrinal Differences of the Old and New School Examined*[16] in defense of the New School position. Simply to list these works, which represent only the *major* polemics of the re-

14. Philadelphia, [1843?].
15. Rochester, N.Y., 1848.
16. Auburn, N.Y., 1855.

newed debates, gives some impression of the vast amount of ver-
biage expended by mid-nineteenth-century denominationalists on
a subject that had been exhausted twenty years previously.

A survey of the general character of these controversies is most
instructive for evaluating the theological position of the New
School denomination. In this regard, the most indicative feature
of the discussion is that all the Old School works deal almost
exclusively with evidences of New School error *prior* to 1837 and
say practically nothing about the current situation in the New
School denomination itself. Each Old School writer used the earlier
works of Barnes, Duffield, and Beman (some added Beecher and
Finney) as their evidence for doctrinal laxity. Lewis Cheeseman,
writing in the 1840s, did mention the triennial Assemblies as an
indication of New School decline; but the polemics of the 1850s
confined themselves to evidence obtained prior to the division.

Nathaniel Rice, Old School author of *The Old and New Schools,*
noted one reason for this approach. The whole purpose of the
debate, he said, was to justify the abrogation of the Plan of Union,
and so the only important question was in the past tense—"Had
our brethren of the New School introduced and fostered in our
church errors and irregularities of dangerous tendency?"[17] Rice's
own expositions of the doctrinal differences were simply republications of articles he had written at the time of the division for
his magazine, the *Protestant and Herald.* The contrast between
those parts of *The Old and New Schools* that were written in 1837
and his preface, written in 1853, is striking. Typical of Old School
sentiments of the 1830s is his evaluation of the dangers of the New
School's doctrine of imputation:

> This doctrine is too absurd to be long maintained. In this age of
> *improvement* it must soon give way to *increasing light:* and New
> Schoolism, more consistent with its own first principles, will deny

17. N. L. Rice, *Old and New Schools* (Cincinnati, Ohio, 1853), p. 9.

that the sin of Adam had any such effect upon his posterity as to render their sinning certain. This will be *Pelagianism full grown.*[18]

By the 1850s, however, Rice had noted in the New School several changes that altered the character of his predictions markedly. So in his 1853 preface he wrote,

> We rejoice to hope and believe, that in the years to come the two bodies will approach nearer together than now—not by the departure of the Old School from the doctrines they have held, but by the gradual purgation which the other body is undergoing, by which its heterogeneous elements are passing off and leaving the true Presbyterian element.[19]

On the New School side, the character of the debates is likewise indicative of the denomination's growing conservatism with regard to the old issues. In addition to reasserting their claim that existing doctrinal differences did not subvert a truly Calvinist and Biblical system, New School apologists now appealed to their own denomination's history as evidence of the harmless tendencies of the disputed positions. Reviewing the controversy the *Presbyterian Quarterly Review* listed some of the Old School's accusations that had been disproved within the first fifteen years:

> They charged that our brethren designed to Congregationalize the Presbyterian Church. Time has written this folly in letters of light, which may be read from the East to the West. . . .
> They charged that the Plan of Union was transferring the Presbyterian Church to Congregationalism. Four hundred Congregationalists, assembled at Albany, in 1852, embracing the leading minds of all New England, have annulled the Plan of Union for an exactly opposite reason. . . .
> They charged our brethren with the design to alter the Confession of Faith. The history of our branch of the Church for fifteen years shows that this charge was utterly erroneous. . . .

18. Ibid., pp. 34–35.
19. Ibid., p. vi.

At the South, Dr. Baxter and Dr. Plumer could only sustain the Excision Acts by imputing universal Garrisonian Abolitionism to our body. The South now sees that this was gross misrepresentation.

. . . They charged disorder and anarchy upon our Synods, Presbyteries and Churches. What are now the relative condition of the two parties in this respect?

. . . They charged our brethren a proclivity to Oberlinism, Arminianism and Unitarianism. Where has our history developed one of these things among us?

. . . They charged men like Lyman Beecher, Cox, Barnes, Duffield and Beman, were trickish, cunning revolutionary spirits aiming to overthrow Calvinistic theology and sound Presbyterianism. What verdict has fifteen years rendered in regard to them?[20]

The New School reviewer's claims required little explication. The history of the New School party as an independent denomination spoke for itself. The Old School could only reply that apostates like Barnes, Duffield, Beman, and Cox were still active in the New School. But there were no new names to add to the list, and the alleged heresies looked less menacing in the lengthened perspective.

Yet the New School apologists were still willing to meet the Old School on its own ground. In each defense they included careful expositions of the disputed doctrines of original sin, imputation, the atonement, justification, regeneration, and ability. In each they reiterated the positions defined in the "Errors and True Doctrines" of the Auburn Declaration, claiming either that the Old School charges were misrepresentations of the implications of the New School position, or that the New School interpretations were superior and more faithful to the Calvinist and Biblical heritage. The Synod of New York and New Jersey, in summarizing the position, duty, and prospects of the church in 1852, depicted the doctrinal position of the denomination as still adhering to the

20. "Division of the Presbyterian Church," *PQR* 1(March 1853):664–66.

fundamentals of Scriptural doctrine. "Our position in respect to doctrine," they declared, "is that of agreement in things *fundamental,* and toleration and forbearance in things not essential, 'endeavoring to keep unity of the Spirit in the bonds of peace.' " But the New School's appeal to fundamentals was not meant to exclude a distinctive Calvinist position. Their Calvinism, they said, was in fact superior to that of the Old School.

> With a creed strictly Calvinistic, we associate views respecting the extent of the atonement, the basis of human obligation, and the nature of the sinner's inability to do the will of God, which furnish advantages for defending the system and justifying "the ways of God to men," which those who differ from us on these points have not. They cannot, as we can, vindicate the sincerity of God in the indiscriminate offer of salvation to all, and press, as we can, the obligations of the impenitent to yield immediate obedience to the Gospel. On these topics, our theology is that of common sense, sound philosophy, and the obvious teachings of inspiration.[21]

The New School men now pointed with considerable pride to their Calvinist tradition. One of their spokesmen characterized the theological attitude that best distinguished the New School tradition in America as "living Calvinism." "Without this element," he said, "Calvinism is but a stalwart skeleton, a sepulchre of departed glory, 'a valley of dry bones, exceeding dry.' " Referring to the vitality of New Side revivalism and the "Log College" tradition in the eighteeenth century, the critic observed: "Leaving out these elements, or crowding them into a corner, resembles the play of Hamlet, with the part of Hamlet omitted; the drama of the Reformation without Luther, or the Revolution, without Washington."[22] By placing their Presbyterian forebears in such illustrious

21. *A History of the Division of the Presbyterian Church in the United States of America, by a Committee of the Synod of New York and New Jersey* (New York, 1852), pp. 216–24.
22. "The Mission of the Presbyterian Church," *PQR* 1(June 1852):21.

company, rather than emphasizing their nondenominational character, New School men now clearly claimed identity as successors to the most heroic tradition of American Presbyterianism.

It is doubtful whether the renewed debate with the Old School contributed much to this tradition of heroism. But the very fact that the New School men were now willing to debate indicates that they were actively searching for a well-defined and positive theological position. If the New School were to compete effectively with the Congregationalists, on the one hand, and the Old School Presbyterians, on the other, it would have to produce a theology that could rival the formidable heritages that each of those denominations claimed.

TRACTS WITH NEW SCHOOL TRADEMARKS

The commencement of publication of doctrinal tracts provided another indication that the denomination was in the process of defining its doctrinal position. The publication committee, situated in Philadelphia and representing roughly the same interests as the *Presbyterian Quarterly Review,* was instructed by the Assembly of 1852 "to superintend the publication of a series of tracts explanatory of the doctrines, government, and missionary policy of the Presbyterian Church."[23] During the next several years the committee produced a series of eleven doctrinal tracts. Three of these tracts are involved treatises on formal theological subjects. Two others defend infant baptism. One is on "Systematic Beneficence," and five explicate the Presbyterian system of government.

The tracts on doctrinal subjects indicate the type of theological discussion that the New School men wished to have identified with their denomination. The first tract is a treatment of *The Extent of the Atonement,* by the late James Richards. This subject had been one of the points of debate with Old School men, though it had not been a major factor in the division. The Old School held to

23. New School *Minutes, 1852,* p. 176.

the dogma of "limited atonement"—that Christ died to atone for the sins of the elect only. Richards' pamphlet is a very able defense of the argument that the benefits of Christ's death are *available* to all men. Such a teaching of a general propitiation, he insists, is not incompatible with Calvinism "unless we wish to be more Calvinistic than John Calvin himself." But Richards' primary interest is Biblical. He seeks to reconcile the Scriptural passages that seem to indicate that Christ died for all men, with those that indicate that only the elect are saved. His solution is to say that the design of the atonement is two-fold, the one ultimate and the other practical. The *ultimate* design of Christ's death, he concedes, *is* with application to the elect in view. But this ultimate design does not necessarily exclude another design, "that *the sacrifice of Christ stood in such a relation to the sins of men, as to open a way for the salvation of all.*" This latter design, in turn, does not necessarily imply that all men will be saved. Rather, it simply provides a practical rationale for preaching the offer of salvation to all men. "To us," Richards concludes, "no maxim appears more certain, *than that a salvation offered, implies a salvation provided.*"[24]

It is easy to see why Richards' study of the atonement was selected to be the first of the denominational committee's publications. His method represents everything that New School men considered best in their approach to theology. First, it is Biblical. Regardless of the merits of his conclusions, his study is a patently sincere attempt to get past the classical formulations of the seventeenth century and to recover the pure Biblical message. Second, his study is consciously placed in a Calvinistic tradition. Richards appeals to Calvin and claims that the Reformer's interpretation of the extent of the atonement was closer to Scripture than the later formulas. Third, Richards' statement mediates between two extremes. On the one hand, he asserts that the atonement was truly vicarious and not merely a governmental display; but, on the other

24. James Richards, *The Extent of the Atonement* (Philadelphia, [n.d.]), pp. 10–21.

hand, he avoids emphasizing that Christ died for the elect to the exclusion of all other considerations. In this respect, his mediating view is the same as that of the Auburn Declaration. Finally, Richards' treatment is typical of the New School approach in that it is practical. His great concern is to explain how the Biblical offer of salvation may be preached effectively to lost and dying sinners.

The second in the New School's series of doctrinal tracts is a discussion of a more controversial subject by a more controversial author. It is a lengthy discussion of justification by faith by Albert Barnes. But this tract, entitled *How Shall Man Be Just with God?*, has the same New School trademarks as Richards' study. It too is largely an exposition of Scriptural passages. At the same time, it is an attempt to express the traditional Calvinist dogma in moderate terms that allow a practical application. So, in treating the crucial question of the imputation of Christ's righteousness to men, Barnes affirms that imputation properly means "the purpose on the part of God . . . to treat those who are themselves guilty, as if they were righteous." But this concept, he warns, should not be presented in misleading legal or literal terms that are contrary to the ordinary experience of men. The transaction involved in the imputation of righteousness is simply "carrying out, on the most elevated scale possible, what is practically occurring every day in common relations and in transactions in life." Barnes therefore describes the doctrine of imputation in common-sense terms that a pastor could easily explain to the man in the pew—as a transaction analogous to the everyday occurrence of the merits of a father being attributed to a son or of credit being extended to a business firm on the basis of the reputation of its backers.[25]

The third of the New School tracts on strictly theological subjects deals with *The Perseverance of the Saints,* a tenet of Calvinism that was not a matter of dispute between the two schools. The author explains that this teaching, while not a fundamental

25. Albert Barnes, *How Shall Man Be Just with God?* (Philadelphia, 1854), pp. 81–88.

doctrine, is a very important one taught in the Word of God. The summary of his argument is purely Scriptural. "There are *express declarations* and *unconditional promises* in Scripture that every saint, without exception, shall be saved. There is no express declaration that any saint has been or ever will be lost."[26]

While not covering the full range of New School teaching, these theological tracts indicate the type of doctrinal statement that the denomination desired. Without exception they claim to be distinctly Biblical and Calvinistic. Yet all are moderate and present doctrines in terms that may be applied practically.

Several of the committee's tracts deal specifically with the subject of Presbyterianism. These indicate not only growing sectarian concern, but also that doctrinal identity was an integral part of the definition of the New School Church. One tract, "A Brief View of Presbyterian History and Doctrine," presents a partisan history of Presbyterianism in America, answering the "old slanders" about the denomination's doctrinal views by reprinting the doctrinal portion of the Auburn Declaration.[27] In another pamphlet, *Presbyterianism Explained,* a major part of the explanation is a discussion of the doctrinal heritage of Presbyterianism, including a summary of each of the characteristic New School doctrines. These doctrines are represented as the essence of the Christian tradition.

> The doctrines of the Presbyterian Church are Calvinistic . . . . They were the doctrines of all the leading reformers,—of the Waldenses, for five or six hundred years before the Reformation, —of Augustine and the primitive Church; and especially are they distinctly exhibited in the Word of God.[28]

The New School now looked to the past as well as to the present for its vindication. Appeals to the theological tradition of the Great

26. Eliphalet W. Gilbert, *The Perseverance of the Saints* (Philadelphia, [n.d.]), p. 34.

27. *A Brief View of Presbyterian History and Doctrine* (Philadelphia, [n.d.]).

28. *Presbyterianism Explained* (Philadelphia, [n.d.]), p. 12.

Awakenings, to the history of American Presbyterianism, and to the Calvinist Reformation, as well as to Scripture, were all standard parts of the New School's program. All these provided the New School with historical depth in an age when Americans, and particularly American denominationalists, felt increasingly compelled to produce a tradition in order to establish a claim to prestige (see Conclusion, below). This trend toward finding identity in the past never completely dominated New School thought. The popular character of the Church still centered on the activities of social reform and Gospel preaching.[29] But in the decade of the 1850s the increase in historical consciousness was unmistakable.

At the same time, the New School's search for relevance continued. The revolutionary changes in American thought that so quickly became apparent after the catalytic and disruptive period of the Civil War had already begun in the 1850s, and men of learning of all schools were giving serious consideration to the meaning of the achievements of the new era.

29. See, for example, Smith, *Revivalism,* pp. 53–54, 185–86, 196–98, 208, 213.

7

New Challenges in
Science and Philosophy

The New School and Science

"Science, in this age, marches with a very confident and aggressive step," wrote a contributor to the *Presbyterian Quarterly Review* in 1853. "It has prescribed no limits on itself, except the universe." New School theologians clearly recognized the claims of natural science as a serious threat to the authority of Scripture. But they did not always agree on the stance that they should assume in meeting these claims. The author of the article in the *Review* warned against those who still preached as though they lived in an age when theologians could be insensible to the demands of science. "We have fallen on a different age," he said, "and we are in no small danger of taking those texts in our preaching where the apostles spoke of the *false* sciences of their day, as the foundation of our discourses in reference to the *real* science of our own times; to the no small merriment or contempt of large classes of our hearers." In this age, he maintained, theologians should study science and stand prepared to acknowledge its legitimate claims.[1]

Christians, however, should not attempt to accommodate Scripture to science by altering the true principles of Biblical interpretation, added the reviewer. They should avoid the temptation to resolve the problem by resorting to a denial of "the entire doctrine of inspiration—maintaining that the Bible *contains* a revelation,

1. "Thoughts on Theology," *PQR* 2(June 1853), p. 10. Albert Barnes is probably the author.

instead of *being* a revelation; or, admitting certain facts as actually existing in the world, to make the whole Bible a *Myth,* to be classed with the beautiful creations of the Grecian Mythology." Scripture, he affirmed, should be allowed to stand on its own merits. Theologians should recognize that "the blowpipe, the telescope, and the microscope pay very little deference to the interpretation of the Bible by theologians respecting the first chapter of Genesis, or the statements of the Bible about the origin of the human race." The theologian should be confident enough in the integrity of Scripture to allow the scientist to continue his investigations unimpeded by the dictates of Scripture. "If we are both right," the reviewer concluded, "we shall harmonize at last; if not, the sooner it is known the better."[2]

No scientific findings were of greater consequence for the theologian in the mid-nineteenth century than those of geology. When the geologist discussed the creation and age of the earth, he dealt with subjects immediately pertinent to Scripture. At first, some American theologians had treated the conclusions of geologists with disdain. When, for example, Yale scientist Benjamin Silliman informed Yale theologian Nathaniel Taylor that the wall of New Haven's Grove Street cemetery contained fossils millions of years old, Taylor is reported to have responded, "God *can* create fossils in stone, and you can't prove that he didn't."[3] But by the 1850s attempts to retain a six thousand year chronology were becoming passé, and theologians were adjusting their interpretations of Scripture to the geological hypotheses with little loss of face. Nevertheless, serious problems remained, and the entire question of the relation of science to theology seemed to focus on the relation of records written in the rocks to those written in the book of Genesis.

The first issue of the *Presbyterian Quarterly Review* set the tone for the extensive discussion of Genesis and geology that was to follow. In an article entitled "Is the Science of Geology True?"

2. Ibid., pp. 10–11.
3. Roland H. Bainton, *Yale and the Ministry* (New York, 1957), p. 107.

the writer observed that the Bible is not a book of science and that it was not meant to anticipate all future inventions or discoveries in philosophy and science. "Men who go to it for an inspired system of astronomy or geology," he suggested, "might as well go to it for a heaven-contrived system of architecture, or agriculture, or navigation; might as well look in the Pentateuch for the telescope, and the steamboat." "The prejudices of many Christians against geology," he advised, "must be surrendered." The writer affirmed that Christians should no longer hesitate to admit that geology had established beyond a shadow of a doubt,

> 1. That the Earth, instead of originating six thousand years ago, had existed through an indefinite period, safely expressed by millions of ages.
> 2. That Creation, taken in its largest sense, instead of being accomplished in one of our weeks, was a gradual work through countless ages.[4]

Nevertheless, even when these conclusions were granted, considerable room for debate remained on the question of the exact method of reconciling Genesis and geology. During the next decade this was the most lively subject for scientific discussion in the *Presbyterian Quarterly Review.* The main phase of the debate centered on the theories propounded by a close associate of the New School, Taylor Lewis, an eminent Dutch Reformed scholar and Professor of Greek at Union College. In a work published in 1855, on *The Six Days of Creation,* Lewis approached the problem from a philological point of view. Examining the derivations of the words in the Genesis narrative, he concluded that the ancient term translated "create" did not mean to bring into existence from nothing, but rather to arrange materials previously existing.[5] So, Lewis argued, the Creation was not a series of sudden supernatural

---

4. "Is the Science of Geology True?" *PQR* 1 (June 1852):84–87.
5. From summary in "The Mosaic Account of Creation Scientific," *PQR* 7 (July 1858):131.

efforts of Almighty power, but a process of gradual developments. Lewis also made a philological study of the word translated "day" in Genesis One, and concluded that the idea of time in the ancient term "day" was wholly subordinate to the idea of a cycle or alteration of two great phenomena, such as light and darkness.[6] This interpretation—that the *primary* meaning of the term "day" was a cycle of indefinite duration—went a step beyond the more popular mid-nineteenth-century explanation that the term "day" simply *allowed* for the long periods of time that geology demanded.

The next year, 1856, Lewis explained some of the implications of his views in a second book, *The Bible and Science: Or, the World Problem.* In this book he made it clear that since science was fallible and the Bible infallible, scientists should listen more carefully to the dictates of revelation. More particularly, they should recognize that Lewis' own philological studies had established that the Bible *did* reveal the basic scientific facts about the process of creation.[7]

The reviewer of *The Bible and Science* defended Lewis' approach to the question of the relation of science to Scripture in no uncertain terms. "Science has reached the end of her peculiar province," he asserted, "when she has produced her classified facts, the materials of our use." Accordingly, only Christians trained in science can draw the proper inferences from the facts that are collected. The Christian must interpret these facts in the light of Scripture; but he may never use them to challenge its authority. "Grant one grain of error in the Sacred Book," the reviewer stated, "and its authority is gone." The Bible claims exemption from error and therefore must be considered the first authority in all scientific questions. Yet in the face of the Biblical claims, "Christian men and Christian ministers are found ready to lose their balance at the discovery of a fossil, or at the superficial suggestion of some

6. "Prof. Lewis' View of the 'Days' of Creation," *PQR* 4(December 1855):473–74.
7. "The Bible and Science," *PQR* 5(March 1857):642–54.

physical explorer." Such an attitude, which encouraged tinkering with Scripture at every new breathing of science, he said, was bound to manufacture infidels by the scores and hundreds. For him, there was only one solution to the question of the relation of the Bible to science—humble faith in Scripture alone. He appealed to

> those who hold forth the Word of Life, to take heed how they bow down before the haughty nod of earthly science. They have a Divine treasure in their hands. Let them beware lest they dishonour it in their "liberality." A "Liberal Christianity" is too often a Christianity brought down to the level of man's corrupt natural taste. When wordly men praise us as "liberal Christians," it is high time for us to examine the foundations.[8]

The editors of the *Presbyterian Quarterly Review* published these remarks only after prefacing the article with the precaution that the antiscientific statements of the reviewer should not be interpreted as suggesting that well-ascertained facts in science are not to be admitted as fixed truth.[9] The contrast between this editorial precaution and the sentiments of the reviewer suggest that there were already two diverse approaches to the question of science and the Bible in the New School. On the one hand, was the approach of the reviewer, assuming a defensive stance behind the wall of Scriptural infallibility; on the other, was the attitude of the editors, boldly accepting the new science with confidence that it would never subvert God's revealed truths.

The pro-science view was championed by Albert Barnes, who had a strong voice in the editorial policies of the Philadelphia magazine. In 1859 Barnes published a full-length statement of his views in *Inquiries and Suggestions in Regard to the Foundation of Faith in the Word of God*. In this book he took the position of the confident. Christians, he declared, have nothing to fear from the disclosures of Science. Science has never demonstrated anything contradictory to Scripture, and by the nature of the case men have

8. Ibid., pp. 651–53.
9. Editorial comments, ibid., p. 642.

every reason to believe that it never will. Barnes based his confidence on an appeal to man's reason. "The teachings of the Bible
commend themselves to man's reason," he said, and "the Bible, in
its moral teachings has commended itself to mankind as being in
accordance with the principles of eternal truth and justice." There
is therefore no need to fear that reason applied to the natural world
will ever undermine the truth revealed in the Word of God. Independent scientific research should, in fact, be encouraged, because "the nearer the approximation which men make in any form
of knowledge to these principles of eternal truth, the more they will
appreciate and love the word of God."[10]

Barnes' *Inquiries and Suggestions* appeared early in 1859, a time
when defenders of Scriptural infallibility could still encourage
independent scientific research as a means of verifying Scriptural
integrity. The greatest challenge of the generation, the findings of
geology, had seemingly been met successfully without hauling
down the masts of an enlightened Christianity. But in 1859 a new
challenge appeared on the scientific horizon that was to force even
Albert Barnes to alter his course.

The Origin of Species did not immediately receive notice in the
Presbyterian Quarterly Review.[11] The first discussion of it appears
in 1862 in an article by Albert Barnes reviewing the liberal trends
in British scientific and religious thought. Barnes's article, entitled
"Readjustments of Christianity," reiterated the general principle
that "in every new age there is some modification to be made of
old opinions and doctrines on all subjects."[12] In the course of his
study, however, he made it unmistakably clear that accommodation

10. Albert Barnes, *Inquiries and Suggestions in Regard to the Foundation
of Faith in the Word of God* (Philadelphia, 1859) pp. 173–75.
11. It did, however, receive an early, unfavorable review in the *American
Theological Review*, under the editorship of New School theologian Henry B.
Smith; see D. R. Goodwin, "Darwin on the Origin of Species," *American Theological Review*, 1st ser. 2(May 1860): 330–44. See also Chapter 8, below.
12. [Albert Barnes], "Readjustments of Christianity," *PQR* 11(July 1862):2.
This article was attributed to Barnes by Davis, "Albert Barnes—1798–1870,"
p. 460.

to the theories of Darwin was one readjustment he was not prepared to make. Barnes prefaced his remarks on Darwin by observing that no opinions are more absurd than those sometimes held by "scientific" men. "With all that there is that is bounded, and fixed, and accurate in true science, yet a collection of the theories advanced and the opinions held by men of 'science' in different periods of the world, would have much more the aspect of wild romance than the Arabian Nights, and would pass in absurdity the wildest legends of the Talmud." He marveled that the general progress of the world had done nothing to restrain men from suggesting such absurdities. He was convinced that Darwin's theory was too fantastic to deserve serious consideration. It went beyond all reasonable demands on men's credulity. "According to this theory," Barnes exclaimed, "elephants, and tadpoles, and men; Bacon, Newton, Plato, the orang-ou-tang and the ape; the lizard [and fifteen more such creatures,] the malt that lay in the 'House that Jack built,' and the rat that ate the malt [etc.] all are derived from the same origin; all are the results of the 'strugglings' of the 'strongest' in the formation of 'species;' all have, in fact, come from one little 'monad,' in its 'struggles' to develope itself." As well as ridiculing the theory, Barnes suggested that it was ironic that the same group of British scientists who had long maintained that it was absurd to think that all men were descended from one pair of first parents now were affirming that all species descended from a single monad. "In the meantime," he continued, "until these 'Doctors shall agree,' and shall inform us which of these theories is to be believed, it may be prudent for the world to act as if the Bible gave the true account of the matter."[13]

New School men had little reason to adopt Darwin's novel theories at this early date, and thus Barnes's reaction should not be interpreted as gross illiberality. His outraged response indicates,

13. [Barnes], "Readjustments of Christianity," pp. 68–71.

however, that there were already signs of the impending realignment of American Protestantism on the new scientific questions. Barnes, for example, stood closer to his old rival Charles Hodge on the great issues of the new era than to the wing of evangelicalism represented by Harvard scientist Asa Gray (1810–88) or Congregationalist preacher Henry Ward Beecher (1813–87), who maintained that evolutionary views could be accommodated to the Christian faith.[14]

As the new era brought increasing challenges to the authority of Scripture, New School men placed greater emphasis on the doctrine of Biblical infallibility. This doctrine, which had been assumed in the debates with the Old School, was now endorsed with remarkable unanimity in the New School Church. Albert Barnes listed it first among the unalterable tenets of the faith in his discussion of "Readjustments of Christianity." It is the established teaching of the Church, he said,

> that the Bible is a book given by a supernatural inspiration of God; that is, that truths are recorded there which in fact have their origin *directly* in the mind of God, and have been imparted by him to the minds of the writers by a direct communication; that those truths are above any natural power of the writers to originate them, to discover them, or to express them; and that in recording them, how ever much they may have been left to their own peculiarities of modes of expression or language, they have

14. Asa Gray, the recipient of Darwin's early outline of the theory of evolution in 1857, defended the doctrine in the *Atlantic Monthly* in 1860, maintaining that it could be held in a form consistent with theism. A gradual evolutionary process, he argued, was compatible with God's creative design. Charles Hodge conceded this, but argued that an integral part of Darwin's view was that the natural causes of change were undirected and hence without design. Charles Hodge, *Systematic Theology,* 3 vols. (New York, 1871–1875), 2:18–19. Cf. [Asa Gray], "Darwin and His Reviewers," *Atlantic Monthly* 6(October 1860):406–25. Henry Ward Beecher, under the influence of Herbert Spencer, later became a popular advocate of Christian evolutionary views.

been so guided by the Holy Spirit as to be preserved from error; that this principle applies to every part of the sacred volume; that the Bible is in fact, and to all intents and purposes, *one book,* whose real author is the Spirit of God.[15]

Barnes presented this statement of his doctrine of inspiration as part of his answer to the challenge of higher critics of the Bible, who used modern historical methods to attempt to discredit the Scriptural accounts. This was another subject on which there was agreement in the New School. Men like Edward Robinson and Albert Barnes had learned from the German methods of Biblical interpretation. Yet they were not willing to accept the conclusions of German critics who challenged the integrity of Scripture. While Barnes refused to make a sweeping condemnation of all German thought, he did maintain that both German Biblical criticism and German philosophical speculations were exceedingly dangerous threats to faith in God's Word.[16]

The New School and Philosophy

In the decade of the 1850s New School theology was experiencing the tensions inevitable to any system that identifies itself by its newness. It was getting old. The modes of philosophical expression that the New School leaders had championed in the 1820s and 1830s already appeared slightly antiquated. The result was an emerging conflict between those who desired to preserve the New School principle of openness to new philosophical interpretations and those who wished to preserve the *content* of the original New School philosophy.

By 1859 the situation had become serious enough for the *Presbyterian Quarterly Review* to publish a call for peace. "Do we Need a New Doctrinal Agitation in Our Church?" asked the New School representative in the title of his article. Presbyterians were

15. [Albert Barnes], "Readjustments of Christianity," p. 32.
16. Ibid., pp. 10–11.

always in danger of division, he warned, and New School men should therefore be particularly careful not to accuse their own brethren of heresy or to make theological mountains out of philosophical molehills. The author attempted to outline the formula for peace. After tracing the history of Reformed doctrine, he observed that "every system of scientific theology has some philosophic germ in it, begins always from some developing metaphysical point, and this, whatever it be, really colours and gives character to the system." The secret for avoiding conflict, then, was to recognize that every such philosophical system could be abused, but that all should be tolerated as long as the essentials of the system of truth were preserved. "Presbyterianism rests on Calvinism," he affirmed. "We have agreed not to go beyond that form of truth. But our compact equally binds us not to disturb men who keep within that enclosure."

The author of "Do We Need a New Doctrinal Agitation?" was not erecting the walls of Calvinism in order to shield the cultivation of error. He explicitly maintained his own opposition to the new philosophy. "We shall be ready to sound the alarm whenever we see real danger," he assured his readers. "If we should be disposed to indicate the direction from which it is likely to come, we should unhesitatingly point to Germany." The speculations of Germany, he charged, appealed to those men in the Presbyterian Church who were hoping to distinguish themselves by being advocates of something original, profound, and transcendent. They were adopted by men who felt that the common-sense methods of looking at the Scriptures and theology were not highly enough spiced for the nineteenth century. Such men, he warned, were in danger of taking the road that led to the critical conclusions of D. F. Strauss (German author of the highly controversial *Life of Jesus*), the speculations of Hegel, and "the practical results in Sunday balls and theatres." But having thus dissociated himself from German views, the author urged toleration of good Calvinists who were more sympathetic than he to the German philosophy.

He cautioned against a party spirit in the New School, and urged
toleration as long as the new views did not lead to actual heresy.[17]

Looking back through the decade we can reconstruct how the
latent party spirit had developed in the New School over the
philosophical question. In 1854 Benjamin J. Wallace, editor of
the *Presbyterian Quarterly Review,* explained the situation in considerable detail. Surveying ten recent publications—including
works by Laurens P. Hickok, Horace Bushnell, Henry James (the
elder) the Unitarian Edmund H. Sears, John Nevin and Philip
Schaff (both of the German Reformed Seminary in Mercersburg,
Pennsylvania), and an edition of the works of Coleridge—the editor attempted to assess the import of the latest trend in American
thought as represented by these men. Adopting the attitude that
where there is so much smoke there must be fire, he suggested that
this immense movement in the "direction of spirituality" demanded serious consideration. Wallace defined "spirituality" as
the emphasis on the spirit or essence of a thing. "In philosophy," he
stated, "it exalts the soul over matter; in religion it seeks whatever
brings God and man into most intimate union; in everything it
searches out life."

Wallace summarized what had happened in American philosophy, observing that

> the philosophy which has mainly prevailed since the beginning
> of the eighteenth century among the Anglo-Saxon race, is the
> Aristotelian or Baconian, that of which Locke and the entire
> Scottish school are representatives. It is the philosophy of the
> golden mean or common sense; the great development under it
> has been that of enterprise and activity in every direction, tem-
> poral and religious.

Now a new philosophy was replacing this common-sense method.
"It is alleged," said Wallace, "that the philosophy of which Plato

17. "Do We Need a New Doctrinal Agitation in Our Church?" *PQR*
7(April 1859):665–69.

is the earliest of the remarkable or well known expounders, and which its advocates represent to be more spiritual, is taking its place." The Presbyterian editor then identified the source of this new Platonic, or spiritualistic, thought that was sweeping the English-speaking world. "No one, we presume, will be disposed to deny the influence of Germany over all the theologizing of the time." This German influence, which was making the Anglo-Saxon world part of its theological colonial empire, was all in the direction of spirituality.

> Germany has no other philosophy than the transcendental. It is not a question there between Plato and the empirical schools; they consider *that* quite gone by; the question is between Spinoza and Kant; and whether Fichte, Schelling and Hegel are legitimate or illegitimate successors of Kant. No one in Germany, at all orthodox, thinks of denying that philosophy now begins at Kant; the question there is, whether the next true movement will develop from him, or from the point which Hegel has reached.

Originally, the spiritualistic influence of German thought had been transmitted to America largely through the medium of Samuel Taylor Coleridge. Wallace's review took note of a recent edition of Coleridge's work edited by William G. T. Shedd, a young New School professor who taught briefly at Auburn before leaving for Andover in 1854. Wallace made no objections to the work of Shedd, but he did object to Coleridge and was ready to point to another source of the dangerous new thought in the New School. "Union College," he wrote, " . . . with Hickok and Lewis on its faculty, bids fair to become a fountain of Coleridgeeanism." Laurens P. Hickok, together with his close associate Taylor Lewis, stood at the center of the new movement in the New School. Hickok, said Wallace, "has written a work on Rational Psychology, and more recently one on Moral Science, both based on this system—and his works have this special advantage, for his cause, that Dr. Hickok's mind is less imaginative than most of the philosophers of this school, which predisposes the shrewd American mind in his favor, as a man of Science."[18] Hickok had left his position at Auburn Seminary in 1852 to become Professor of Mental and Moral Science and vice-president of Union College. But he remained in very good standing in the New School Presbyterian Church, subsequently defeating George Duffield in the election for Moderator to preside over the crucial slavery debates at the Assembly of 1856.

Benjamin Wallace pointed out the dangers of the trend toward German thought, but, in the spirit of the New School, refused to condemn the new ideas *per se.* The next year the *Review* published a favorable notice of Hickok's works,[19] and in 1856 it included an article by Hickok himself.[20] But, while urging tolerance, Wallace hoped to meet the problems raised by spiritualism in traditional New School terms. In his 1854 article he asked the question— What should be done for theology under the influence of this "ground-swell of spiritualism?" His answer was "that in theology we need GOOD COMMON SENSE. It is this excellent quality which teaches us the grand outlines of Calvinism.[21] As for the Church itself, the proper response to the new philosophy should be to combine the theoretical and the practical. The theoretical spiritualism of the philosophers should be transformed into the practical revival spirit that had given birth to the New School. "Has that mode of revival spirit which swept in such mighty power over our church, spent its force?" Wallace asked. In this practical spirit was the common ground on which the New School could stand united in the face of the impending theological debates. "We are like those who watch for the morning," the editor of the *Presbyterian Quarterly Review* concluded, "our souls break for their longing after God; and while knowing the doom that rests upon

18. "Religion and Philosophy," *PQR* 2(March 1854):655–87.
19. "Dr. Hickok's Works: The Rule of Right," *PQR* 4(December 1855): 435–69.
20. Laurens P. Hickok, "Theology and Philosophy Possible," *PQR* 4(March 1856):529–60.
21. "Religion and Philosophy," p. 693.

those who, though anointed captains, will not lead in the great
battle of life, we ponder anxiously and yet hopefully the deep
words: HE SHALL BAPTIZE YOU WITH THE HOLY GHOST AND
WITH FIRE."[22]

The Challenge for Theology

The prayers for a return to the New School spirit of unity in
revivals and practical reforms were answered in part by the great
revival of 1858, by their crusade in the Civil War, and finally by
the reunion with the Old School. But in the meantime New School
men were facing a series of problems in trying to define their
theological position. First, they had the problem of whether the
New School would have a distinctive theology at all. The characteristic teachings of the early New School theology no longer
seemed wholly adequate to many in the 1850s. At the same time,
considerable sentiment continued in the denomination in favor of
avoiding theological debates, emphasizing rather unity in social
and religious action. In the 1850s the trait that best distinguished
New School from Old School Presbyterians was zeal for social
reforms—a trait that created at least some danger that activist
sentiments would submerge the theological emphases. Yet, as New
School men were forced to assume the responsibilities of denominationalism in the 1840s and 1850s, it became increasingly
apparent that they must maintain a vigorous formal theology if
they were to compete successfully with the Old School and the
Congregationalists. In such an undertaking New School theologians were faced with several important restrictions. The tradition of their movement demanded that their theology be distinctly
Biblical and Reformed on the one hand, yet mediating and practical
on the other. Their denomination's claim to constitutionality demanded that their theology be traditional in its content, while the
spirit of the age demanded that it be relevant to contemporary

22. Ibid., p. 698.

cultural, intellectual, and scientific achievements. Maintaining all these balances was a difficult assignment. Yet a complex and unsettled atmosphere is often most productive of genuine creativity.

The New School theologian who preeminently met the demands of this situation was Henry Boynton Smith (1815–77). A New Englander, Smith came into the New School Presbyterian Church in 1850 when he accepted a call to be Professor of Church History at Union Theological Seminary in New York City. Union Seminary had been founded in 1836 by a group of New School ministers, led by Absalom Peters, as an intellectual center "around which all men of moderate views and feelings, who desire to live free from party strife, and to stand aloof from all extremes of doctrinal speculation, practical radicalism, and ecclesiastical domination may cordially and affectionately rally."[23] Yet, as with many united evangelical projects of the earlier era, the seminary had failed to distinguish itself after the Presbyterian schism. When Henry B. Smith came to Union, Edward Robinson of the Department of Biblical Studies was his only colleague of any note. Within the next two decades, however, Smith's influence was decisive in transforming the institution into an important center for theological study. Working in the context of the New School climate of opinion, he also established himself as one of the leading American thinkers of his day. James Hastings Nichols rates Henry B. Smith with Charles Hodge, Horace Bushnell, Edwards A. Park, John Nevin, and Philip Schaff as "among the first half-dozen theologians of their generation."[24] Smith was easily the first among New School theologians, and as such deserves attention as the most influential representative of later New School thought.

23. George L. Prentiss, *The Union Theological Seminary in the City of New York: Historical and Biographical Sketches of Its First Fifty Years* (New York, 1889), p. 8.

24. James Hastings Nichols, *Romanticism in American Theology: Nevin and Schaff at Mercersburg* (Chicago, 1961), p. 3.

8

The Mediating Theology of
Henry B. Smith

The decision to leave the pleasant security of his Professorship of
Mental and Moral Philosophy at Amherst College for the un-
certainty of Union Seminary, New York City, and New School
Presbyterianism was a difficult one for Henry Boynton Smith. As
well as involving a cut in salary, a supposed hazard to his health,
and entirely new social connections, it meant identifying himself
with an institution that he considered to be of slight academic
standing, where concern to produce useful ministers often outweighed zeal for theological science. Furthermore, he noted, "the
theological position is not defined. It stands somewhere between
Andover and Princeton, just as New School Presbyterianism
stands between Congregationalism and consistent domineering
Presbyterianism, and it will be pressed on all sides." In 1850 it was
"still a problem" whether the theology of Union would be "resolved into these two" or "consolidated on its own ground." But
Smith seems to have recognized that his talents were well-suited
to the position of Professor of Church History at the New School
seminary. He accepted the "more arduous" task with the observation that at least it would allow him to be "a little more free."[1]

During the quarter century that Smith taught at Union, he
used this freedom to define the theological position of the semi-

1. Henry B. Smith in a letter to George Stearns, September 17, 1850, in
Henry Boynton Smith: His Life and Work, ed. Mrs. Henry B. Smith (New
York, 1881), p. 159 (hereafter cited as *Smith*).

nary. In 1855, on the occasion of his election to the more prestigeous Chair of Systematic Theology, he outlined the basic principle of his own thought. "To mediate between our extremes is our vital need," he declared, "and such mediation can only be found in Christ, and not in an ethical system. As the central idea of the whole Christian system is in mediation, so should this be the spirit of our theology, the spirit of our lives."[2] Unity through mediation in Christ was the dominant and recurring theme of Smith's life and work. It was the controlling principle of his philosophy and theology, the basic motif of his work as a church historian and a systematic theologian, and his compelling motive as the chief architect of the reunion of Old and New School Presbyterians.

Henry Smith's thought was attuned to the needs of mid-nineteenth-century Reformed theology long before he came into the New School Church. His Christocentric principles grew directly out of his own youthful religious experience. A native of Maine, he was raised in a Unitarian home and attended Bowdoin College, where he was known as a free thinker "in danger from convivial habits."[3] According to his own account, his dissatisfaction with trinitarian Christianity was wholly intellectual. But during the spring of his senior year he experienced a radical change of heart. Under the influence of the piety of the poet Longfellow, who then taught at Bowdoin, and the intellectual persuasion of Thomas G. Upham, his teacher of Mental and Moral Philosophy, Smith committed himself to the crucial tenet of trinitarian Christianity with the fervor of a convert. "I know nothing," he wrote at the

2. Henry B. Smith, "The Idea of Christian Theology as a System, Inaugural Address Delivered on Occasion of His Induction into the Chair of Systematic Theology in the Union Theological Seminary, New York, Sabbath Evening, May 6, 1855," in *Faith and Philosophy: Discourses and Essays by Henry B. Smith, D.D., LL.D.,* ed. George L. Prentiss (New York, 1877), p. 6.

3. Cyrus Hamlin in a letter to Lewis F. Stearns, n.d., in Lewis F. Stearns, *Henry Boynton Smith* (Boston, 1892), p. 10.

time of his conversion, "but that Christ is my Redeemer and has atoned for my sins."[4]

Smith's commitment to the service of Christ, made when he was eighteen, had a decisive influence on his thought for the rest of his life. By the time he was twenty-one he had already arrived at the basic principle of his theological method. Writing on his twenty-first birthday (November 21, 1836), he summarized his ambitions as a theologian in the context of the religious controversies of New England. "I cannot find religious truth in the Old School or the New," he said. "I find it only in the doctrine of redemption. My object is to make and harmonize a system which shall make Christ the central point of all important religious truth and doctrine."[5] Smith was evidently evaluating his past and future. In the previous two years he had begun formal theological study but had found little to satisfy him. In 1834 he had enrolled at Andover Seminary to study theology with Leonard Woods, but a serious illness had forced him to leave before the year was completed. The next year he had resumed his studies, this time at Bangor Seminary in Maine, where Enoch Pond, a disciple of Nathaniel Emmons, was in charge of the Theology Department. After a year at Bangor he had returned to Bowdoin to assume a position as tutor. At this point, then, he was evaluating the prospects for his future as a theologian. Without desiring to uproot the conservative New England tradition in which he had been trained, Smith sought a more vital statement of the Biblical message.

The opportunity to expand his theological horizons beyond the boundaries of the New England debates presented itself within the next two years. At the end of his year of teaching at Bowdoin, he suffered a physical collapse that prompted him to go to Europe

4. Henry B. Smith in a letter to his parents, April 9, 1834, in Smith, *Smith,* p. 15.

5. Henry B. Smith in a letter to Daniel Goodwin, November 11, 1834, in Smith, *Smith,* p. 32.

for a complete rest. After spending the winter of 1836–37 re-cuperating in Paris, he traveled to Germany where he began two years of study. Study in Germany was still relatively uncommon for American students of divinity. For many American Protestants the Transcendentalist movement in New England was sufficient proof of the dangers necessarily inherent in German thought, and prejudice against all German ideas was becoming almost an article of faith in many areas of American theology. Henry Smith was one of the first American theologians to venture deeply into the supposed dark forests of German philosophy and to return to his native country with his Reformed faith intact.

The character of Henry Smith's reception in Germany indicates something of the novelty of his adventure. He spent the first year of his study at the University of Halle, which was then experi-encing an evangelical revival under the influence of Friedrich August Gottreu Tholuck (1799–1877). Tholuck, who came to Halle in 1826 to turn the university away from rationalism, stood at the center of the vigorous evangelical party in Germany. This party had appropriated much from Schleiermacher, Hegel, and Moravian Pietism in order to preserve a remnant of Christian thought in the face of the assault of radical German philosophy. When Smith arrived in Germany, Tholuck soon adopted him as one of his closest personal friends. Through Tholuck's influence, Smith quickly gained acceptance in the circle of some of the leading German thinkers of the day. During the second year of his study, spent at the University of Berlin, he cultivated valuable close friendships with Ernst Wilhelm Hengstenberg (1802–69), the conservative Biblical scholar; Johann August Wilhelm Neander (1789–1850), the famous church historian; and the widow of the philosopher Hegel. Smith's letters of this period read like pages out of a history of nineteenth-century Germany theology. They are filled with references to his conversations with many of the most prominent thinkers in the German theological world and indicate that he had become thoroughly familiar with nearly every aspect of German evangelical philosophy and theology.[6]

At first, he passed through a period of intense struggles with doubts and unbeliefs generated by the German challenges to his faith.[7] By the second year, however, he had reconciled his admiration for German thought with his New England principles. In August 1839 he wrote,

> As to the unfavorable influence of German philosophy, I cannot, of course, judge of myself, how much I have changed; but I have not the conviction that study here has had any other effect than that of making my views more deeply grounded, and of developing them more clearly. If I thought that my heart was losing ground, that I were losing my simple reverence for the Scriptures, and my simple faith in experimental religion, I would not, could not hesitate—I would come right home.[8]

When Smith did finally come home the next year, he was probably a decade ahead of most of his contemporaries in the moderate and conservative camps of Congregationalism and Presbyterianism in his comprehension of German thought. Accordingly, nearly a decade passed before his qualifications were fully recognized. At first, he could not even find permanent employment. For a year he held a temporary instructorship at Bowdoin. Then, after another year of waiting, he accepted a call to a country pastorate at West Amesbury, Massachusetts. He remained in this position until 1847, when he received the appointment to Amherst.

The real turning point in Smith's career came as a result of an address he delivered before the Porter Rhetorical Society at Am-

6. Various letters from Europe, March 18, 1838 to April 8, 1840, in Smith, *Smith*, pp. 45–84.

7. Stearns, *Henry Boynton Smith*, p. 57.

8. Henry B. Smith in a letter "to a friend," Berlin, August 11, 1839, Smith, *Smith*, p. 74.

herst in 1849. Horace Bushnell, then approaching his zenith, had delivered the annual address the previous year. Speaking on "Dogma and Spirit," Bushnell had urged emancipation from the dogmas of the competing theological parties and return to the spiritual life of early Christianity. The controversial Hartford pastor was a formidable man to follow on any platform. It was particularly difficult for Smith since he sympathized with much of Bushnell's criticism of the scholasticism of the New England systems. But Bushnell, he believed, held a one-sided view that emphasized the spirit at the expense of the dogma. In Smith's view, the spiritual life of faith and the formal intellectual discipline of philosophical theology were complementary and should be balanced. He therefore accepted the challenge that Bushnell's address had provided, choosing as his subject "The Relations of Faith and Philosophy."[9]

Smith's address proved the turning point in his career in very practical terms. William Adams, one of the directors of Union Seminary, was in the audience and was directly responsible for Smith's nomination to the Professorship of Church History the next year.[10] At the same time, the publication of the lecture in *Bibliotheca Sacra* in November 1849 was a major factor in establishing Smith's reputation as one of America's outstanding thinkers.[11] All the essential elements of his theological method are contained in the address, and much of his career at Union Seminary was devoted to developing the principles he enunciated at Amherst.[12] An examination of its contents reveals why Smith's thought was well-suited to the needs of New School theology.

9. Stearns, *Henry Boynton Smith,* pp. 114–17.

10. William Adams, in the *New York Evangelist* (September 9, 1880), quoted in Stearns, *Henry Boynton Smith,* pp. 138–39.

11. Stearns, *Henry Boynton Smith,* pp. 117–18.

12. Smith himself observed near the end of his career that he had never gone much beyond this address; see editor's Introductory Note, in Henry B. Smith, *Introduction to Christian Theology,* ed. William S. Karr (New York, 1883), pp. iv–v.

"The Relations of Faith and Philosophy" describes the impending philosophical challenge to American orthodoxy, defines the essential terms of the conflict, and then proposes a positive solution. Faith and philosophy come into conflict, Smith argues, because they are essentially diverse human activities. "The one is a simple act of trust; the other a reflective process. . . . The former says, I must believe in order to know; the latter, I must know in order to believe, and then, it not seldom adds, there is no need of believing." Faith rests upon authority. "That authority is divine and decisive; it is the very word of God recorded in Scriptures." Philosophy, on the other hand, "is the product of human thought." It rests its authority on the principles, laws, and systems which men observe and develop. The tendency of all philosophy is to assume the universality of its principles. In its most extreme form it leads to a pantheism that claims to stand triumphant over Christianity. It accepts the alternative, faith *or* philosophy. In the mid-nineteenth century it presents "the great alternative of our times—the choice between Christ and Spinoza." The natural tendency of faith is also to accept this disjunctive alternative of faith *or* philosophy but then to judge philosophy by its abuses, concluding that all philosophy is subversive.[13]

Neither of the alternatives in the disjunctive proposition is tenable, according to Smith. Rather, "our ground should be, that faith and philosophy are not inherently opposed, but inherently at one." The suggestion that there can be faith without philosophy ignores the fact that faith claims to present man with the most rational account of the origins and order of the universe and that as soon as faith makes this claim, it must be prepared to enter into philosophical discussion.[14] Likewise, the claim that there can be philosophy without faith is equally untenable, he asserts. It ignores the limits inherent in the nature of philosophy. Philosophy is a

13. Henry B. Smith, "The Relations of Faith and Philosophy," *Faith and Philosophy,* pp. 4–12.
14. Ibid., p. 12.

mode of human knowledge. It is not the whole of that knowledge, but only a mode of it. It is the mode of knowing things rationally, of knowing them in their causes, their relations, and their ends, and of knowing them in the harmony and completeness of a system. "It being only such a mode of knowledge, the materials, the substance, the facts must, from the nature of the case, exist before the philosophy, and be taken for granted by the philosophy, and be the limit and the test of the philosophy."[15] Here is where faith and philosophy converge. Faith also rests on something external to itself. Both faith and philosophy are modes of dealing with facts that have a real existence independent of man's knowledge of them. This realism is an essential part of Smith's system. In another place, he calls it "the life of theology."[16] According to Smith, the Calvinist doctrine of God's eternal decrees implies that "all that is . . . pre-existed in the divine mind in idea and purpose," and that "all true knowledge is a participation in these ideas."[17] Faith and philosophy are both modes of dealing with these facts of reality. They converge when both accept as their assumptions the reality of the existence of a personal God, and the possibility of a revelation. Through revelation men may know the facts of redemption. They are revealed in Scripture, "which gives us both the facts and the divine interpretation of them." Faith and philosophy complement each other, as they are both means by which men may properly respond to the most important realities they can know.[18]

Once men grant the assumption of the existence of a personal God and the possibility of revelation, they receive confirmation that the Scriptural revelation is the correct one through the internal testimony of the experience of their own hearts, the evidences of the power of Christianity in history, and the compelling

15. Ibid., pp. 18–19.
16. Smith, "The Idea of Christian Theology as a System," p. 129.
17. Ibid., p. 24.
18. Smith, "The Relations of Faith and Philosophy," pp. 20–23.

solutions to the great questions of human destiny that Christian revelation provides.[19]

When philosophy grants the Christian assumptions, it complements faith by allowing men to reach a more rational understanding of the universe and of their own situation. But philosophy does not always grant such an assumption. It may claim to undermine the cardinal points on which revelation rests. "And here," says Smith, "is where philosophy can be met only with philosophy. It is as unphilosophical for faith to be dogmatic here, as it is for philosophy to be dogmatic in the face of recognized reality." The only way to meet skepticism is to expose the principle that lies at the heart of all modern infidelity. That prime falsehood is the principle "that we have given a rational account of things when we have reduced them to abstract ideas, or great principles; to laws, whether physical or ideal; that physical causes, antecedents and consequents, are the great end of philosophic inquiries; in short, that law and system are sufficient to account for the energy, the order, and the end of the universe." The limits inherent in skeptical philosophy must thus be exposed and contrasted with the verities of Christian revelation. Man's actual belief in these verities is not dependent on scientific analysis or rational proof, but on his God-given ability to recognize truth. The starting point of Christian apologetics is that man was created in the image of God and therefore is endowed with native belief and the capability of recognizing the truth of God's revelation as it speaks to his own needs. "Man was made for God," says Smith, "and all man's powers, in their right use, tend toward their great Author. Here is the actual stronghold of such belief against all skeptical systems."[20]

Christians can not be content, however, to rest their faith solely in the simple realities that they recognize as true in their own

19. Ibid., pp. 20–21.
20. Ibid., pp. 24–26. Cf. Henry B. Smith, *Apologetics: A Course of Lectures,* ed. William S. Karr (New York, 1882), p. 75.

hearts. Rather, once they have recognized the reality of God and the truth of his revelation, they must use the methods of philosophy to give a systematic form to their faith. Here is Henry B. Smith's answer to Horace Bushnell's attack on systematic theology. We need systematic theology, he declares, "for systematic theology is the combined result of philosophy and faith; and it is its high office to present the two in their most intimate conjunction and inherent harmony." Systematic theology is the field on which faith and philosophy must be reconciled. "Simple faith," he says, "might have been sufficient for the first ages of the church, though it was not; we live in an age of controversy, surrounded by minds drenched with objections to orthodoxy, among people who, whatever else they have asked, have always asked a reason; to defend our faith, to commend our faith, we need systematic theology."[21]

While the Amherst professor criticized Bushnell's attacks on systematic theology, he agreed that the New England and Presbyterian schools of thought were no longer wholly adequate expositions of the faith for the mid-nineteenth century. In "The Relations of Faith and Philosophy" Smith repeated in mature form the observations that he had sketched on his twenty-first birthday. He described each of the three major schools in the American Calvinist camp—the Old School Presbyterian, the Hopkinsian, or Edwardsean (old school in New England), and the New Haven (new school in New England). Each he found to be wanting. Smith did not suggest that the content of the systematic theology of these schools was erroneous, but only that their controlling principles gave each of them a character that no longer spoke adequately to the needs of the modern age. All theological systems, he said, are based on some ultimate principles by which the arrangement and even the definitions of the doctrines are controlled. "Consciously or unconsciously, they are under the power of some dominant idea, which determines the shape of the separate parts." The doctrines of the Old School Presbyterians, he ob-

21. Smith, "The Relations of Faith and Philosophy," p. 27.

served, are based on the Westminster Standards and are controlled by the principle of divine sovereignty modified by the idea of a covenant relation. New England theology has its basis in the same general idea of divine sovereignty, but modified in the old school (Edwardsean or Hopkinsian) by an articulate and abstract system of divine decrees, and in the new school (New Haven) by an emphasis on conforming Christianity to the principles of ethical truth and common-sense dictates of mental science.

Now we have fallen upon other times, Smith continues. We are being asked new questions for which the old theories about sovereignty, virtue, and free agency can give no definite response. "The questions of our time . . . do not bear upon the point, whether the doctrines of the Christian system are in harmony with the truths of ethics or mental philosophy; but rather upon the point, what are its essential characteristics?"

A new controlling principle, then, is needed for systematic theology. But where, Smith asks, is it to be found? It would be unphilosophical for philosophy to import its own principles into the Christian system. Rather, "to get at a living Christian theology, we must have the central principle of Christianity itself." And what is that central principle? It is the revelation of Jesus Christ. "He is the centre of the Christian system, and the doctrine respecting Christ is the heart of Christian theology."

In Jesus Christ, Christian faith and philosophy converge and complement each other. "Let us come to Jesus," Smith exhorts. "The best and the fullest inward experience is that which centres in Christ; and the centre of the experience is then identical with the centre of divine revelation." At the same time that Christ forms the center of man's faith, he gives him all that philosophy aims after, and in more perfect form. Only in the principle of the mediation of Christ can man answer the most perplexing question of philosophy—how can finite man come to know his infinite Creator? "The highest idea which man can frame," Smith concludes, "is that of the unity of divinity with humanity; this is the very verge of a possible conception of the human intellect; and in the Person of our Saviour we have this idea realized in all its fullness, and with such a marvellous adaptation to human sympathies that they are made the very means of drawing us within the hallowed sphere of the glories of divinity."

Henry Smith readily acknowledged that he had imported aspects of his Christocentric principles from the evangelical party in Germany. German Protestantism, he observed, had erected the bulwark of the doctrine of Christ against the assaults of rationalism and pantheism. Since this doctrine was in fact central to the Christian religion, it was simply unjust to condemn either it or *all* of German theology merely because they were subject to abuses. In the name of Christian charity, Smith commended German theologian Frederic Schleiermacher for making the love of Christ central to his theological system. Smith by no means agreed, however, with Schleiermacher's emphasis on the principle that the feeling of dependence was the germ of all religion. He repudiated Schleiermacher's low view of many of the historical facts of the life of Christ and disclaimed any sympathy with the German thinker's vague doctrine of the atonement. But Smith was not willing to reject a good principle simply because it happened to be associated with errors. Nor was he willing to condemn Schleiermacher himself. "Many were his errors," Smith remarked, "but much was his love to our blessed Lord." Orthodoxy can afford to be generous, he maintained, and should be ready to appropriate the best insights of any school of thought.[22]

It is not difficult to see why "The Relations of Faith and Philosophy" established Henry Smith's reputation as a theologian and attracted the attention of New School Presbyterians. He had proposed an intelligible synthesis of New England and German thought, mediating between the extremes of each. The content of his system reflected the instruction of Leonard Woods and Enoch

22. Ibid., pp. 31–46.

Pond; but Smith expressed the traditional New England theology in terms of the vital Christocentric principles that he had appropriated from Tholuck and the German evangelicals. Yet at the same time that he embraced a central tenet of German evangelical thought, he asserted the inherent impotency of the challenge of post-Kantian philosophy to Christian theology. He had developed the essentials of a modern Christian apologetics and proclaimed Christ as the center of the Christian system. Through his emphasis on the doctrine of Christ, he had proposed a basis for a renewal of the waning hope for evangelical unity.

When Henry B. Smith's name was proposed for the vacant Chair of Church History at Union Theological Seminary, however, there were some in the New School denomination who suspected that he was doctrinally unsound. They knew that he had studied in Germany and that he had publicly defended Schleiermacher. This was enough to raise the question of his entire orthodoxy. But Smith satisfied Union's Boards of Directors; and after he came to New York quickly gained the confidence of his colleagues in the New School Church.[23] Nevertheless, an aura of suspicion of his German training seems to have persisted for a few years. New School men suspected German Biblical scholarship as well as German theology. In 1855 the Synod of New York and New Jersey, of which Smith was a member, directed him to preach before the Synod on the subject of the inspiration of Scriptures. This assignment was apparently intended to be a means of testing Smith's orthodoxy on this subject.[24] If it were, Smith's discourse likely dispelled any lingering doubts about his essential soundness.

Smith's sermon, "The Inspiration of Scripture," indicates that his whole system was firmly rooted in a confidence in the veracity of the Biblical records. It may also provide a clue to the reason

23. George L. Prentiss, *The Union Theological Seminary in the City of New York*, pp. 68–69.

24. Stearns, *Henry Boynton Smith*, pp. 196–97, says "tradition has it that there was an intention of testing his orthodoxy on this important subject."

why Smith had so few real followers in the next generation. Even Smith's biographer, Lewis F. Stearns, writing in the 1890s, felt it necessary to apologize for his subject's high view of Scriptural inspiration.[25] At Union Seminary, where Smith's name was most revered, higher critical methods of Biblical interpretation were adopted soon after his death; so Smith and his followers no longer stood on common ground. And in those areas of American Presbyterianism where reverence for Scriptural infallibility persisted, Charles Hodge and Princeton Seminary were considered the great bastions of orthodoxy, while Smith was once again suspect because of his associations with Union and his generous estimates of German thought. By neglecting Smith, conservative Presbyterians lost what is certainly one of the better statements of the doctrine of Scriptural infallibility made in the nineteenth century.

Smith's sermon on inspiration begins with a description of the importance of the subject. "The Protestant position of the supreme authority of the Bible stands or falls with the evidence for its infallibility." The doctrine of Scripture is central to Protestantism because of the Christocentric character of the Bible itself. "All in it centres in one person—that of the Redeemer; and has respect to one object—that of redemption of the race from sin."

The Union professor then turns in characteristic fashion to a precise definition of the distinctions that must be made between the terms involved. The basic distinction is that between inspiration and revelation. Inspiration, he says, is a recording process and presupposes revelation. It is not the revelation itself, but rather the guiding and controlling principle by which a record of God's revelation is preserved. The object of inspiration "is the communication of truth in an infallible manner, so that, when rightly

25. Ibid., pp. 198–99. *The Inspiration of the Holy Scriptures* was also omitted from his collected addresses, *Faith and Philosophy,* published posthumously in 1877 under the editorship of Union Theological Seminary professor George L. Prentiss.

interpreted, no error is conveyed." Yet when Scripture says that Holy men of God spake as they were moved by the Holy Spirit, it does not imply a mechanical view of inspiration by dictation. Rather, inspiration involves a *combination* of human and divine, with the constant supremacy of the divine. The writers of Scripture used their own language and all their own faculties in producing the inspired records; but they were preserved from error by the Holy Spirit. Erroneous theories of inspiration fall into two categories, according to Smith. The one asserts only the divine aspect and leads to a dictation theory. The other denies the divine element and claims that the Bible is solely a human work. Each is an equally unsatisfactory extreme. The only tenable position is the mediating view that affirms *both* the human and the divine aspects of inspiration. Here, Smith's doctrine of Scripture is directly parallel to his doctrine of Christ. The Bible "has the same relation to all other books that the person of the Son of God has to all other men." Furthermore, the whole Bible is the Word of God pointing toward the revelation of Christ. "The Bible," he states, "not only contains, but is the Word of God."

Smith next turns to answering the critics of infallible inspiration of Scripture. Here, he was well-qualified to face his foes, because he had been in Germany at the height of the furor that followed the publication of D. F. Strauss's radical *Life of Jesus* in 1835. Strauss had asserted that the defenders of Biblical authority argued in a circle, defending the doctrine of the inspiration of Scripture from the statements of Scripture itself. No amount of human testimony, Strauss had said, can establish a divine fact. But, Smith replied, such a statement is based on an arbitrary assumption about the impossibility of divine communication to men. Once it is seen that this assumption is arbitrary, it is possible to establish a doctrine of Scriptural infallibility on the basis of the manifest credibility of those who witness to its integrity— the apostles of Christ. These are witnesses "worthy of credit," and therefore we may accept their claims to inspiration.

Smith supports his argument for the credibility of the Scriptural witnesses by reversing the critical arguments based on the supposed discrepancies in the Gospel accounts. The differences in detail only demonstrate that the Gospel writers were real witnesses who recorded what they saw and remembered. These witnesses, Smith notes, did not claim to have any special faculties of observation. Lapses of memory are perfectly consistent with the integrity of an account and even lend plausibility to it. Paul, for example, admits in 1 Corinthians 1:16 that he can not remember how many people he baptized on a certain occasion. So the presence of differences in details sustains, rather than disproves, Scriptural infallibility. "Inspiration itself then," says Smith, " . . . not only allows, but must often demand differences in details, according to the observation and experience of the writers, guarding against error, but leading them to say what they had heard and seen."[26]

Smith's defense of Scriptural infallibility was expressed in terms that reflected his historical training. It was founded on his judgment of the credibility of the witnesses based on an examination of the integrity of their accounts. While never denying the supremacy of the divine element in inspiration, he approached the Scriptural books as genuinely human documents that must be treated with the normal historical tools.

Smith was well-equippel to use such historical tools. In Germany he had attended lectures by the historian Leopold von Ranke and had read his works.[27] In addition, he had studied extensively with Neander, the Church historian. George Bancroft, the most renowned American historian of the time, was a warm admirer of Smith's abilities. After Smith's death Bancroft wrote of him: "I

26. Henry B. Smith, *The Inspiration of the Holy Scriptures,* "A Sermon Delivered before the Synod of New York and New Jersey in the First Presbyterian Church, Newark, New Jersey, October 17, 1855" (New York, 1855), pp. 3–31.

27. Henry B. Smith in a letter "to a friend," Berlin, June 30, 1839, in Smith, *Smith,* pp. 70–71.

do not think we have had in any time a man who more fully understood the canons of history, and I know that he was looked to by the best German theologians as the ablest and most trustworthy authority for all that was passing in America within his sphere of observation."[28] When Smith assumed the post as Church historian at Union, Bancroft wrote his friend, "In Church history you have no rival in this hemisphere."[29]

In his inaugural address, delivered at the time of his appointment to the Chair of Church History at Union, Smith outlined his philosophy of history. Church history, he maintained, must be approached as a science, in the same way that other aspects of human history are approached scientifically. "The history of the church falls under the conditions and laws, and has the dignity of all history." The task of any historian is not merely to provide an account of kings and wars, but also to describe the development of the human race, basing the description on a scientific examination of the facts. "The greatness of history," the young historian asserted, "consists, . . . essentially, in these two things: that it is a body of facts, and that these facts are a means of leading us to a knowledge of the great realities of human welfare, and of the actual development of the race under the pressure of vital interests." When history is considered in this perspective of human progress, Church history assumes a particularly vital role because it deals with the most significant aspect of such progress—man's relation to God and his Kingdom. Church history is "the record of the progress of the kingdom of God, intermingled with and acting upon all the other interests of the human race and shaping its destiny." In the history of the Church of Christ, man's progress is most clearly manifested. Christianity provides men with the highest principles of human rights and human welfare. Through

28. George Bancroft in a letter to George L. Prentiss, February 2, 1878, in Stearns, *Henry Boynton Smith*, p. 174.

29. George Bancroft in a letter to Henry B. Smith, n.d., in Smith, *Smith*, p. 167.

the influence of the Church, men find the best means for the reform of society. And the history of the Church "gives us the most
elevated and inspiring view of the ultimate destiny of the human
race." It looks forward to the consummation of the Kingdom of
God.

The reform of society, important as that may be, is not, however, the primary goal of God's kingdom, according to Smith.
It is always subservient to the greater purpose of redeeming men
from sin. The focal point of Smith's philosophy of history is the
same as that of his faith and of his theology. It centers in God's
revelation to man through Jesus Christ. This revelation is made
in history and "centres in the Person and Work of our Lord, who
is the living head of a new creation." Church history deals with
the progress of man in relation to the history of redemption. "And
the history of the church tells us how far the redemptive purposes
of God have been accomplished in the actual course of human
events."[30]

Smith acknowledged that he had patterned his view of Church
history after the design outlined by Jonathan Edwards in his
projected "History of Redemption." Edwards' great work was to
encompass all of Biblical theology and Church history, interpreting it in relation to the redemptive work of Christ.[31] Referring to
the unfinished enterprise, Smith maintained that Edwards' emphasis on the centrality of redemption in history should still be
the controlling principle for the study of Church history.

Smith, however, was no more successful than his great pre-
decessor in completing a major historical work. His principal
work in Church history, *History of the Church of Christ in Chrono-*

30. Henry B. Smith, "Nature and Worth of the Science of Church History,
An Inaugural Address, Delivered before the Directors of the Union Theological Seminary, February 12, 1851," in *Faith and Philosophy,* pp. 54–68.
    31. Ibid., p. 60.

logical Tables, though an impressively complete basic chronology, was, like Edwards' history, only an outline.[32]

Smith's work in Church history was curtailed when after five years at Union he accepted the Chair of Systematic Theology in 1855. Moving from Church history to systematic theology meant for him, however, only turning from one aspect of the history of redemption to another. In his inaugural, as in his Church-history inaugural five years earlier, he reiterated the major theme of all his work—redemption through Christ. Analyzing what is meant by redemption itself, Smith arrived at the controlling principle of his systematic theology—the principle of mediation. "This redemption," he said, "centers in the person and work of Christ, the one mediator between God and man. In his mediation is, then, to be found the central principle of this divine economy." This principle of mediation gives vitality to a theological system. "It gives us a fact and not a theory, a person and not an abstract doctrine."

As in his earlier treatment of the same subject in "Faith and Philosophy," Smith in this second inaugural used his mediatorial principles to criticize one-sided or abstract theological systems. Throughout the history of theology, he said, the tendency has always been either to place a too exclusive emphasis on divine sovereignty, on the one hand, or to make God simply an indefinite extension of human wants and needs, on the other. New England and Old School Presbyterian covenant theology would fall into the first category, Schleiermacher into the second. But

32. Henry B. Smith, *History of the Church of Christ in Chronological Tables* (New York, 1859). Smith's other contributions to the field also indicate that his primary interest was to provide adequate basic tools for the study of Church History in America. Much of his work consisted in translating and editing several major German historical works, including Johann Karl Ludwig Gieseler (1792–1854), *A Text-book of Church History* (New York, 1865–68), and Karl Rudolf Hagenbach, *A Text-book of the History of Doctrines* (New York, 1869).

here, Smith took the opportunity to single out the principal source of the New School's theological poverty—the preoccupation of later New England theology with ethical theory.

In Smith's view, Nathaniel Taylor and the New Haven divines were clearly the chief offenders, but few of the supposed followers of Jonathan Edwards were totally exempt from his accusations. Smith's admiration for Edwards himself seemed unbounded. But the disciples of Edwards, he maintained, had violated both the spirit of Edwards' thought and the letter of the Westminster Confession. Edwards' leading works were all expositions of various aspects of the same problem: *"man in his relation to divine grace."* His principal disciples, however, each had emphasized one aspect of his work at the expense of all others. In doing so, they reduced the great questions of man's relation to divine grace to abstract ethical theories. Slogans such as "divine efficiency," "disinterested benevolence," and "moral government" became the stock in trade of the New England pulpit.

Speaking in 1855, Smith could claim that he need not even pause to debate whether or not the extreme emphases on these doctrines were a deviation from the wise tradition of Calvinist theology. The most objectionable of these views, in his account, were those that used the Scottish philosophy to construct an ethical theory on the principle of contrary choice and then made all other theological considerations subservient to that principle. Such a scheme (clearly New Haven's) was an ethical theory and not a theological system. "Ethical truth," he said, "has a relative value in the Christian scheme." It is a superficial affair compared to the great truth of Christ's mediation and can not be made the controlling principle. "Nor can such an ethical system satisfy man's profoundest wants or solve the real problems of his destiny."[33]

Smith's criticisms of the New Haven theology were nearly as cutting as those of the Old School Presbyterians and assumed

33. Smith, "The Idea of Christian Theology as a System," pp. 132–60.

much of the same ground. But rather than condemning the ethical theorists primarily for their departures from the principles of divine sovereignty as stated in the Confession, he attacked them for neglecting the principle of Christ's redemptive work as the only means of reconciling fallen men to a sovereign God. In constantly reasserting this mediatorial principle, Smith's purpose was irenic rather than polemic. He called for a more balanced emphasis, not for a total repudiation of everything associated with the one-sided views. Through the principle of Christ's mediation, Smith hoped to reconcile the extremes of American Reformed theology.

Rapport with the Old School was not immediately forthcoming. Charles Hodge's *Princeton Review,* which could be relied on to be thoroughly critical of anything not taught at Princeton, praised Smith for his repudiation of the New Divinity, but remained suspicious of his philosophical principles. Hodge, presumably the author of the journal's notice of Smith's address, used common-sense principles of Biblical interpretation himself.[34] He therefore objected to Smith's approach to systematic theology on the basis that Smith's realistic philosophical principles would lead to a denial of man's distinct individuality.[35] Hodge, however, had very little basis for criticizing Smith when it came to particulars. The best he could do was claim that the New School theologian had misinterpreted Jonathan Edwards' doctrine of imputation of Adam's sin. Smith claimed that he stood with Edwards in teaching that the imputation of sin was mediated on the basis of man's oneness and union with Adam. Hodge objected, saying that such a oneness was taught in only a single isolated passage in Edwards and that everywhere else Edwards taught the doctrine of "imme-

34. Ahlstrom, "Scottish Philosophy," pp. 257–72. Cf., for example, Charles Hodge, "On the Nature of the Atonement," *The Spruce Street Lectures* (Philadelphia, 1841), p. 175; and Charles Hodge, *Systematic Theology,* 1:56.
35. "The Charge and Inaugural Address Delivered on the Occasion of the Inauguration of the Rev. Henry B. Smith, D.D. into the Chair of Systematic Theology in Union Theological Seminary, New York, May 6, 1855" (New York, 1855), *Princeton Review* 27(October 1855):700.

diate imputation" of sin.[36] Hodge was eventually reconciled to Smith at the time of the Presbyterian reunion, though the differences in their philosophical assumptions remained. In 1855, however, at the height of the revived Old School–New School debates, Hodge readily unpacked his old stock of objections to even the most conservative of the New England teachings.

Henry Smith was willing to buck the tide of denominationalism in the 1850s. His zeal for the unity of all the parties of American Calvinism, together with his abilities as a theologian, soon brought him to a position of unquestioned leadership in the New School Presbyterian Church. His most ambitious project of the decade was an attempt to restore some of the old ties between New School Presbyterianism and Congregationalism through a new interdenominational theological review. In 1859 Smith accepted the editorship of the newly established *American Theological Review.* Immediately, he was accused of deserting Presbyterianism. But even this, he considered a good sign. "The *Review* is assailed terribly," he wrote to a New School friend, "which shows that it was needed."[37]

In the second issue of the *American Theological Review* Smith undertook to state its principles and to defend its objectives. The chief object of the *Review,* he said, was not ecclesiastical, but theological. It was intended "to represent what is familiarly known as the old school of the New England theology." Whatever reservations Smith may have had about New England theology, he now explicitly claimed the conservative Edwardsean tradition as his own. This theology, he said, had provided the marrow and the strength of the Congregational and Presbyterian Churches in America. Describing the tradition, he wrote: "It was represented

36. Ibid., p. 702. The doctrine of "immediate imputation" teaches that the guilt of Adam's sin is imputed to his posterity *antecedent* to the corruption of their hearts that arises from natural generation. "Mediate imputation" teaches that the guilt is *consequent* to the depravity of man's heart.

37. Henry B. Smith in a letter to George L. Prentiss, March 25, 1859, in Smith, *Smith,* p. 201.

by such names as the elder Edwards, Bellamy, Smalley, Hopkins, Burton, and Dwight; among those nearer to our times, it has been ably advocated by Griffin, Woods, Tyler, and Richards. It has been intermediate between the extreme views and tendencies on either hand." On these principles Smith called for theological unity, suggesting that the old denominational disputes could well be left to take care of themselves.[38]

The *American Theological Review,* published in New York and Boston, resembled in content and format its Philadelphia counterpart, the *Presbyterian Quarterly Review.* Smith's nondenominational journal too surveyed the major theological, intellectual, and scientific developments of the day and from much the same perspective. In 1860, for instance, the *American Theological Review* contained an extensive critique of Darwin by D. R. Goodwin, president of Trinity College in Connecticut. Goodwin took the position that, even admitting Darwin's facts, and though he should add to these facts a hundred-fold, his conclusions would not follow scientifically.[39] Henry Smith himself opposed Darwin's materialistic assumptions until the end of his life. But, characteristically he refused to condemn all theories of development through evolution simply because of their misapplication to the question of the origin of the human race. Progress was an integral part of Smith's theological system, and he consistently affirmed that there was a proper place for the theistic "law of growth."[40]

In the pages of the *American Theological Review,* Smith set the tone for the defense of the faith. Surveying the new trend in English religious thought toward accommodating Christianity to naturalistic scientific assumptions and radical Biblical criticism, he took an unequivocal stand, much like that of Albert Barnes in treating the same subjects in the *Presbyterian Quarterly Review*

38. "The *American Theological Review,*" *American Theological Review,* 1st ser., 1 (May 1859):327–30.
39. Goodwin, "Darwin on the Origin of Species," pp. 326–27.
40. Smith, *Apologetics,* pp. 170–94.

(see Chapter 7, above). Smith argued that Christianity was founded on the exclusive presuppositions of a divinely inspired revelation and a personal God. Only with these claims, he said, could it withstand the attacks of infidelity. "As soon as it abandons these cardinal positions, it abandons its claim to supremacy and ultimate authority, and is resolved into some more general movement, into some philosophical generalization." The attempts to defend Christianity by methods that compromised these fundamental principles, he asserted, were not admissible into a truly Christian apologetics.[41]

The duplication of the efforts of New York and Philadelphia Presbyterians of the New School in their theological quarterlies did not last long. When Benjamin J. Wallace, the editor of the *Presbyterian Quarterly Review,* died in 1862 the two journals were merged as the *American Presbyterian and Theological Review,* under the editorship of Smith and James M. Sherwood—one of his New School associates in the New York City area. It was clearly a New School Presbyterian enterprise, having professors from Union, Lane, and Auburn and several Philadelphia ministers as its associate editors. Smith, who already occupied the most important theological chair in the New School, now controlled its most influential publication. The same year, 1863, he was elected moderator of the General Assembly.

Henry Boynton Smith's rise to leadership in the New School came at the most critical juncture in the denomination's history. In 1863 the New School Church was wholeheartedly committed to the cause of preserving the Federal Union. The trend toward denominationalism in the 1850s was suddenly submerged by the spirit of nationalism. At the same time, Northern loyalty brought the Old School closer to the New and talk of cooperation, and even reunion, was in the air. The theologian from New England now had his best opportunity to apply his mediating principles to a practical ecclesiastical situation.

41. "The New Latitudinarians of England," *American Theological Review,* 1st ser., 3 (April 1861):313–15.

The coming of the Civil War also changed the character of the New School denomination. The war revitalized the evangelical Protestant vision of the Church as moral leader of society. The New School spirit of national revival and militant reform emerged with all its fervor. The crusade to save the nation and end slavery was suited well to New School ideals, and within the denomination national and Christian objectives were virtually identified.

In order to understand the character of this New School response to the war, it is necessary first to consider another aspect of the mid-nineteenth-century evangelical outlook that contributed directly to their crusading zeal.

9

The Kingdom of Christ and
the American Nation

Stand up, stand up for Jesus!
Ye soldiers of the cross;
Lift high his royal banner,
It must not suffer loss:

"Stand up, stand up for Jesus" is undoubtedly New School Presbyterianism's best known contribution to the American religious
heritage. Written at the height of the great revival of 1858 by
New School pastor George Duffield, Jr. (1818–88), of Philadelphia, the hymn quickly gained the popularity it has retained ever
since. Its rapid acceptance is indicative not only of the character of
popular theology in the New School Church but also of the spirit
of much of American Protestantism in this era.

The Christocentric emphasis of the first stanza of the younger
Duffield's hymn is no more incidental to its message than it was
to the systematic theology of Henry B. Smith. Indeed, the season
of revival that flourished in Philadelphia, New York, and other
American cities during the winter of 1857–58 was, according to a
contemporary report, marked particularly by the extent to which
the preacher emphasized the Cross of Christ: "One thought—one
feeling is absorbing this work. It is the *Cross of Christ*. Not somewhat that grows incidentally from the atonement; not somewhat
that tends thither; but the Cross itself. The nearer the speaker gets
to the Cross, the more he carries his hearers with him."[1] Duffield

1. "The Revival," *PQR* 7 (January 1859):504–05.

himself believed in preaching the Gospel in its simplest terms. "The way of life is a very short one" he wrote in a popular tract. "There are but two steps to it. FIRST, the sinner 'comes to himself,' (Luke xv: 17) and sees *what he is,* viz.; a sinner. SECONDLY, he comes to Christ (Matt. xi: 28) and sees what He is, viz.; a savior (I Tim. i: 18, iv: 10)."[2] In the doctrine of the Cross evangelists of all schools found new possibilities for cooperation during the revival.[3] Presbyterians of both Schools, Methodists, Baptists, and Low Church Episcopalians joined together in daily noonday prayer meetings and found practical unity in the proclamation of the Gospel message.

Among Duffield's closest friends and associates in the revival was Dudley A. Tyng, son of Stephen H. Tyng—a leader of the Low Church party in the Protestant Episcopal Church. Though not yet thirty, the younger Tyng proved one of the most effective evangelists in the revival. At one of the noonday meetings in Philadelphia he preached before a gathering of five thousand men, at least a fifth of whom, it was claimed, committed themselves to Christ. A few weeks later Tyng was fatally injured when his arm caught in a cornshelling machine. Reportedly, his dying words were, "Tell them to stand up for Jesus." The next Sunday, Duffield took the words of his Episcopal friend as the theme for his famous revival verses.[4]

"Stand up, stand up for Jesus" soon became one of the most popular hymns sung by the Union armies during the Civil War.[5] No doubt, it was readily accepted because its military imagery appealed to fighting men, but there was also much in its message appropriate to the popular Northern Protestant view of the cause

2. George Duffield, Jr., *The Pastor and Inquirer: Or. What It Is to Repent and Believe the Gospel* (Philadelphia, [n.d.]), p. 24.

3. "The Revival," p. 507.

4. E. E. Ryden, *The Story of Christian Hymnody* (Rock Island, Ill., 1959), pp. 534–37; Edward S. Ninde, *The Story of the American Hymn* (New York, 1921), pp. 215–22.

5. Ninde, *American Hymn,* p. 200, from a letter of Duffield's.

of the Union. Northern spokesmen of all denominations, and virtually all New School Presbyterians (see Chapter 10, below) characteristically identified the advance of the Kingdom of Christ with the preservation of the nation. It is a safe conjecture that many evangelical Americans saw a temporal as well as a spiritual meaning in the concluding lines of Duffield's first stanza:

> From victory unto victory
> His army he shall lead,
> Till every foe is vanquished
> And Christ is Lord indeed.

The confidence of nineteenth-century Americans in progress through reform and struggle was well-rooted in their Protestant heritage. Their acquaintance with apocalyptic imagery was reflected and reinforced in the words of the most famous war hymn, "His truth is marching on." Expectations of the millennial age were by no means confined to extremist groups. The approaching spiritual reign of Christ was confidently preached in many of the most respectable pulpits of the nation. American progress was considered a sign of the approach of the second advent of Christ, and the approach of the advent was urged as a reason to hasten earthly progress.

Confidence in the progress of the Kingdom of Christ in America was not limited to any particular denomination. Though Protestants did not always agree on just what was meant by the coming Kingdom, their disagreements did not necessarily follow denominational lines. Among New School Presbyterians most of the major views were found. But in almost all views it was clear that the spiritual, moral, and even material progress of the nation should be interpreted in the perspective of the consummation of all history in the reign of Christ. In its teachings about the millennium, American Protestant theology bore directly on contemporary views of the nation's destiny. The teachings in the New School Presbyterian Church on the ultimate progress of the Christian nation therefore deserve more careful examination as preparation for considering the relation of evangelical thought to Northern ideology during the Civil War.[6]

Progress toward the Millennium

By far the most prevalent apocalyptic view among American Protestants in the Civil War era is known technically as "postmillennialism." It teaches that Christ will not come again until *after* a millennium of prolonged progress on earth and special spiritual blessings. In the writings of the day this view was often designated "Spiritualist" because its advocates believed that the promised Kingdom of Christ would be manifested in the reign of the Holy Spirit over the hearts of his people. The millennial kingdom, which was expected to last for an indeterminate time (some said a literal thousand years), was not to be an entirely new age. Rather, it would be an extension of the spiritual kingdom that Christ had introduced at the time of his first advent, when he had established his Church as the agency through which the Holy Spirit would be made manifest. The millennium would be marked by a great revival of Christianity and the conversion of all the nations of the world, so that the numbers of the saved would far exceed those of the lost. It was also expected to bring radical social-reforms, including the cessation of wars, the end of enslavements and oppressions, triumph over all forms of vice, and a great extension of learning and the arts. After this would be the Second Coming and Judgment by Christ, the creation of "a New Heavens and a New Earth," and the everlasting reign of Christ over his people.[7]

6. This is not to imply that the millennial views were the *cause* of evangelical patriotism during the Civil War, but to clarify something of the character of their loyalty.

7. "Millennarianism," *PQR* 2(June 1853):21–25; "History of Opinions Respecting the Millennium," *American Theological Review*, 1st ser., 1(November 1859):655.

In 1859 the nondenominational *American Theological Review* characterized these views as "the commonly received doctrine."[8] They were firmly rooted in the English Puritan and New England tradition of American theology and were found particularly in the writings of Jonathan Edwards, Samuel Hopkins, and Joseph Bellamy.[9] Their appeal to American revivalists and reformers is evident. The New England emphasis on the outpourings of the Spirit during the seasons of revival was intimately related to the belief that at some time, when the world was properly prepared, the new age would be initiated by the greatest of all awakenings. The zeal of New England reformers increased as they saw the reforms of the present age as preparation for the great age when the Spirit would triumph over evil. The campaigns for Sabbath reform, temperance, and antislavery were all part of the program to prepare the nation for the advent of the great millennial age. Belief in the progress of America and in American virtue was often part of a larger confidence in the triumph of Christ's Kingdom. As Timothy L. Smith observes, "clergymen identified the popular American mission with the Christian hope."[10]

New School Presbyterians expected the millennium to grow out of nineteenth-century revival and social reform. Lyman Beecher, who did more than anyone to set the tone for New School reform, had called, as early as 1812, for a moral reformation, declaring that "if we endure a little longer, the resources of the millennial day will come to our aid." He predicted that the time of the millennium was drawing near.

8. "History of Opinions Respecting the Millennium," p. 655.

9. Ibid. See also C. C. Goen, "Edwards' New Departure in Eschatology," *Church History* 28(March 1959):25–40.

10. *Revivalism,* p. 236. In pp. 225–37, Smith gives the best brief survey of the relation of millennial views to social reform during this era. Cf. Charles C. Cole, Jr., *The Social Ideas of the Northern Evangelists, 1826–1860* (New York, 1954), pp. 232–33; and Bodo, *The Protestant Clergy and Public Issues,* pp. 251–52.

Many are the prophetic signs which declare the rapid approach of that day. Babylon the great is fallen.[11] The false prophet is hastening to perdition. That wicked one hath appeared, whom the Lord will destroy by the breath of his mouth and the brightness of his coming.[12] The day of his vengeance is wasting the earth. The last vial of wrath of God is running out. The angel having the everlasting Gospel to preach to men has begun his flight; and, with trumpet sounding loud, and waxing loud, is calling to the nations to look unto Jesus and be saved.[13]

Absalom Peters, writing in 1837, used almost the same imagery to urge the necessity of missionary zeal and benevolent reforms (see the opening page of Chapter 5, above), indicating the prevalent belief that the signs prophesied in the book of Revelation were being fulfilled in the nineteenth century. Seth Williston of New York state, another New School minister, expressed similar sentiments in a volume on the millennium written in 1849. Williston emphasized the special responsibilities of the American nation. America had been especially chosen to receive the blessings of God, he said, because "the only true religion which is to be found in our world—the only scheme which reveals the true God and his Son Jesus Christ . . . is in our hands." But this blessing, he said, also involved special obligations for the nation, namely, that America must have become a nation of Christians. Before they can preach the Gospel to all nations, said Williston, Americans must become disciples of Christ who conform their hearts and lives to the doctrines and precepts of the Gospel.[14]

New School confidence in the progress of the Kingdom of

11. "Babylon the great" almost always refers to the papacy. Here, Beecher is probably referring to Napoleon's arrest of the pope.

12. This most likely refers to Napoleon himself.

13. Lyman Beecher, "A Reformation of Morals Practical and Indispensable," in *Works*, 2:110.

14. Seth Williston, *Millennial Discourses: Or, a Series of Sermons Designed to Prove That There Will Be a Millennium of Peace and Holiness; Also to Suggest Means for Hastening Its Introduction* (Utica, N.Y., 1849), pp. 185–88.

Christ had a direct effect on the denomination's zeal to promote social reforms. In the annual "narrative of religion" in 1840, for example, the New School Assembly declared, "With the general progress of religion in the church, the standard of morality in the world appears to be rising." The narrative went on to note that lax principles of infidelity were losing ground, outward respect for the Sabbath was increasing, checks on licentiousness were multiplied, and that the principles of the cause of temperance were being more and more extensively adopted. It concluded with the exhortation that still more vigorous efforts should be made.[15]

Certainly the most engrossing of New School efforts to increase the evidences of the influence of the Kingdom of Christ and the Church in America was the antislavery campaign. According to Albert Barnes, the New School discussed this subject more thoroughly than did any other denomination.[16] The presence of the Southern minority during its first twenty years accounted for the vigor of the debates in the New School Assembly and for the element of restraint in most of the official New School pronouncements. But the New School antislavery leaders continued to press for decisive denominational action. Every New School Assembly from 1846 to 1857 passed resolutions deploring the existence of the slave system, many urging that the synods and presbyteries do all they could to eliminate this evil from the land.[17] Finally, in 1857, the Presbytery of Lexington, responding to the pressure, declared that some of its ministers, elders, and church members owned slaves as a matter of principle,[18] thus justifying withdrawal from the Church. With the subsequent exodus of about ten thousand Southern members, the denomination at last faced the era of national crisis solidly united in the cause of abolition.

Albert Barnes, who was one of evangelicalism's leading spokes-

15. New School *Minutes, 1840,* p. 27.
16. Barnes, *The Church and Slavery,* p. 120.
17. *New Digest,* pp. 276–95.
18. New School *Minutes, 1857,* p. 404.

men against slavery and reputedly "Philadelphia's most famous citizen,"[19] advocated a strong official stand for abolition as a necessary part of the Church's witness to the world. In 1857, presenting an extended defense of his denomination's position that the evils inherent in the slave system were contrary to the Bible and to the spirit of Christianity, he said, "It is impossible not to reflect on the noble position which the Christian church would occupy if the sentiments which have been advocated in this essay should become the practical sentiments of the church at large." Attacks on the Church for upholding such a system would cease, and Christians could then stand united in opposing patent violations of the laws of God. The Church, therefore, must purge itself of moral inconsistencies, Barnes urged, so that it could witness effectively to the power of the Gospel over the lives of men.[20]

New School confidence in progress seemed unbounded. All the signs in mid-nineteenth-century America appeared to point toward continued advance in every field of human knowledge and Christian endeavor. New School men felt assured that the Church would be purified and that eventually its efforts in missions and reforms would meet success on every front. To them, the remarkable development of the American nation and culture confirmed the Biblical promises of the approach of the Kingdom of Christ. In 1850 Albert Barnes wrote in connection with the advance of learning.

> Our last thought is that the world is growing *better* than it was. . . . We would have every man adopt it as settled truth . . . —that our own country is making advances—that the church is increasing in numbers, in purity, and in knowledge—and that there is sure and steady progress toward the universal triumph of Christianity, and of civil and religious liberty.[21]

Even as subdued a scholar as Henry Boynton Smith shared this

19. Smith, *Revivalism*, p. 214.
20. Barnes, *The Church and Slavery*, p. 194; cf. ibid., p. 117.
21. Albert Barnes, "The Position of the Christian Scholar," *Biblical Repository*, 3rd ser., 6(October 1850), p. 625.

unwavering confidence in progress in human history. One of his prerequisites for a philosophy of history was that it "give us an adequate law of progress in the development of the race." Such a philosophy, he said, must take into account the "law of growth" in every living thing.[22] Smith accounted for this progress in terms of faith in the coming of the Kingdom of God. In his first inaugural at Union, for example, he announced, "In the whole history of man we can trace the course of one shaping, o'mastering and progressive power, before which all others have bowed, and that is the spiritual kingdom of God, having for its object the redemption of man from the ruins of the apostasy."[23]

Premillennial Views

During the middle decades of the nineteenth century, a second view of the millennium was gaining ground among American evangelicals.[24] Premillennialism taught that the second coming of Christ to earth will *precede* the millennial age. According to this view, as it was usually held in England and America in the mid-nineteenth century, Christ would physically return to earth and set up a political empire, reigning in Jerusalem for one thousand years.[25] At the time of Christ's coming there would be

22. Henry B. Smith, "The Problem of the Philosophy of History," *PQR* 3(June 1854):10.

23. Smith, "Nature and Worth of the Science of Church History," p. 57.

24. A third view is called "amillennialism." It does not predict an earthly millennium or period of worldwide peace of righteousness but holds that the eternal order of things will immediately follow the Second Coming and Judgment Day. This view was defended in the *Princeton Review* 22(April 1850):328–33, as the historic doctrine of the Church. But some members of the Princeton party accepted the postmillennial views, as in the article "Modern Millennarianism" 25(January 1853):66–83, written in opposition to premillennial doctrines. Several leading premillennialists—most notably, James H. Brookes—were members of the Old School Church, although their views were opposed at Princeton.

25. Premillennialists appealed to John Cotton and Cotton Mather as predecessors who taught the basic aspects of their views in America. See George

a series of miraculous events. There would be localized conflagrations and judgments of the wicked nations. The saints of all ages would be raised from the dead; living saints would be caught up into the clouds in the "Rapture"; their bodies would be transformed; and together with the resurrected saints they would reign with Christ on earth for a thousand years. During this thousand years many of the Scriptural prophecies would be literally fulfilled. The Jews would return to Palestine, and all the world would be converted to Christ. The personal reign of Christ in the world would thus be a prelude to the eternal age.[26]

The appearance of vigorous advocates of these views on both sides of the Atlantic aroused increased discussion of all millennial teachings. The Millerite movement of the 1840s created nationwide excitement over an extreme form of premillennialism. But the more moderate premillennialists of the same era were careful not to identify themselves with the advocates of William Miller's widely discredited prophecies,[27] and premillennialists could be found in most of the respected American denominations.

Several prominent New School ministers were among the early champions of the premillennial (or "millenarian," as it was more frequently called) movement in nineteenth-century America. George Duffield, Sr., the father of the hymnwriter and one of the outstanding defenders of the New School, was one of America's leading spokesmen for the millenarian views. In 1842 Duffield, then a pastor in Detroit, published an extensive defense of his interpretations of the Biblical prophecies concerning the second

---

Duffield, *Dissertations on the Prophecies Relative to the Second Coming of Jesus Christ* (New York, 1842), p. 264. See also C. Norman Kraus, *Dispensationalism in America* (Richmond, Va., 1958).

26. The exact nature and order of these events were not fully agreed upon by premilliennialists. This summary is based on a review of several premillennial works, including George Duffield's *Dissertations,* in "Millenarianism," pp. 21–25.

27. Duffield, *Dissertations,* pp. 158–59.

coming of Christ. In this work he argued that the millennium is to be regarded "not as the consummation of the present evangelical dispensation, but as a new dispensation, to be miraculously introduced as all the former dispensations were, and to possess its own distinct and peculiar attributes."[28] Opposing the postmillennial teaching that the millennium would be an expansion of the present age of the Spirit, Duffield vigorously affirmed the premillennial return of Christ and the establishment of a temporal kingdom.

The hallmark of Duffield's system was Biblical literalism. Literal interpretations of the Biblical prophecies (particularly those in the books of Daniel and Revelation) were an essential part of the millenarian movement of his day. Among the writings that Duffield recommended were those found in a magazine called *The Literalist,* published in Philadelphia from 1840 to 1842.[29] And a large part of Duffield's own work was a defense of literal, rather than spiritualizing or symbolic, interpretations of the Biblical prophecies.[30] He believed, for example, that in the year 1792, the 1,260 prophetic years "very probably" had ended and that the 75 years before the millennium had begun; so, he said, the coming of the Lord in the clouds of heaven was certainly imminent in the mid-nineteenth century.[31]

Defenders of the postmillennial views objected to the interpretations of Duffield and other millenarians on two principal grounds. First of all, most of the leading conservative Biblical scholars objected to such thoroughgoing literalism. According to the *Presbyterian Quarterly Review,* the majority of English and American

28. Ibid., p. 161. Precise dispensational schemes for dividing eras of world history and Biblical revelation were often associated with nineteenth-century premillennialism; see Kraus, *Dispensationalism.*

29. Duffield, *Dissertations,* p. 163. Strict Biblical literalism was almost always characteristic of nineteenth-century premillennialism; see Kraus, *Dispensationalism,* p. 57.

30. Duffield, *Dissertations,* pp. 32–167.

31. Ibid., p. 406.

interpreters (including, for instance, Albert Barnes) were un-willing to admit that the language of the prophecies describing Christ's Kingdom could be interpreted in literal or physical terms. The only literal interpretation on which most of them agreed was that the book of Revelation predicted the overthrow of the papacy. Even on this point, however, they disagreed as to whether the 1,260 days mentioned in the Apocalypse as the length of time before the overthrow of the beast was properly interpreted as 1,260 years or as symbolizing an indefinite period of time.[32] Other scholars, influenced by German methods of interpretation, discarded all attempts to read the Apocalypse as a precise revela-tion of future events. This group maintained that much of the imagery referred to the first-century political and religious situa-tion. Moses Stuart, who carried on a lengthy debate with Duffield in the 1840s, ridiculed all ideas of the Apocalypse being "an out-line of Church History, down to the end of the world."[33] And in the New School itself, Calvin Stowe testified in 1843 to the "utter groundlessness of all millennial arithmetic."[34]

The second major objection to the millenarian scheme was a practical one. Postmillennialists, who were confident in the con-tinuing progress of the present era, frequently repeated the accusa-tion that premillennialism implied a pessimistic outlook for the world that would discourage missionary and reforming efforts.[35] If the era of the conversion and spiritual renewal of the world was to be delayed until another dispensation, they argued, there was little point in striving to accomplish those ends in this age.

Postmillennialists believed that only their own views provided a proper rationale for missionary zeal. In referring to the post-millennial doctrines the *American Theological Review* stated,

32. "The Apocalypse," PQR 2(March 1853):540–41.
33. Quoted in ibid., p. 533.
34. Calvin E. Stowe, *A Letter to R. D. Mussey, M.D., on the Utter Ground-lessness of All Millennial Arithmetic* (Cincinnati, Ohio, 1843).
35. "History of Opinions Respecting the Millennium," p. 655; "Millenar-ianism," pp. 39–40.

"It is under the influence of these views, that the great missionary enterprise, in all its departments, has been projected and thus far prosecuted."[36] Seth Williston, the New School minister who defended postmillennial views in *Millennial Discourses,* noted that "Missionary Discourses," would have been an equally appropriate title for his book.[37] Zeal for missions pervades every page of Williston's work, and indeed it is evident that he considered missionary efforts as the primary means by which Christians could help hasten the introduction of God's Kingdom. Social and moral reforms, and even technological achievements, he said, were signs of a "grand moral revolution" that could be further advanced by the universal promulgation of the Gospel.[38] Missions abroad and revivals at home were always considered the greatest of all reforms by New School men, and they were urged with the hope that they would help advance the coming of the millennial age.

Premillennialists answered the accusation that their views would dampen such missionary and reforming spirits by pointing out that they themselves drew no such implications from their beliefs. The fact was, they said, that they pursued exactly the same goals but for slightly different reasons. "We mean not to insinuate that Missionary efforts, and other labors of benevolence, should be relaxed," George Duffield, Sr., maintained in his defense of premillennialism. "The groans of a world perishing in its corruptions call for quickened, multiplied, effort, and for zeal irrepressible and inextinguishable. The Gospel of the kingdom must be preached, in all the world, for a witness unto all nations: and then shall the end come!"[39] Here was the rationale for premillennial missionary efforts. Such efforts were considered among the most important signs of the approaching end. Alfred Byrant,

36. "History of Opinions Respecting the Millennium," p. 655.
37. Williston, *Millennial Discourses,* p. ix.
38. Ibid., p. 137.
39. Duffield, *Dissertations,* p. 382.

another New School minister from Michigan, listed them first among nine such precursors of the advent. "One prominent premonitory sign," he wrote, "which will indicate the near approach of the end of the present dispensation, and the coming of our Lord, will be the preaching of the gospel unto all nations as a witness."[40]

Samuel H. Cox, New School pastor in New York state, former professor at Auburn, and Moderator of the General Assembly of 1846, found an ideal opportunity to defend the implications of his premillennial views for missions when he was asked to speak before the American Board of Commissioners for Foreign Missions in 1849. Having worked out a mathematical scheme of revealed dispensations consummating in the millennium,[41] Cox attacked scholars (such as Stuart and Stowe) who had ridiculed such millennial arithmetic. His appeal was to the American Protestant prejudice against Germany. "Where in the mean time leave they the millennial arithmetic of the Holy Ghost?" he asked. "They lose it—in Germany." Cox then outlined his own scheme, starting with the commonly held doctrine that the revealed lifetime of the papacy was to be 1,260 years.[42] But much more than the overthrow of the papacy, he claimed, was explicitly revealed in the prophecies:

> When this grand obstacle to the truth is removed, others will soon follow in course: as the fall of Islam, or the ruinated delusion of the prophet of Arabia; the conversion of the Jews to

40. Alfred Bryant, *Millenarian Views: with Reasons for Receiving Them* (New York, 1852), p. 206. Duffield, *Dissertations,* p. 397, lists this as one of eleven such signs.

41. Kraus, *Dispensationalism,* pp. 30–31, lists Cox as a precursor of later American dispensationalism, a form of premillennialism closely identified with the fundamentalist movement of the twentieth century.

42. George Duffield, Sr., who held the same view, admitted that there were difficulties in knowing where to begin to count, since the date of the rise of the papacy could be placed at A.D. 533, 538, 606, or 756; in Duffield, *Dissertations,* p. 385.

the true Messiah; the universal propagation of the gospel and
its ascendency among the nations; the ages of the long-desired
millennium, the earth being full of the knowledge of the glory
of God, and all flesh rejoicing together in his salvation. *And the
Lord shall be king over all the earth; in that day shall there be
one Lord, and his name one.*[43]

Cox described the hope for the coming millennium in confident
terms that are difficult to distinguish from those held by postmillennialists. Like them, he urged it as a primary motive for missionary zeal. "We must see to it that the gospel of the kingdom
is preached to all nations," he exhorted the American Board of
Commissioners for Foreign Missions.[44] More than likely, the
commissioners did not need to be told.

Much other common ground remained for premillennialists and
postmillennialists in interpreting world history and the signs of the
times. George Duffield, for instance, claimed that Scripture revealed that Christ would appear during a season of great increase
in knowledge and wealth; though it would also be a time of increased apostasy. Duffield also shared the old New England prejudice against France and the French Revolution. "Ever since the
French Revolution," he said "the peculiar signs, both moral and
political, which it is predicted shall mark the time of the end, have
been developing." He had a clear notion of the source of the
increase in infidelity, which he attributed to the French. "This
demon, proceeding out of the mouth of 'the dragon,' appeared
first, and acted a most conspicuous part, in that prime intellectual
juggler Voltaire."[45]

Duffield read the signs of the nineteenth century, indicating an
increase in the forces of both good and evil, as a prelude to the

43. Samuel Hanson Cox, *The Bright and the Blessed Destination of the
World,* "A Discourse before the American Commissioners for Foreign Missions"
(New York, 1849), p. 16; cf. ibid., p. 13.

44. Ibid., p. 38.

45. Duffield, *Dissertations,* pp. 402–05.

great final conflict in the millennial age. The increase in adversities was therefore no reason for the Christian to relax his efforts to convert the world. Rather, it gave him all the more reason to enter the battle against the forces of evil. As the father of the hymnwriter stated, the Christian "feels that as he enters the service of Christ, he enlists as a soldier, commences a warfare, and that both the service and the war are for life."[46]

As the competing theories of the millennium were debated in mid-nineteenth century, millennial imagery became increasingly familiar to American Protestants. The rapid acceptance of the younger Duffield's hymnodical presentation of his father's view is one indication of the power of such imagery. The only other New School hymnwriter of any prominence was Nathan S. S. Beman, the evangelist and New School leader from upstate New York. Beman's hymns contain as much millennial imagery as Duffield's. One of his hymns, "Hark!—the judgment-trumpet sounding," is unmistakable in its apocalyptic terminology. Another, "Jesus! We Bow Before thy Throne," is headed, a "Prayer for the Millennium." Its terms are apparently postmillennial. The third verse, for example, reads:

> Lord! arm thy truth with power divine.
> Its conquests spread from shore to shore.
> Till suns and stars forget to shine,
> And earth and skies shall be no more.[47]

The differences between the millennial views in the pre–Civil War era appear to have been less important than the similarities of the militant apocalyptic imagery shared by most American Protestants. George Duffield, Jr., was presumably a premillennial-

46. Ibid., p. xii.
47. Three of Beman's hymns are found in the *Social Psalmist: Or. Hymns, Selected for the Private Use and Social Meetings of Evangelical Christians* (New York, 1843). Beman was the compiler of this book, which was later used as the basis of the New School's hymnal.

ist, but there is nothing in his hymn that would be objectionable to a postmillennialist. The other verses of the hymn, as usually sung, are indicative of the militant spirit of American Protestantism in this age.

> Stand up, stand up for Jesus,
>   The trumpet call obey;
> Forth to the mighty conflict
>   In this His glorious day:
> Ye that are men, now serve Him
>   Against unnumbered foes;
> Your courage rise with danger,
>   And strength to strength oppose.
>
> Stand up, stand up for Jesus,
>   Stand in His strength alone;
> The arm of flesh will fail you,
>   Ye dare not trust your own:
> Put on the gospel armor,
>   Each piece put on with prayer;
> Where duty calls or danger,
>   Be never wanting there.
>
> Stand up, stand up for Jesus,
>   The strife will not be long;
> This day the noise of battle,
>   The next the victor's song:
> To him that overcometh
>   A crown of life shall be;
> He with the King of glory
>   Shall reign eternally.

10

The Civil War:
The Flag and the Cross

In the second half of the nineteenth century, observes Sidney E. Mead, American Protestants had two religions. The first was the pietistic orthodoxy of the denominations; the second was the religion of the democratic society and nation. During the era beginning with the Civil War, he says, "there occurred an ideological amalgamation of this Protestantism with 'Americanism,' and . . . we are still living with some of the results."[1]

In New School Presbyterianism this amalgamation of Protestants and Americanism had roots deep in the tradition of the movement and was immediately evident when Civil War broke out. In theological terms the New School's response to the war may be described as an identification of the doctrines of the Church's mission to prepare the world for the millennium and to call the nation to its covenantal obligations with the patriotic dogmas that the Union must be preserved and slavery abolished.[2] The conception of America as the nation divinely chosen to usher in the millennium was well-entrenched in American Protestantism. When the crisis arose, New School men instinctively turned to it for vindication of the Northern cause. In November 1860, Roswell

---

1. Mead, *The Lively Experiment*, p. 134; cf. ibid., pp. 135–36.
2. Vander Velde, *The Presbyterian Churches and the Federal Union,* presents an excellent account of New School patriotism during the war. The present study is intended only as a supplement to that account, emphasizing particularly the ways in which New School patriotism was expressed in terms of the doctrines of the millennium and the covenant.

D. Hitchcock, Professor of Church History at Union Seminary, expressed it in clear terms.

> But we are Americans. . . . We are here, by the ordering of Providence, in charge of the final theatre and the final problems of history. . . . It is for ourselves to say, . . . whether, . . . by those sturdy moral virtues begotten only of a positive Christian belief, we may not hold our ground here, puissant and respected amongst the nations of the earth, till the trumpet of God's providence announces the final triumph of universal justice, freedom, truth and love.[3]

From the outset of the war New School Presbyterians were united in maintaining that it was the duty of Christians to help preserve the federal government.[4] Albert Barnes, for instance, looked upon the Constitution as a gift of God. "To the formation of that constitution, and to the constitution itself," he said, "we now look with gratitude, with pride, as the chief, the crown of the blessings which God has given the land."[5] Nathan S. S. Beman went further, saying that the principles of equality of men and their inalienable rights embodied in the Declaration of Independence, could be traced as much to the apostle Paul as to Thomas Jefferson.[6]

The New School doctrine of the divine mission of the nation was intimately involved with their doctrine of the national covenant. The conviction that the American people had special responsibilities under the terms of a covenant with God had been a

3. Roswell D. Hitchcock, "The Laws of Civilization," *American Theological Review*, 1st ser., 2(November 1860):594–95.

4. Vander Velde, *The Presbyterian Churches and the Federal Union*, pp. 337–75.

5. Albert Barnes, *The Conditions of Peace*, "Thanksgiving Discourse, November 27, 1862" (Philadelphia, 1863), p. 11.

6. Nathan S. S. Beman, *Thanksgiving in the Times of Civil War*, "Nov. 28, 1861" (Troy, N.Y., 1861), p. 16. The traditional New School common-sense interpretations of the nature of man may account for some of their loyalty to the common-sense—and perhaps Lockean—principles of the American Revolution. The connection between these aspects of American theology and American political thought might be a useful area for further investigation.

common teaching since the days of the Puritans. It had been an important aspect of the patriotic sermons during the Revolutionary era. Perry Miller argues that this covenant concept had lost much of its force by the time of the Civil War.[7] But if New School preaching of the war years is representative, the covenant ideology still lingered in American Protestantism, continuing to shape men's opinions.

A recurring theme in New School Civil War sermons is the parallel between ancient Israel and modern America. According to Old Testament teaching, nations are subject to special blessings and curses depending on their obedience to the laws of God as stipulated in the covenant. New School ministers believed that America was subject to such divine judgments. Those of them who were confident in the nation's continuing progress, i.e. postmillennialists, maintained that the United States was an essentially righteous nation and was therefore especially blessed by God. Even at the height of the war, Albert Barnes affirmed his belief that America was still both the most virtuous and the most prosperous nation in the world.[8] But America, like all nations under the terms of the covenant, was subject to judgment for its sin.[9] Here, Barnes declared, the greatest national sin was slavery. This evil, he charged, was fastened upon Americans by their English forebears. It had threatened to corrupt the whole nation, and now it brought on the national disaster. "We have not been able to remove it," Barnes stated, "and when we failed for want of power, or want of will, or both, God took the matter into his own hands."[10] The war was God's judgment on slaveholders and was his means of purging the nation of its greatest sin.

Thomas Brainerd (1804–66), one of Albert Barnes' associates

7. Perry Miller, "From the Covenant to the Revival," in *The Shaping of American Religion,* ed. Smith and Jamison pp. 322–68.

8. Barnes, *The Conditions of Peace,* pp. 18–19.

9. "There may be, and probably will be, providential judgments on anti-Christian nations *before* the Millennium," said the postmillenial reviewer in "Millenarianism," p. 22.

10. Barnes, *The Conditions of Peace,* p. 18.

in Philadelphia and the Moderator of the 1864 New School Assembly, went farther, depicting the war as a judgment on *all* the national sins. "Ingratitude, Sabbath-breaking, profanity, intemperance, gambling, . . . who doubts that all these cry to heaven for judgment against us?" Brainerd asked. "No wonder God is disciplining us by national disasters." Only repentance would provide true national security. "The nearer we approach to holiness," the New School minister urged, "the fewer will be our disasters and the more certain our triumphs."[11]

Thomas Brainerd's sermon was preached on the national Fast Day, April 30, 1863. During the Civil War crisis President Lincoln gave official notice to the doctrine of the nation's responsibilities to God by declaring days of "Fasting, Humiliation, and Prayer." According to covenant theory and national tradition, these fast days were the necessary counterpart to thanksgiving days. In New School churches they were solemnly observed with sermons on the nation's sins. On the first such fast day, January 4, 1861, George Duffield, Sr., of Detroit preached on "Our National Sins to be Repented of." His sermon indicates that premillennialists were, if anything, more conscious than their postmillennialist brethren of God's direct judgment for specific national sins. Duffield listed the sins for which God was punishing the nation in the sectional crisis. These included slavery, *all* the normal vices,[12] and oppression of Indians and Mexicans. Turning to the parallel between ancient Israel and modern America, Duffield quoted the curses embodied in the Old Testament law

11. Thomas Brainerd, *Patriotism Aiding Piety,* Fast Day Sermon, April 30, 1863 (Philadelphia, 1863), pp. 18–20.

12. Among the vices that he lists as deserving God's "retributive judgments" are intemperance, disrespect of truth, falsehood and frauds, desecration of the Sabbath, contempt for compacts and oaths, profanity, licentiousness, lawlessness, oppression, polygamy among the Mormons, adultery sanctioned by divorce laws, avaricious extortion, and swindling. George Duffield, *Our National Sins to Be Repented of and the Grounds of Hope for the Preservation of Our Federal Constitution and Union,* Fast Day Sermon, January 4, 1861 (Detroit, 1861), p. 9.

and surmised that the national crimes justified God's retribution. But there was still possibility for national repentance, and the fast day was one means of expressing such contrition. "Our only hope," Duffield said, "is in the effusion of the Holy Spirit, which the Lord Jesus Christ has power to grant, by which to turn the heart of this people back unto him again."[13]

On the same fast day, Duffield's son expressed almost identical sentiments before his congregation in Philadelphia. George Duffield, Jr., listed almost exactly the same sins in his plea for national repentance.[14] Duffield, Jr., was intensely patriotic. At the outbreak of the war he preached a sermon, "Courage in A Good Cause," in which he identified the cause of the nation and the cause of God in explicit terms. "A war such as God approves," said Duffield, "he considers as his own cause, and to help it by all proper means, is to COME UP TO THE HELP OF THE LORD."[15] In the published version of this sermon he appended a discourse by his great-grandfather, George Duffield, the chaplain to the Continental Congress during the Revolution, thus providing a precedent from 1776 for his own sentiments of 1861. Two days after the younger Duffield preached his patriotic sermon, he followed his great-grandfather's example by volunteering for the chaplaincy of a Philadelphia regiment.[16]

The tradition of the national covenant called for thanksgiving days as well as fast days. On the first such thanksgiving day during the war, November 28, 1861, Nathan S. S. Beman of Troy, New York, preached on the subject "Thanksgiving in the Times of Civil War." In this sermon the venerable New School evangelist

13. Ibid., pp. 1–35.

14. George Duffield, Jr., *The God of Our Fathers,* Fast Day Sermon, January 4, 1861 (Philadelphia, 1861).

15. George Duffield, Jr., *Courage in a Good Cause: Or, the Lawful and Courageous Use of the Sword,* Sermon, April 21, 1861 (Philadelphia, 1861), p. 5.

16. Ibid., p. 4. Apparently, he was not accepted, since he was listed as pastor of a church in Adrian, Mich., the next year.

made a powerful application of the parallel between God's covenant with Israel and America's national covenant. "We must stand around the Ark of our civil and political Covenant," he proclaimed, "and never surrender it into the hands of the Philistines." Beman was as certain as the Duffields that the Lord was on the side of the Union, and he was confident in the success of the righteous cause. "Let our armies go forth then, to the battle with brave hearts, and strong hands, and fearless steps, in the name of God and freedom, and my faith shall wait quietly for the result— while the old Flag of the nation is given to the breeze."[17]

The General Assembly of the New School Church, meeting in May 1861, expressed confidence that its members would "ever keep the Cross above the Flag."[18] But from the other pronouncements of the Assembly it was clear that the two were to be borne on the same flagstaff. Among the resolutions adopted on the state of the country was the declaration "That this Assembly . . . cherish an undiminished attachment to the great principles of civil and religious freedom, on which our National Government is based; . . . and, by the preservation of which, we believe that the common interests of evangelical religion and civil liberty will be most effectively sustained."[19] Not only were the principles of the Constitution identified with the cause of the Kingdom of God, but enlisting in the Union Army was marked as an evidence of discipleship to Christ. In the "Narrative of the State of Religion" the Assembly declared with approval, "Large numbers of the members of our churches have enlisted to fight their country's battles, feeling that the time has come, when those of the followers of the Prince of Peace who have no swords should sell their garments and buy them."[20]

The Assembly made these declarations when the war was a month old. A year later, the resolutions adopted by the Assembly

17. Beman, *Thanksgiving in the Times of Civil War*, pp. 45–46.
18. "Narrative of the State of Religion," New School *Minutes, 1861,* p. 484.
19. New School *Minutes, 1861,* p. 447.
20. Ibid., p. 484.

indicated that the identification of the causes of the cross and the flag was almost complete. The Assembly explicitly declared the federal government to be an agency for the salvation of the world: "We deem the Government of these United States the most benign that has ever blessed our imperfect world; . . . we revere and love it, as one of the great sources of hope, under God, for a lost world."

The next resolution is even more remarkable. It lifts the cause of the Union to the level of cosmic history: "Rebellion against such a government as ours, . . . can find no parallel, except in the first two great rebellions—that which assailed the throne of heaven directly, and that which peopled our world with miserable apostates."

Unlike these two parallels, the source of the evil that led to the Southern rebellion could be specifically identified. The Assembly declared "that in our opinion, this whole insurrectionary movement can be traced to one primordial root, and to one only— African Slavery."[21]

The Assembly expressed faith and urged prayer: "We have great confidence in Abraham Lincoln . . . and . . . we will ever pray, that the last sad note of anarchy and misrule may soon die away, and the OLD FLAG OF OUR COUNTRY, radiant with stripes and brilliant with stars, may again wave over a great, and undivided, and happy people."

Finally, the commissioners to the Assembly expressed contrition and offered their lives in complete sacrificial service: "We here, in deep humiliation for our sins and the sins of the nation, and in heartfelt devotion, lay ourselves, with all that we are and have, on the altar of God and our country . . . "[22] There was one altar for two religions.

The same summer, at perhaps the darkest moment of the war,

21. Other resolutions stated that even advocates of international peace joined in support of putting down the rebellion and condemned all Northern apologists for the Southern cause.

22. New School *Minutes, 1861,* pp. 23–25.

George L. Prentiss, a prominent New School minister from New York, expounded a similar Northern Protestant view before the Phi Beta Kappa Society at Dartmouth College. Prentiss, a close friend of Henry B. Smith, clearly explained the basis of Protestant patriotism in terms of covenental and millennial theory, and Smith considered the address important enough to reprint in the *American Theological Review.* The language that Prentiss used indicates that he *assumed,* rather than had to demonstrate, the parallel between Old Testament Israel and modern America. He summarized his challenge to the New England students in the words of Moses' challenge to Israel's first covenant breakers (Exodus 32:26): "Who is on the Lord's side?" This challenge, which was nothing more than a call to "help put down this rebellion," was explicitly framed in terms of the curses of the Old Testament covenants. "And those who hold back and shirk . . . " said Prentiss, "deserve the malediction pronounced against Meroz; *Curse ye Meroz,* said the angel of the Lord."

Prentiss considered the Confederate rebellion against the federal government a rebellion against God himself because it violated the sovereign Union that God had ordained. "It ruthlessly puts asunder that Union and Liberty," he said, "which Almighty Providence, on the day when they so happily joined hands in the presence of the jubilant nation, surely intended should be one and inseparable, then and forever." He equated the rebellion with religious heresy. The American people, Prentiss stated, "have marked it with an anathema such as the Christian Church has put upon an open denial of God. It is like atheism, and subverts the first principles of our political worship as a free, order-loving, and covenant-keeping people."

Even during these dark days of the war Prentiss expressed his confidence that the Northern armies would eventually triumph, adding his conviction that God was on their side. "Reason and religion, then, alike impel us to acknowledge reverently the hand of God in this crisis," he asserted. The war was part of the judgment of God's Eternal Providence against the wicked, and therefore it promised ultimate triumph for the righteous.

The war itself, as well as the temporary defeats of the Union armies, had, according to Prentiss, made Americans reevaluate their unquestioning faith in the progress of the nation toward the "millennial days" of general peace and brotherhood. But, because they knew that God was on the side of the Constitution, loyal Americans could be assured that the divine judgments were only means by which God was achieving even greater things through his chosen nation. Here, nationalism, covenantal theory, New School reform, and millennialism coincide. All four are present in Prentiss's optimistic description of the outcome of the crisis:

> And while the Union is all in all, the very ark of the covenant, to us and our children, it is everything to the race. It is freighted with better hopes for freedom and humanity than any other nation in existence. . . . If still united, we shall cross the threshold of 1900 a hundred millions strong; and if we fight this battle successfully, what battles for truth and justice and freedom and all good things shall we not *then* be able to fight?

Prentiss looked forward to a greater society in the twentieth century, not only as the inevitable outcome of the epic struggle, but as an explicit foreshadowing of the fulfillment of the millennial promise. He concluded his address, speaking of the war,

> It is a true Apocalyptic contest, full of mysterious seals and vials of tribulation; but it is in the hands of Him who in righteousness doth judge and make war. Let us not doubt that in due time he will bring forth judgment unto victory. "Then," to conclude in the glowing words of Milton, " . . . Thou, the eternal and shortly-expected King, shalt open the clouds to judge the several kingdoms of the world, and distributing national honors and rewards to religious and just commonwealths, shalt put an end to all earthly tyrannies, proclaiming thy universal and mild monarchy through heaven and earth.[23]

23. George L. Prentiss, "The National Crisis," *American Theological Review,* 1st ser., 4(October 1862):674–718.

As the Civil War progressed toward its consummation, with the Union armies trampling the Southern vintage, American Protestants seem to have given increased attention to millennial themes. In 1864 and 1865 nearly every number of the *American Presbyterian and Theological Review* contained a major article on the subject. Edwin F. Hatfield of New York City, who contributed a series of three such articles, indicated some of the reasons for this interest. Several of the popular premillennial interpretations of the Biblical prophecies had predicted that either the coming of the millennium or a great turning point in history would take place between 1864 and 1869. The Civil War stirred excitement concerning such literal interpretations of the Biblical prophecies and added plausibility to them. Hatfield systematically attacked these views, claiming that their Biblical arguments were unsound and that modern premillennialists did not hold an historic Christian position.[24] The publication of Hatfield's articles, together with several other treatments of the same subject, indicate that the editors of the *American Presbyterian and Theological Review* resisted the trend toward disillusionment with the world's progress.

With the Union victory, the party of the hopeful in the New School could reassume its stance of unqualified optimism. In an article appearing in the *American Presbyterian and Theological Review* in January 1865, Conway P. Wing, a New School pastor from Carlisle, Pennsylvania, asserted confidently, "We have very little doubt that, at this moment, causes are in operation which only need be intensified and extended to secure the coming of Christ's kingdom." Wing predicted that this progress toward the Kingdom would continue through the uninterrupted manifestations of the conquering power of the Holy Spirit. It would bring an age of unprecedented development of the Church, the state,

---

24. Edwin F. Hatfield, "The Messiah's Second Advent," *American Presbyterian and Theological Review*, 2d ser., 3(April 1865):195–202; ibid., 2(July 1864):411–51.

science, and the importance of the individual man.[25] A year later, William Adams of New York summarized the lesson that many in the New School had learned from the victory of the Northern armies. "Whoever may doubt, whoever may falter, whoever may oppose, we as individuals, and as a nation, are identified with that kingdom of God among men, which is righteous, and peace, and joy in the Holy Ghost."[26]

The report of "The Committee on the State of the Country" to the New School Assembly of 1866 goes so far as to equate explicitly the cause of the Church and the cause of the nation, describing them in both convenantal and millennial terms. In a preamble to a statement advocating radical reconstruction, the report expresses thanks to God for the blessings brought by the war, acknowledging "that He has purged and enlightened our national conscience in respect to our national sins, especially the sin of slavery: and has also made us to recognize more fully than before the reality of Divine Providence, the sureness and justice of retribution for national guilt, and the grand fact that a nation can be exalted and safe only as it yields obedience to his righteous laws." The report goes on to praise the ministers and the churches of the New School for the "singular unanimity and zeal" with which "they upheld our rightful Government, . . . identifying the success of the Nation with the welfare of the Church." Not only are Church and nation identified, but, says the report, "our American Christianity has been vindicated, . . . our Christian benevolence enhanced . . . ; while . . . He has also, in these latter days, rained down spiritual blessings in abundant measure upon many churches all over the land."[27]

The experience of the Civil War restored much of the original

25. Conway P. Wing, "Christianity and Civilization," *American Presbyterian and Theological Review*, 2d ser., 3(January 1865):105–09.

26. William Adams, "The War for Independence and the War for Secession," *American Presbyterian and Theological Review*, 2d ser., 4(January 1866):92.

27. New School *Minutes, 1866*, p. 263.

character of the New School movement. The New School party
in the Presbyterian Church had originally represented the activist
strain of American Protestantism. Its distinctive theology had developed in the milieu of reform and revival. It was an integral part
of the "Evangelical united front" and was the direct outgrowth of
the crusade of evangelical Protestants to save the nation from
apostasy and corruption. During the years of its ecclesiastical independence, however, the New School Church had moved in the
direction of denominationalism. Its theology and its polity had
become distinctly Presbyterian and constitutional in their emphases. By 1860 it had all the marks of a Presbyterian denomination and was becoming increasingly parochial in its outlook. But
the Civil War reversed this trend. The crusade to preserve the
Union and free the Negro seemed to vindicate the earlier New
School principles, restoring its wider national objectives.

In equating the goals of Protestantism and patriotism, the New
School revealed an extravagant dedication to the nation. Many
believed America to be God's chosen nation and supported the
Northern cause, with the confidence that the war was not only
a judgment for national sins, but also a divinely sanctioned means
of purging the covenant people. Not only would God provide
victory for his covenant-keeping people; he also promised even
greater blessings in the approaching millennial age. So, New
School spokesmen, with the exception of some premillennialists,
believed that they fought not only to restore the status quo ante
bellum, but also to ensure progress toward the nation's provi-
dentially ordained mission to bring peace and brotherhood to the
world. The victory of the Union armies appeared to confirm these
theoretical conclusions. Now, the New School looked to the post-
war era with assurance that the Church would play an unprecedented role in shaping the national destiny.

In the Old School the war disrupted the pattern of denominationalism even more dramatically. In 1861 the Old School alliance
between North and South was destroyed when the churches in

the Confederate States withdrew to form a separate denomination. The same year, the Assembly in the North broke its traditional silence on political issues, adopting the famous "Spring Resolutions" affirming that the churches under its care should do all in their power to strengthen, uphold, and encourage the federal government.[28] Throughout the war, the great majority of Old School Presbyterians in the North displayed an unquestionable loyalty to the Union.[29]

Civil War patriotism and the Southern exodus made the Old School more like the New. Conversely, the New School's strong denominational organization, developed in the antebellum years, gave it a character more like that of the Old. Evangelists from the two denominations had cooperated briefly and unofficially during the revival of 1857–58; but, until the war, prospects for widespread cooperation appeared dim indeed. Ministry on battlefields and in hospitals, as well as desire for unity on the home front, however, changed the situation. Disputes over moral depravity, limited atonement, and mediate imputation lost much of their urgency in the midst of national crisis.

In 1862 the Old School made an unexpected move. The Assembly reversed its twenty-five-year-old policy of nonrecognition of the New School and proposed an exchange of fraternal deledates.[30] Suddenly the door leading to possible reunion was unlocked.

28. *Minutes of the General Assembly of the Presbyterian Church in the United States of America, 1861*, Old School (Philadelphia, 1838–69), pp. 329–30 (hereafter cited as Old School *Minutes*).

29. See Vander Velde, *The Presbyterian Churches and the Federal Union*, pp. 21–336, for an excellent and comprehensive account of Old School patriotism.

30. Old School *Minutes, 1862*, pp. 633–34.

II

Presbyterian Reunion:
A Question of Orthodoxy

"We have met to consult for the peace and unity of the church, while the nation is aflame with the blaze of civil war, and every battle of the warrior is with garments rolled in blood," declared Henry Boynton Smith, the retiring Moderator, before the New School General Assembly of 1864. Sensing that he must use the unique opportunity provided by the war for promoting Presbyterian reunion, Smith urged that the unity of the Church should be no less important than the unity of the nation. "Our nation is now vindicating its unity by the costliest sacrifices," he proclaimed. "Let the church of Christ heed the lesson, scrutinize the disease and inquire for the remedy."[1]

Henry Smith recognized that hope for reunion of Northern Presbyterians had been aroused only because of the patriotic fervor generated by the Civil War. He was convinced, however, that out of conflict should come progress. Through the war, he told the Assembly, the nation would be purged of its greatest evil —the bondage of one race by another. Both Church and state would emerge from the war better unified and better prepared for the millennial age. Then, said Smith, "may we extol and magnify that exalted justice tempered by an infinite love, which laid upon us such bitter and costly sacrifices for our discipline and

1. Henry B. Smith, "Christian Union and Ecclesiastical Reunion," in *Faith and Philosophy*, pp. 295, 267. The best general account of both the reunion and its relation to the Civil War is in Vander Velde, *Presbyterian Churches and the Federal Union*, pp. 479–522.

welfare, that we might be purified in the furnace of affliction, and prepared for the coming of the Son of man."[2]

Regardless of how much the catalytic influence of the Civil War hastened the restoration of Presbyterian ties, however, the reunion would not have been feasible without a substantial alteration in the theological situation since the 1830s. By the 1860s all the other major contributing factors in the division had been removed. The slavery issue, the Plan of Union, differences in form of government, and the question of cooperation with voluntary societies were all matters of the past. But suspicion concerning theological differences remained. During the first three years of formal negotiations for reunion, from 1866 to 1868, the question of the meaning of subscription to the Westminster standards was the only major issue on which the two Schools could not readily agree. Finally, in 1869, this issue was resolved as well.

The rapid culmination of the Presbyterian reunion raises an intriguing question, what happened to the doctrinal issues that had been so divisive? Had the wave of Northern nationalism that followed the Civil War led the Old School to forsake its tradition of theological conservatism and to unite with a denomination that still tolerated subversion of the Presbyterian standards?[3] Or, had the doctrinal position of the New School changed sufficiently so that the Old School men could be assured that the reunited Church would not shelter heresy?

From an examination of the evidence produced during the reunion discussions, it is possible to gauge the extent to which the New School had, in fact, become more conservative theologically since 1837.

There were four groups of witnesses to the character of the New

2. Smith, "Christian Union and Ecclesiastical Reunion," p. 294.
3. This is the interpretation usually offered by conservative Presbyterians, who trace twentieth-century theological liberalism to the influence of the New School. For example, Edwin H. Rian, *The Presbyterian Conflict* (Grand Rapids, Mich., 1940), p. 16, says that the reunion "brought together two parties who disagreed fundamentally as to doctrine."

School theology during the reunion period. First, there were the members of the New School Church itself, who were virtually unanimous in their enthusiasm for the reunion. These men claimed, as the New School had always claimed, that the denomination was essentially orthodox. Reiterating that the ministers of the denomination had never departed from the terms of the Auburn Declaration, they asserted that the Church had become increasingly conservative in recent years. Although these men knew more than anyone else about the actual conditions in the New School, their testimony must be qualified by the consideration of their strong partisanship to the reunion.

The second group of witnesses to the character of New School theology was a large element in the Old School denomination who favored the reunion from the outset. This group included the new generation of Old School ministers who had emerged since the division,[4] and a politically "radical" Western element who had been enthusiastically loyal to the Union during the war.[5] As outspoken advocates of reunion, they tended to accept New School claims to orthodoxy at face value and to seek evidence to support that claim. Their estimate of the character of the theology of the New School must also be accepted with caution.

The testimony of a third group of witnesses is somewhat more reliable. This was a large minority in the Old School who opposed the doctrinal terms of reunion as proposed in 1867 and 1868, yet supported the terms proposed in 1869. The presence of this element is the most conclusive evidence that the reunion was not entirely the result of a relaxation of doctrinal vigilance in the Old School.

4. William Adams, "The Reunion," in *Presbyterian Reunion: A Memorial Volume, 1837–1871* (New York, 1870), p. 247.

5. Vander Velde, *Presbyterian Churches and the Federal Union*, p. 594, says that this group controlled the Old School Assembly of 1866, when it took its first positive steps toward reunion. Vander Velde provides a most thorough discussion of the identification of the messages of both Churches with the cause of the Union and the effect of the war on the reunion itself.

Finally, a small minority in the Old School opposed the terms of reunion till the end. This group included some men who had been hesitant to take a strong stand in support of the Union before and during the Civil War, and who favored reunion with the Southern Church.[6] It also counted in its numbers several of the leading participants in the division of 1837, such as Robert J. Breckinridge. Some of its most influential spokesmen were Old School leaders who put doctrinal matters above all else. Among these were Charles Hodge and Samuel J. Baird, the author of the doctrinally oriented *History of the New School,* published in 1868 in opposition to the reunion. For whatever reasons this group may have opposed the reunion, they could be expected to uncover any and all evidence of extant heterodoxy in the New School Church. If the doctrinal unsoundness of the New School at the time of the reunion could have been convincingly established, it certainly would have been by these men. An examination of their arguments against the reunion is, therefore, another important test of the accuracy of the New School claim that the doctrinal issues that had once divided them from the Old School had all but disappeared.

In attempting to define the final doctrinal position of the New School, the testimony of all four of these groups must be considered in the context of the negotiations for reunion.

In 1866, having exchanged fraternal delegates for three years, the two General Assemblies appointed a joint committee, which reported the next year with a proposed basis for reunion. The terms of subscription to the Westminster Confession were clearly the crucial issue. The committee had proposed that in the reunited Church the Confession "shall continue to be sincerely received and adopted 'as containing the system of doctrine taught in the Holy Scriptures'; and [in] its fair, historical sense, as it is accepted by the two bodies in opposition to Antinomianism and Fatalism on

6. Ibid., pp. 501–02.

the one hand, and to Arminianism and Pelagianism on the other. . . . "[7] While this statement was acceptable to the New School and to most of the Old School, the militant minority in the Old School opposed to the reunion objected to it on the ground that the very basis of the dispute between the two Schools had always been disagreement over the meaning of the "fair, historical sense" of the Confession and of the subscription formula, "as containing the system of doctrine taught in Holy Scripture." As a concession to this minority the Old School Assembly of 1867 gave the proposal only tentative approval.[8]

With definite action postponed for a year, the antireunion Old School minority launched its counterattack. Charles Hodge, a reluctant supporter of the division of 1837 now took the lead in opposing the reunion. Using the pages of his powerful *Princeton Review,* he attacked the proposed terms of reunion unmercifully in an article that was reprinted and distributed as a tract. Even the usually irenic Henry B. Smith was scandalized by the review. "The general tone of discussion was manly and conciliatory, until the publication of an article in the *Princeton Review,* in July," he observed.[9]

Hodge in his controversial polemic had built his case against reunion on the accusation that "a latitudinarian principle of subscription . . . is now urged upon us." The New School, he argued, interpreted the formula accepting the Confession "as containing the system of doctrine taught in the Holy Scriptures" in a way unacceptable to the Old School. Here, as elsewhere, Hodge was careful to repudiate the rigid confessionalism that often has been attributed to him. He conceded that a man could be a good Calvinist or Augustinian while disagreeing with the Confession on cer-

7. Adams, "The Reunion," p. 257; cf. ibid., pp. 255–62.
8. Charles Hodge, "The General Assembly," *Princeton Review* 39(July 1867):496–97.
9. Henry B. Smith, "Presbyterian Reunion," *American Presbyterian and Theological Review,* 2d ser., 5(October 1867):633; cf. Adams, "The Reunion," p. 262.

tain nonessentials, such as the doctrines concerning worship, the Sabbath, the civil magistrate, vows, marriage, the Church, communion of the saints, the sacraments, and the future state. Furthermore, he granted that differences in philosophical explanation of even essential doctrines should be allowed. But the New School, he maintained, had always gone beyond even such broad restrictions, interpreting the subscription formula as requiring nothing more than acceptance of the essential doctrines of religion or of Christianity. If the reunion proposal that the Confession be adopted "as it is accepted by the two bodies" meant that this New School interpretation would be permitted, Hodge argued, then the Old School would be sacrificing the principles for which it had always stood.

The question that remained, however, was whether the New School actually held such a lenient interpretation of the subscription requirements. Here, Hodge rested his case primarily on evidence from the disputes of the 1830s. He pointed out also that the New School Church had never disciplined any minister for holding the New Haven doctrines—doctrines that Old School men agreed *did* subvert the essential system of the Confession. This, he maintained, meant that they tolerated subscription to something other than the Reformed system of doctrine. To prove this point, Hodge made the most vulnerable assertion of his article. "Yet it is undeniable, and we presume universally admitted, that these doctrines are publically avowed and taught by not a few of their ministers." While Hodge made it clear that he did not rest his case on the prevalency of heresy, but only on its *tolerance,* he certainly implied that such heresy was as prevalent as ever.[10]

Hodge's article cited no specific contemporary evidence of the existence of questionable New Haven views in the New School. In the next issue of the *Princeton Review* his closest associate in the quarterly's publication, Lyman Atwater, attempted to provide

10. Hodge, "The General Assembly," pp. 505–18.

such evidence. Atwater (1813–83), Professor of Mental and Moral Philosophy at Princeton College, had been born in New Haven and baptized in Nathaniel Taylor's Center Church on the New Haven Green but then had practically made a career out of criticizing his former pastor's theology. Since 1843 he had contributed nine major articles to the *Princeton Review* attacking the New Haven teachings.[11] In October 1867 he contributed his tenth. This time the immediate subject of his attack was one of the old spokesmen for the New School, George Duffield, Sr.

In 1863 Duffield had written an article for Andover's *Bibliotheca Sacra* on the "Doctrines of the New School Presbyterian Church," as part of a series the quarterly was running on the theologies of various denominations. The differences between the Old and the New School, Duffield argued, "are differences in philosophy, not in faith." According to Duffield, New School Presbyterian theology could not be identified exactly with the New England systems any more than it could with the Old School theology. Citing the Auburn Declaration as representative of the mediating position that the New School had always assumed, Duffield reiterated in detail his own views on imputation, original sin, regeneration, justification, the atonement, human ability, and divine sovereignty, claiming as he always had that his views were simply explanations of the accepted system of doctrine.[12]

Atwater reviewed Duffield's statements on each point and repeated the usual Old School charge that Duffield actually subscribed to the New Divinity of Nathaniel Taylor. "Dr. Duffield has put it beyond all doubt, that the doctrinal scheme known as 'New Divinity,' which was the main cause of the disruption of our church, and the protection of which was a chief end of the New-school secession, prevails, though we trust it does not predominate,

11. *Princeton Review* Index Volume, 1829–1871, pp. 95–96.
12. George Duffield, "Doctrines of the New School Presbyterian Church," *Bibliotheca Sacra and Biblical Repository,* 20(October 1863):571–634.

in that body now."[13] Atwater used this evidence to repeat Hodge's argument that the real question in the discussion of reunion was whether views such as Duffield's should be tolerated in the reunited Church.

Henry B. Smith was outraged. The same month that Atwater's article appeared in the *Princeton Review*, Smith used the pages of his *American Presbyterian and Theological Review* to reply to Hodge's accusations. Smith's article, almost certainly the most bitter he ever wrote, reflects little of his usual tone as a champion of peace and mediation. "In all the heat of fierce controversies, thirty years ago," he said, "no more reckless or distorted representations of the New School positions were ever penned, than have just appeared in the *Princeton Review*." If the position of the New School were actually as Hodge described it, then talk of reunion would be pointless.

Turning to the specific charges, Smith maintained that Hodge had misrepresented both the New School's view of subscription and the intention of the proposal of the joint committee on reunion. The New School, he said, had "uniformly repudiated" the principle ascribed to it by the *Princeton Review*, i.e. that "system of doctrine" referred only to the essentials of Christianity. Furthermore, he pointed out, "the Report of the Committee is so far from adopting the lax principle of subscription, that it is wholly inconsistent with it." The New School, he said, actually held a view of subscription virtually identical with Hodge's. The words of the ordination vows meant just what they said. Adoption of the "system of doctrine" meant adoption of the Reformed or Calvinistic system, as distinct from the Lutheran, the Arminian, the Antinomian, the Pelagian, and the Roman Catholic. "No one can honestly and fairly subscribe to the Confession who does not accept the Reformed or Calvinistic system." To charge New School men with

13. Lyman Atwater, "Dr. George Duffield on the Doctrines of New-school Presbyterians," *Princeton Review* 39(October 1867):674.

holding any other view, Smith asserted, was charging them with the immorality of not sincerely making their ordination vows.

As to the accusation that the New School still sheltered heresy, Smith was even more definite. Hodge, he said, had distorted New School teachings. He had described the most extreme implications of the New Haven theology as though they were representative of New School views. Yet the New School men themselves, Smith insisted, had always explicitly disavowed any such extreme implications of the New Haven doctrines and would not accept those who held them. "If any one so holds the fact of man's freedom and ability as to deny the doctrines of God's omnipotence, and of original sin, he of course could not accept our Confession of Faith, and would be rejected by our presbyteries." "Does the *Princeton Review* know of any such, who have been accepted?" Smith asked. "We do not." If the *Princeton Review* could not substantiate its charges, it should withdraw them. "The *Princeton Review* has said what, in common courtesy, it must take back."[14]

Charles Hodge replied to Smith's article in the next issue of the *Princeton Review,* moderating his tone considerably, though not actually conceding his basic point. First, he showed that the New School had in the past *claimed* to demand subscription to only the essentials of Christianity.[15] Second, he said that New School tolerance of New Haven views could be established by the presumptive evidence that they had freely admitted graduates of the New Haven seminary into their presbyteries. Atwater's article on Duffield, he said, established the same point. But this, he claimed, had been his only point. He stated that he did not believe that Duffield's views represented the views of one-tenth of the New School or that one presbytery in ten would accept into its ministry a man who

14. Smith, "Presbyterian Reunion," pp. 634–57.

15. Charles Hodge, "Presbyterian Reunion," *Princeton Review* 40(January 1868):59. Hodge quotes, for example, from *Division,* p. 216, "Our position in respect of doctrine, is that of agreement in things *fundamental,* and toleration and forebearance in things *not essential,* 'endeavoring to keep the unity of the Spirit in the bonds of peace.' "

held to the New Haven system. "We only say that the New-school as a body, as an organized church, has up to the present time, tolerated in its ministry those who openly proclaim themselves its adherents."

Hodge evidently had been impressed by Smith's article and now was willing to concede all that he could. Smith's statement of the New School's position on reunion, he said, alters the aspect of the case. "He assures us that it is perfectly willing to accede to the principle of subscription for which the Old-school contend. . . . The Old-school have never demanded more than this. And they have no right to demand more." If Smith's views truly represented those of the New School he had no objections to the reunion.[16]

Charles Hodge had been impressed by another event that occurred between the publication of his first and second article on the reunion. In November 1867 he had been present at "The Presbyterian National Union Convention" in Philadelphia, a meeting well-attended by representatives of the two Schools and including delegations from five smaller Presbyterian denominations.[17] Ostensibly, the convention, which had no official standing, was to consider possible union of all the Presbyterian churches in the country. Actually, in fact, the more realistic subject of the pending reunion of the two largest denominations became its principal concern. During the discussion of a possible doctrinal basis for a general Presbyterian union, Henry B. Smith suggested that the usual subscription formula be modified simply by adding: "It being understood that this Confession is received in its proper historical, that is, the Calvinistic or Reformed sense." Smith clearly had Hodge's criticisms in mind when he proposed this amendment.

16. Ibid., pp. 61–79.
17. These were the United Presbyterian Church, the Reformed Presbyterian Church (New Side), the Cumberland Presbyterian Church, the Reformed Dutch Church, and the Southern Presbyterian Church (nominally represented). For an account of the Minor Presbyterian Churches in this era, see Vander Velde, *Presbyterian Churches and the Federal Union*, pp. 5–13, 379–424.

His design was to allay some Old School suspicions and to persuade the New School to accept such an explicit interpretation of the meaning of subscription. In this, he succeeded. Delegates from both Schools endorsed his proposal, and it was clear that it would be carried to the official joint committee on reunion. Furthermore, the warm spirit of brotherhood at the convention made a deep impression on some of the most recalcitrant in the Old School.[18]

Charles Hodge's apparent change in his estimate of the New School was remarkable. Their endorsement of the clause guaranteeing adherence to the Reformed system had appeared so complete, he observed, that the Old School could ask for nothing more. "And," said Hodge, "if the New-school Assembly and Presbyteries will sanction what their representatives did on the floor of the Convention, the doctrinal basis of union may be considered as satisfactorily adjusted."[19]

By the time the joint committee of the two Schools met again in the spring of 1868, however, the New School representatives were unwilling to concede the issue so completely. Rather than accepting the Smith amendment with no other qualifications, they at least wanted to retain the phrase, "as it is accepted by the two bodies," from the original proposal. As a result, the committee adopted a statement qualifying the standard subscription formula with both the Smith amendment *and* the words, "It is also understood that various methods of viewing, stating, explaining, and illustrating the doctrines of the confession, which do not impair the integrity of the Reformed or Calvinistic system, are to be freely allowed in the United Church, as they have hitherto been allowed in the separate Churches."[20]

The committee's proposal, which now went to the two General Assemblies, meeting in May 1868, was now sufficiently complex that the resulting complications seem hardly surprising. The New

18. This account is based on Adams, "The Reunion" pp. 263–65.
19. Hodge, "Presbyterian Reunion," p. 82.
20. Adams, "The Reunion," pp. 265–68.

School Assembly accepted the proposal with little difficulty; but in the Old School the conservative party remained unpacified. While conceding "a decrease of objectionable views . . . during the last thirty years,"[21] they rested their case on the fact that the views of the older men, such as Barnes, Beman, and Duffield, were still tolerated in the New School Church.[22] The majority, however, voted to adopt the joint committee's proposals and to send it down to the presbyteries, three-fourths of which had to approve for final adoption. Fifty-eight commissioners (including Charles Hodge) of the defeated minority in the Assembly entered a strong protest against this action. While denying opposition to reunion itself, they attacked the *proposed terms* of reunion. They also expressly disavowed any intention of imputing error or insincerity to the mass of New School men. They objected, however, that the current proposal would allow former New School men to claim the precedent that their Church had tolerated men holding New Haven views.[23]

In answer to this protest the Old School majority in the Assembly declared their reasons for confidence in the New School. On the matter of tolerance of doctrinal error, they affirmed that the Auburn Declaration was "an authoritative statement of the New-school type of Calvinism, and as indicating how far they desire to go, and how much liberty they wish in regard to what the terms of union call 'the various modes of explaining, illustrating, and stating' the Calvinist faith." The majority also asserted that they were firmly convinced that the instances of laxity in doctrine in the New School were exceptional cases and that no views that actually impaired the integrity of the Reformed system would be tolerated in the reunited Church. As evidence of the trend toward orthodoxy in the New School, they noted that all three of

21. *Report of the Proceedings of the General Assembly of the Presbyterian Church in the United States of America* (Philadelphia, 1868), p. 28.
22. Vander Velde, *Presbyterian Churches and the Federal Union*, p. 515.
23. "Protest," Old School *Minutes 1868*, pp. 658–61.

the New School theological seminaries fully and firmly taught Westminster Calvinism and combated and refuted the alleged errors.[24] On this last point the committee answering the protest had some good evidence. Its chairman was William G. T. Shedd, an Old School man who had held the Chair of Sacred Literature at Union Seminary in New York since 1863. Even the protesters conceded the soundness of the seminaries. One of their number, Dr. John Backus, declared before the Assembly, "I have but little doubt that Auburn, and Union, and Lane are becoming orthodox."[25]

Still, the majority in the Old School Assembly acknowledged that these dissidents had honest misgivings about the terms of reunion. In order to conciliate them, the Assembly subsequently passed a resolution qualifying its approval of the Joint Committee's terms. This resolution stated that the Old School would *prefer* to drop both the current amendments and to base the reunion on acceptance of the standards in simple terms of the traditional formula—"the Confession of Faith shall continue to be sincerely received and adopted as containing the system of doctrine taught in Holy Scriptures"—with no qualifications. This, they contended, would be more expressive of mutual confidence.[26]

This action only caused confusion. The New School Assembly had adjourned by the time it received the Old School's new suggestion. The result was a year of frustration for the advocates of reunion. The Old School presbyteries, holding out for a simpler formula, decisively defeated the longer amended proposal, which was the only official action before them. Nothing could be done until the Assemblies met again in 1869.[27]

Now, however, in 1869, accord was quickly reached. The two Assemblies adopted overwhelmingly (in the New School unani-

24. "Answer to the Protest," ibid., pp. 663–64.
25. *Report of the Proceedings of the General Assembly* (1868), p. 106.
26. Old School *Minutes, 1868,* p. 631.
27. Adams, "The Reunion," pp. 293–97.

mously and in the Old School 285–9) the simple unamended formula. Opposition was slight in the presbyteries as well. All the
New School presbyteries and 126 of 129 voting Old School presbyteries approved. The Church was reunited.[28]

The question that the overwhelming approval of the reunion
by the members of the Old School suggests is, what happened to the
formidable opposition of the previous year? Or, more basically,
how could the vast majority of the members of the Old School,
which was widely reputed to be the strictest of the major denominations in America on matters of doctrine, be so completely reconciled to the body they had consistently opposed for nearly a generation? The refusal of a substantial minority to approve the doctrinal terms of reunion proposed at the Assembly in 1867 and 1868
indicates that many in the Old School were still unwilling to forsake the principles for which they had sacrificed the unity of their
Church in 1837. Yet by 1869 this opposition had nearly disappeared, as all but nine of the dissenters joined the rest of the Assembly in expressing confidence in the doctrinal soundness of the
New School.

Lyman Atwater, now the junior editor of the *Princeton Review*
and a vigorous opponent of the reputed errors of the New School,
was one of the strict Old School men who had changed his mind
during the course of negotiations with the New School. In an
article appearing soon after the Assemblies of 1869, he explained
why.

When Atwater had arrived at the Old School Assembly of 1869,
he had not been sure that the two Churches were ripe for reunion.
He was convinced, however, that if there were a reunion it must
be on the basis of the standards, without qualification. In the course
of the Assembly he became convinced that both bodies were ready
for the reunion on terms that would not sacrifice the principles for

28. Vander Velde, *Presbyterian Churches and the Federal Union*, p. 516.

which the conscientious in the Old School had always stood. He therefore concluded that he ought not to continue to oppose what might be the leadings of Providence and the Spirit of God.

Atwater had described the basis for his newfound confidence in the New School in a speech before the Old School Assembly. First, he said, the old contributing factors in the division, such as questions of cooperation with Congregationalism and the voluntary societies, had been removed. The only remaining question was whether there might still be an element of heterodoxy in the New School. "On this point," he said, "I have long been happy to observe a change for the better going on among them." He was confident that New School theology was sound because of his knowledge of the orthodoxy of the New School seminaries. At Auburn, he noted, he knew the Professor of Theology, Edwin Hall, personally and was assured of his "doctrinal soundness." In fact, reliable testimony from a critical Old School source indicated that in the whole region around Auburn in upstate New York "there had been a complete revolution since that time and the days of the New Divinity and New Measure revivalists: and that the New School body in this region was now every whit as sound and orthodox as our own."

Atwater was even more certain of the soundness of Union Seminary in New York City, particularly because of the influence of Henry B. Smith, who rivaled Atwater himself as an opponent of the New Haven views. He observed that Union graduates were thoroughly imbued with Smith's views and that they were received for ordination without objections in Old School presbyteries. Similar confidence could be placed in Lane Seminary in Cincinnati, Atwater continued. Here he referred to recent testimony before the Assembly that at Lane opposition to the New Divinity was so firm that "in fact, they *out-Princeton* Princeton itself." Lyman Atwater, who had seldom been "out-Princetoned" by anyone, accepted this verdict.[29]

29. Lyman Atwater, "The Late Assemblies on Re-union," *Princeton Review* 41 (July 1869):430–36.

The opinion of the junior editor of the *Princeton Review* on the changed conditions in the New School Church had much to commend its reliability. Atwater was one of the last in the Old School to change his mind but eventually experienced the same revolution in feeling that was common to the vast majority of the Old School men during this period. He, and apparently the majority in the Old School, approved the reunion only when entirely assured that they were sacrificing none of their principles on subscription and that the New School was essentially reformed.

Charles Hodge, still the senior editor of the *Princeton Review*, continued to oppose the reunion until the end. Hodge did not attend the Assembly of 1869 and was not satisfied that his original objections to the reunion proposals had been adequately answered. In a short statement following Atwater's defense of the reunion in the *Review*, Hodge reiterated his old arguments. Again his only objection was, not that the New School was unorthodox, but that the New School Church had always *tolerated* some questionable theological views and that this spirit of tolerance could be expected to continue after the reunion.[30]

Another die-hard dissenter was Samuel J. Baird, whose *History of the New School* appeared in 1868 as a bitter denunciation of the attempts for reunion. In criticizing the doctrinal stand of the New School, he wrote, "It is asserted that our New School brethren have changed on the doctrinal question. The only question that has ever divided us, on that subject has been the propriety of tolerating and shielding error."[31]

The attacks of Hodge and Baird are significant for what they did not say. Neither of them denied that the New School had, in fact, become doctrinally more sound. Had it been possible, they undoubtedly would have uncovered new evidence of New School heterodoxy. Yet their only objection was to the New School's standard of tolerance.

30. Charles Hodge, "The New Basis of Reunion," *Princeton Review* 41 (July 1869):465–66.
31. Baird, *New School*, p. 17.

The testimony of all the major parties in the reunion discussions confirms the conclusion that the New School had become more orthodox during the period of its independence. In 1869 the only doctrinal differences that any of the interested parties noted were those left over from the controversies of the previous generation. As to more recent developments—such as the new science, new philosophy, or Biblical criticism—no one at the time distinguished any substantial difference in the attitude of the two Schools. Opponents of the reunion in the Old School pointed only to men such as Albert Barnes and George Duffield, Sr., who had once been accused of heresy and yet were still tolerated in the New School Church.

Tolerance was, perhaps, a real issue. But, aside from the views of these few men of the older generation, New School orthodoxy was not questioned.

In the preamble to the Plan of Reunion the mutual confidence of the two Assemblies was clearly expressed with the words, "Each recognizing the other as a sound and orthodox body, according to the principles of the confession common to both." This clause was inserted at the insistence of George W. Musgrave, chairman of the Old School delegation on the joint committee. At the Assembly, Musgrave, pastor of the Tenth Presbyterian Church in Philadelphia, spoke in defense of the Plan of Reunion in what was considered one of the most able and remarkable discourses of the whole proceedings.[32] It summarizes the testimony of many of the old guard in the Old School, and is still remarkable,

> Why, Sir, the change of circumstances is almost radically entire. There were causes in operation from 1828 up to 1838, which we had good reason to dread, and which were undoubtedly corrupting and revolutionizing the church of God. I have never said, because I have never felt, as some men have said and doubtless felt—I have never said that I regretted the part I took in the

32. "Basis of Reunion," *Princeton Review* 41 (July 1869):449.

early conflict. . . . I will rebuke heresy now, as I did then. . . .

Sir, the circumstances are different. . . . All I ask is for a man to be a good Calvinist, and a thorough Presbyterian, and a sound Christian, and I don't care from what quarter he comes. . . . Some men like to repeat that remark of Whitfield, that there will be no Presbyterians and no Methodists, etc., in heaven. Well, sir, I don't know any more about heaven than Whitfield did, as I have never been there. I don't know exactly what form of worship they have, but I have an idea that it will be Presbyterian. . . .

But certain I am of this, or more certain I should say, that we will all believe the doctrines of Paul, when we get to heaven. I believe what Augustine and John Calvin taught; but I would not like myself to say that we will all be Calvinists in heaven. But I will say this, that we will all believe in accordance with the revelation which God gave through the Apostle Paul, and by that I understand Calvinism; and therefore I think that we shall all have that system of doctrine in heaven.[33]

33. Ibid., pp. 457–59.

Conclusion: The Evangelical Mind and Mid-Nineteenth-Century America

New School Presbyterianism is significant for understanding mid-nineteenth-century America not because it was so unusual, but rather because it was not. Measured by most gauges, whether intellectual, theological, religious, political, or social, the movement stood near the center of the cultural spectrum. Moreover, as part of the larger evangelical awakening, New School Presbyterianism was representative of many of the characteristics of that most successful religious movement of the era. The account of the distinctive concerns of the New School may be balanced therefore with an analysis of the broader relationships between the evangelical mind in general and the mid-nineteenth-century American climate of opinion.

Both the great success, and eventually the failure, of American evangelicalism may be attributed in large measure to its strong identification with nineteenth-century values. The relationship between the religion and the culture was, of course, reciprocal. Evangelicals, through their vigorous and comprehensive campaigns, doubtless left an indelible imprint on nineteenth-century American life. Their firm commitment to revivalism, moral reforms, and the fundamentals of Biblical Christianity changed the character of both the religion and the culture itself. In fact, evangelicals seem to have succeeded in rescuing the nation from at least a substantial portion of the infidelity and immorality that their progenitors had feared at the opening of the century. At the same time, nonetheless, their success was due in part to their willingness to allow their message to be accommodated to the spirit of the culture. Either way—whether the evangelicals shaped the culture or the culture shaped the evangelicals—the result was a close identification of Protestant and American values.

The broad characteristics of the evangelical mind therefore parallel those of the American mind in general in the mid-nineteenth century. Ralph Gabriel has long since pointed this out in his classic study of *The Course of American Democratic Thought,* and his generalizations still provide a useful framework on which an elaboration of the similarities between evangelical and American values can be built. In his characterization of nineteenth-century Americanism, Gabriel suggests three primary articles of the democratic faith: the existence of God-ordained natural and moral law, the importance of the freedom and responsibility of the individual, and the mission of America. Each of these played a major role in the development of the evangelical mind.[1]

Evangelicalism, Natural Law, and Moral Law

The Enlightenment concept that seems to have made the deepest impression on the American mind of the nineteenth century was the idea of a God-ordained natural law. Basic to the eighteenth-century reformulation of this ancient concept was the application of the Newtonian model for physical laws to all areas of experience. Natural law in every area was assumed to be—like the laws of physics—fixed, orderly, and universal. Moreover, because it was perfectly rational, it could be discovered by human reason. In America it was of particular importance that these assumptions were applied to moral law. The nation itself defended its independence on the principle (to which everyone from deists to Calvinists subscribed) that a higher moral law superseded the laws of corrupt men and governments. With the relative isolation of the

1. Ralph Henry Gabriel, *The Course of American Democratic Thought* (New York, 1956), pp. 14–39.

American intellect after the Revolutionary era, there was little advance on such popular doctrines. For a time, particularly during the first several decades of the nineteenth century, the American mind appeared almost fixated in its acceptance of the rationalism and moralism of eighteenth-century thought.

Evangelicals of the early national era shared these assumptions and helped to weld them solidly to the American Protestant outlook. "The Moral Government of God," a concept suggesting that God was a benevolent and enlightened despot who clearly revealed thoroughly reasonable moral laws, increasingly became a central concern of New England's moderate theologians. Joseph Bellamy had introduced this theme, and Samuel Hopkins had elaborated on it and transmitted it to nineteenth-century evangelicals.[2] Both Lyman Beecher and Nathaniel Taylor, for instance, made "moral government" the principal organizing theme of their theological lectures. God's moral laws, nearly everyone agreed, were ordered and rational and therefore could be best understood through science. Francis Wayland, Baptist president of Brown and author of the century's most popular text on "moral science," argued, for example, that "as all relations, whether moral or physical, are the result of His enactment, an order of sequence once discovered in morals is just as invariable as an order of sequence in physics."[3] Reason was always essential to such scientific discovery. "Truth and Reason are so intimately connected that they can never with propriety be separated,"[4] stated Princeton Seminary's Archibald Alexander in a typical nineteenth-century defense of Christianity. Taylor of Yale put it even more strongly, insisting that reason and common sense were as reliable as the Word of God itself (see Chapter 2, above).

2. See Haroutunian, *Piety,* pp. 90–94.
3. Francis Wayland, *The Elements of Moral Science,* ed. Joseph L. Blau (Cambridge, Mass., 1963), p. 18.
4. Archibald Alexander, *Evidences of the Authenticity, Inspiration, and Canonical Authority of the Holy Scriptures* (Philadelphia, 1836), p. 10.

Scottish Common Sense provided the primary philosophical rationale for evangelical rationalism and moralism during the New School era. According to Herbert W. Schneider, "The Scottish Enlightenment was probably the most potent single tradition in the American Enlightenment,"[5] and the Common Sense philosophy doubtless contributed considerably to preserving the Age of Reason in America even when it was being forgotten elsewhere. The evangelical colleges, which dominated American higher education and where this philosophy was particularly popular, played a major role in perpetuating this Enlightenment tradition. Through its affirmation of man's ability to perceive God's natural order and moral law, Common Sense philosophy supplied evangelicals with both a popular intellectual defense of the faith and a clear rationale for moral reform.

Even when American philosophy after about 1830 began slowly to drift from such late-Enlightenment rationalism toward romanticism and idealism, there was no great crisis within the evangelical camp. Though the newer philosophies emphasized nonrationality, subjectivity, intuition, and process in historical development more than Common Sense philosophy, they were turned to much the same practical uses as the common-sense methods. In the New School, for instance, Laurens P. Hickok one of the pioneers of German idealism in America, created only a mild stir with this new philosophy (see Chapters 5 and 7, above). The reason was that, despite his attacks on the "false systems of nature" of New England's Edwardsean theologians, Hickok's conclusions were much the same. While he maintained that "philosophical knowledge" rests on "those a priori conditions which give the necessary and universal laws to experience" and that "Nature" may be "comprehended in a pure Spontaniety,"[6] his idealism was intended to provide only a new explanation of the traditional affirmations—that there is a God-ordained universal law and that men can compre-

5. Schneider, *History of American Philosophy*, p. 216.
6. Quoted in Schneider, *History of American Philosophy*, pp. 380, 382.

hend it. Hickok, furthermore, used his method to defend traditional morality, and his own text on "Moral Science," except for its idealistic presuppositions, was "as a whole . . . conventional."[7]

The evangelical philosophers' confidence in man's ability to comprehend God-ordained natural and moral law had its counterpart on the popular level of evangelical activity. Common sense was particularly popular among the reputedly practical and realistic American people, and the philosophy of that name only claimed, after all, to be an affirmation of what was already universally believed. Not only the theologians, but the popular evangelists as well, insisted on the reasonableness of the doctrines they preached.

Nevertheless, the strong elements of rationalism apparent at every level of evangelical discourse were often tempered by the more conspicuous strain of emotionalism that characterized the revivals. The "religion of the heart" was a popular form of romanticism with some definite anti-intellectual overtones (cf. Introduction, above). The revivalists themselves, however, would hardly have conceded that they had abandoned rationality. As Finney maintained, everyone could agree on intellectual propositions; the danger was that these propositions would be grasped by the mind *only* and not with the heart.[8] New School evangelicals affirmed the importance of the rational intellect even more clearly. Albert Barnes's criteria for a preachable theology, for example, were careful Scriptural exegesis, common sense, and a proper relation to the spirit of the age (see Chapter 5, above). Even when unorthodox—in fact, *especially* when unorthodox—evangelicals displayed a firm commitment to the American faith that rational men could discover God's natural and moral law.

---

7. Schneider, *History of American Philosophy*, p. 379; cf. ibid., pp. 379–85. The warm acceptance in New School circles of Henry B. Smith, whose thought clearly reflected the influence of German philosophy, illustrates the same points (cf. Chapter 8, above).

8. Miller, *Life of the Mind in America*, p. 25.

Evangelicalism and the Free Individual

The second fundamental tenet of the American democratic faith, says Ralph Gabriel, was the importance of the "free and responsible individual." This doctrine was closely related to the faith in natural and moral law. As individuals better understood fundamental law, they reputedly became more mature morally, and hence they should be more free from the restraints of civil government.[9] Such confidence in the individual was supported by the major popular and academic philosophies of the day. Confidence in the individual was basic to Jeffersonianism; individual introspection was the ultimate court of appeal in Common Sense philosophy; and the free individual was exalted extravagantly in the popular romanticism (as well as in the more esoteric Transcendentalism) of the Jacksonian era.

The importance of American individualism for understanding American evangelicalism is clear. The great debates in American intellectual life during the first half of the nineteenth century focused on the question of the nature of man. In evangelical Protestant circles, where Calvinism and optimistic individualism were each strongly represented, such controversies were particularly intense. The question of whether men had the natural ability to do good was the major ideological issue that divided the New School from the Old in the 1830s. In general America's evangelicals seemed to be moving away from the Calvinist emphasis on inborn depravity and toward more optimistic doctrines. The revivalists' emphases on the individual's acceptance of the Gospel and on high standards of personal morality, as well as the individualistic doctrines that permeated the American climate of opinion, made such a trend nearly inevitable. Moreover, even evangelicals of moderate persuasions, as in the New School, optimistically affirmed that men's moral standards (if not their natures) were steadily improving.

9. Gabriel, *Democratic Thought*, pp. 19–21.

The experience of the New School Presbyterians, nevertheless, indicates that the collapse of the Calvinist outlook during the first half of the nineteenth century was not nearly so complete as is generally supposed. Doubtless by mid-century the "one-hoss shay" of Oliver Wendell Holmes had long since disintegrated in the vicinity of his home town, Cambridge, Massachusetts; but in other areas of the country the conveyance could be seen in prominent places for many years to come. Among New School Presbyterians, at least, Calvinism survived the challenges of the thoroughgoing optimism of the era, resisting the doctrines of extreme confidence in man found both among the perfectionists, on the one hand, and among the Unitarians and Transcendentalists, on the other.

In the more practical area of religious organization individualism also had an important, though mixed, effect. The tendency of American thought in general since the early eighteenth century had been away from the Puritan ideal of corporate responsibilities in a unified society and toward affirmation of the individual's right to choose voluntarily his beliefs and affiliations. In religious life this trend was paralleled by the revivalists' emphasis on voluntary acceptance of the Gospel and was manifested to some extent by the appearance of those sects and denominations that reflected an individual evangelist's peculiar creed. Although the basic pattern of American denominationalism developed more because of American diversity than because of such individualism, the character of every denomination was clearly influenced by individualistic doctrines. Particularly important was the idea that the Churches, like any other American institution, were subject to the will of their constituents. They therefore had little binding power over their members, who felt relatively free to leave when dissatisfied. Evangelical Protestants in the early nineteenth century were accordingly almost always Low Church, sharing the general American distrust of authority and tradition and emphasizing instead free democratic organization. The "united front," though an attempt to reestablish Christian unity, was one of the strongest manifestations of this antichurch trend among evangelicals. Its interdenominational agencies were voluntary societies that individuals could freely join or leave and were virtually free of traditional theological or ecclesiastical restraints.

The history of New School Presbyterianism, however, indicates a slight reversal of this anti-church trend. The division of 1837–38 had been one instance of a more general conflict between denominationalism and interdenominationalism in America. Yet very shortly after mid-century, denominationalism had triumphed in the New School—one of the branches of Protestantism most closely identified with interdenominational cooperation.

This renewed concern for the importance of the organized Church was accompanied by a complementary new concern for tradition in New School thought. The later works of New School theologians indicate a conscious attempt to define the theology of the Church in terms of the denomination's own history, the tradition of Presbyterianism in America, and the larger history of Christian dogma. This rise of historical consciousness, best exemplified in the work of Henry B. Smith, reflects a more general tendency toward romantic traditionalism in American thought of the antebellum era.[10] In the American Churches this tendency is best indicated by the High Church movements that flourished in the 1850s;[11] but the development of a slight trend in the New School suggests that the recovery of tradition and authority affected even Low Church and reputedly individualistic organizations.

Although its influences in some areas must be qualified, the American doctrine of the free and responsible individual was a major factor in shaping the evangelical mind. Perhaps its most

10. For a useful interpretation of this renewal of interest in the past in the midst of the age of hope, see R. W. B. Lewis, *The American Adam: Innocence, Tragedy, and Tradition in the Nineteenth Century* (Chicago, 1955), pp. 159–73. Henry B. Smith's close friendship with George Bancroft suggests the New School's kinship to this trend.

11. Nichols, *Romanticism in American Theology*, provides the best account of the spirit of this movement.

lasting impact was its contribution to the peculiar quality of American moralism. As Stanley Elkins suggests, "the individual in America has historically insisted upon his right to define sin for himself."[12] While the idea of corporate and national guilt persisted into the Civil War era, the evangelical message more often reinforced the American predilection to define sin in individualistic terms. Common Sense philosophy contributed to this tendency by insisting that each individual is endowed with the ability to perceive the first principles of morality. Evangelicals characteristically appealed to the consciences of individuals as the best means for social reform. Much of the antislavery campaign was conducted on this principle.[13] James G. Birney, one of the evangelical promoters of the American Anti-Slavery Society, for example, represented the typical approach when he advised that agents in the field "insist principally on the *sin of slavery,* because our main hope is in the consciences of men, and it requires little logic to prove that it is always safe to do right."[14] The other moral issues for which evangelicals campaigned most vigorously were almost invariably presented to the individual as such an absolute choice between right and wrong. That the temperance crusade quickly turned into a campaign for *total abstinence* is the best illustration of the evangelical penchant for dealing almost solely in moral absolutes in their efforts to awaken the consciences of individuals.[15]

Such programs suggest another manifestation of the individualistic moral outlook; that is, the evangelicals emphasized those sins that were clearly definable and observable individual acts. The

12. Elkins, *Slavery,* p. 162.

13. Cf. ibid., especially pp. 140–222, where Elkins suggests that the emphasis on reform through individuals rather than through institutions contributed to the failure of antislavery leaders to find a peaceful solution.

14. Quoted in Dwight L. Dumond, *Antislavery Origins of the Civil War in the United States* (Ann Arbor, Mich., 1959), p. 35.

15. It suggests also the nineteenth-century opposition to anything that reduces the individual's rational control over himself. One consequence of drinking was that it would impair a person's ability to use his common sense.

revivalists particularly centered their attacks on such visible sins and demanded strict abstinence from them as evidence of conversion. Prohibitions on all sorts of observable activities such as drinking, smoking, dancing, Sabbath-breaking, card playing, and theater attendance thus become indelibly associated with Protestantism in this tradition. Though the roots of most of these concerns could be traced to seventeenth-century Puritanism or to eighteenth-century Methodist Pietism, they were certainly strengthened by nineteenth-century influences as well. The emphasis in Nathaniel Taylor's theology that sin is an *act* (and hence the responsibility of only the individual involved) is at least symptomatic of this trend. Likewise, the exorbitant personal ethical demands of the perfectionist wing of evangelicalism undoubtedly contributed further to the American Protestant tendency to define sin in terms of observable actions of free and responsible individuals.

Evangelicalism and the Mission of America

The most striking parallels, observes Ralph Gabriel, between the Protestant and the American faith "were the religious counterparts of the mission of democratic America."[16] This theme requires little elaboration here, as it is conspicuous in the account of New School millennialism and Civil War patriotism. Evangelicals unquestioningly identified the future of America with revivalism, reform, and the millennial hope. Examples of such identification could be multiplied almost indefinitely,[17] and these equations of religious and patriotic goals provide the clearest illustrations of the evangelicals' readiness to accommodate their message to the spirit of their age and nation.

One of the major impulses that drove American evangelicalism after 1800 was, as Perry Miller maintains in "From the Covenant

16. Gabriel, *Democratic Thought*, p. 34.
17. See, for instance, ibid., pp. 34–35; Miller, *Life of the Mind in America,* especially pp. 66–72; and Miller, "From the Covenant to the Revival."

to the Revival," a fervent desire to create a new religious national-ism. This fervor, says Miller, was a reaction to the three-fold challenge presented by the skeptical rationalism of the Revolu-tionary era, the rapid expansion into the West, and the disestab-lishment of the churches. "If this configuration posed a threat of centrifugal force," he goes on, "then that had to be countered by the centripetal power of the Revival."[18] The campaigns for na-tional moral reform had much the same purpose. American evan-gelicals by the early nineteenth century were reconciled to dis-establishment as a legal fact, but they did not abandon the principle underlying establishmentarianism—that theirs should be a Christian nation. In effect, the evangelical movement in the first half of the nineteenth century was an attempt to found an unofficial American establishment, and by the second half of the century it was clear that in some respects it had succeeded. As American Protestantism entered the Gilded Age, there was little to distinguish its aspirations and values from those of the re-spectable American middle class.

Its success took political form as well. Prior to 1860 (except for some brief indulgence in Know-Nothingism) evangelicals had not been predominantly inclined toward any particular major political party. The professional reformers, who had the most direct interest in political affairs, had in general remained un-committed politically. With the advent of Republicanism, how-ever, this situation seems to have changed as that Party became "a refuge for reformers."[19] The Civil War reinforced the identifi-cation of Christian reform and Republicanism. If there was any truth to the later remark that the Democrats were the Party of "Rum, Romanism, and Rebellion," then the Republicans, by espousing the opposites, were championing three causes very close to the hearts of America's evangelicals.

18. Miller, "From the Covenant to the Revival," p. 354; cf. ibid., pp. 322–68.
19. Clifford S. Griffin, *Their Brothers' Keepers: Moral Stewardship in the United States, 1800–1865* (New Brunswick, N.J., 1960), p. 239; cf. ibid., p. 240.

Evangelical thought apparently contributed to Republican economic theory as well. According to Common Sense philosophy, one of the self-evident moral principles was that each individual had a right to accumulate and to own property. Ralph Gabriel cites the works of presidents Noah Porter of Yale, James McCosh of Princeton, and Mark Hopkins of Williams to indicate the widespread influence of this doctrine. Together with the traditional Protestant emphasis on stewardship, he argues, Common Sense philosophy made a substantial contribution to the rapidly secularized "gospel of wealth" of the industrial tycoons in the Gilded Age.[20]

Though evangelicals did not usually condone the political and economic excesses associated with the post–Civil War era, their contributions to Republican ideology further illustrate the extent to which they had succeeded in incorporating many of their values into the mainstream of American life.

The Perils of Success

Yet the price of success was high. How high it was may be gauged by comparing the relationship of the Churches to American culture at the beginning and at the end of the period under study. In the early decades of the nineteenth century the American Churches clearly represented the Church militant, standing arrayed against a secular nation and challenging its citizens to repent and be saved. But by the end of the Civil War era, though their primary message appeared much the same, the denominations had almost merged with the culture. The Kingdom of God and the nation were virtually equated. Rather than remaining a force for revolution, evangelical Protestantism, now firmly institutionalized, was fast becoming synonymous with the middle class *status quo*.

Ironically, then, the same factors that contributed to American

20. Gabriel, *Democratic Thought,* pp. 155–58.

Protestant success fostered its weakness. The pattern of merger between religion and culture is evident from the study of evangelical thought. In their zeal to communicate the Gospel the evangelicals had accommodated their message to the temper of their American audience, and much of their accommodation was also a concession. The result was that some of the doctrines of the essentially humanistic American democratic faith were presented as though they were an integral part of the evangelical Christian message. Common Sense philosophy again provides the most notable example. The dictates of common sense were above all humanistic. Man's ability to do good, his freedom, and his ability to discover the principles of morality were among its primary lessons. Both man and moralism were exalted. As Joseph Haroutunian remarks concerning the religious thought of this era, "Having lost its social basis, Christianity tried to manufacture a modern equivalent. It absorbed the moralism of the new age, and drenched its theology with humanism."[21]

Reliance on eighteenth-century Enlightenment philosophy also weakened the apologetic of nineteenth-century American Protestants. James Ward Smith in "Religion and Science in American Philosophy" argues persuasively that American Protestant acceptance of science in the pre-Darwinian era was essentially a "superficial accommodation"—that is, an acceptance of the corpus of scientific discovery without either taking seriously the scientific method of inquiry or challenging its speculative basis.[22] Among nineteenth-century American evangelicals, where the rationalistic arguments of Bishop Butler and William Paley were still in style, Smith's analysis fits exactly. In the New School, for instance, the new geology generated considerable discussion, but few problems. The new discoveries could be adequately incorporated into the traditional argument from design with no serious reevaluation

21. Haroutunian, *Piety,* p. xix.
22. James Ward Smith, "Religion and Science in American Philosophy," in Smith and Jamison, eds., *The Shaping of American Religion,* especially pp. 409–25.

of the implications of the scientific method. Such, of course, was not the case with Darwinism, and the New School Presbyterians along with most American Protestants were poorly equipped to face the scientific challenges of the next era.

The accommodation of theology to the American temper also weakened the evangelicals' intellectual defenses. The content of their theology changed relatively little during this era, and judging from the New School example, the trend was away from doctrinal innovation; but the role played by theology in the American Churches appeared to be changing. Early in the century evangelicals of the Reformed heritage had fought for their theological rights. Their doctrinal views were intimately bound to their practical concerns, and they expended much intellectual energy in justifying their position. After mid-century, theological investigation continued, perhaps on a higher plane. Henry B. Smith, for example, was only one of a half-dozen major Reformed theologians during the era. Yet theology seemed less relevant to the activities of the Church. Doctrinal controversy had proved a disruptive force during the early decades of the century. Moreover, it was clearly becoming less popular with the American constituency. Controversial theology in most denominations was going out of style. It was being submerged by religious activism. This activistic tendency, which had its roots in the earlier evangelical campaigns, had become dominant by the end of the century. The decades bridging the turn of the century were, as Winthrop Hudson describes them, "an era of crusades—'movements' they were called—which served to channel the unusual moral idealism and superabundance of zeal generated by the churches into a host of good causes." But, as Hudson also concludes, the great malady of the Church in this age "was the theological erosion which had taken place during the nineteenth century."[23]

23. Hudson, *American Protestantism,* pp. 124–25, 132. See also Mead, *The Lively Experiment,* p. 15, who draws the same conclusion.

Intellectually, then, evangelical Protestantism had not been as well prepared to face the post–Civil War era as its external prosperity might have suggested. Success had bred considerable complacency. Though it had not consciously repudiated the intellect, its concessions to Common Sense humanism, its Victorian moralism, its unblushing patriotism, its activism, and its aversion to theological debate had all inadvertently contributed toward leading the Church away from the careful theological discipline that had once been characteristic of its heritage.

Epilogue: The New School Presbyterian Tradition in the Twentieth Century—Fundamentalist or Liberal?

The relative peace that followed the Reunion of 1869 lasted only until the 1890s. Then a new era of Presbyterian controversy arose. At first the major issues were the question of Biblical infallibility and the renewal of efforts to broaden slightly the denomination's confessional standards. By the early decades of the twentieth century these issues were eclipsed by challenges of the liberal theology to major tenets of the traditional faith, including the deity of Christ, the reality of the supernatural, and the superiority of Christianity to other religions. In reaction, a strong fundamentalist movement emerged in Presbyterianism. This movement represented an alliance of stereotyped revivalistic and sometimes anti-intellectual fundamentalism of the William Jennings Bryan variety, with Old School style theological conservatism represented best by J. Gresham Machen of Princeton Seminary. The outcome of the protracted controversy was a victory for moderates willing to tolerate theological liberalism in the Church, and the eventual exclusion of Machen and a few of his followers, who formed the Presbyterian Church of America (subsequently the Orthodox Presbyterian Church) in 1936.

The parallels between the Presbyterian schisms of 1741, 1837, and 1936 make almost irresistibly neat history, and, in general, interpreters have pointed to the essential continuities between the New Side, the New School, and twentieth-century theological liberalism.[1] Such an interpretation, though occasionally useful, is somewhat misleading. Viewing New School Presbyterianism in the context of the wider evangelical movement, it becomes clear that, despite its undeniable affinities to the tolerant doctrinal position of theological liberalism, the New School had nearly as great affinities to twentieth-century fundamentalism. The emphases in the New School on revivalism, moralistic reformism, strict Biblicism, a relatively low view of the Church, a form of millennialism, and a tendency to emphasize fundamentals as a means of unifying the Church against rationalism and corruption—all suggest characteristics of the later fundamentalist movement.

The most striking illustration of the similarities between nineteenth-century New Schoolism and twentieth-century fundamentalism is found in the sequel to the Presbyterian division of 1936. In 1937 the newly formed Presbyterian Church of America itself was divided over a complex set of issues remarkably similar to those of 1837. The majority in the new denomination, led by J. Gresham Machen until his death, January 1, 1937, and then by his immediate associates at Westminster Seminary, took clearly Old School positions on each of the issues. The minority, which withdrew to form the Bible Presbyterian Synod, was led by the militant fundamentalist, Carl McIntire.[2] McIntire, who had envisaged the Presbyterian Church of America as part of a wider "twentieth century Reformation," soon found that he was not at home in a strict Old School tradition. The specific programs for which he fought were (1) tolerance of a doctrine (dispensational

1. For examples, see Smith, *Presbyterian Ministry,* p. 264; Rian, *The Presbyterian Conflict,* p. 23; C. Gregg Singer, *A Theological Interpretation of American History* (Philadelphia, 1964), p. 66; and Lefferts A. Loetscher, *The Broadening Church: A Study of Theological Issues in the Presbyterian Church since 1869* (Philadelphia, 1957), p. 18. Loetscher, however, cautions against too close an identification of the New School and later liberalism, pp. 18, 27.

2. McIntire subsequently gained a national reputation as a radio speaker and as the organizer and principal exponent of numerous anti-Communist and fundamentalist activities.

premillennialism) that the majority in the Church considered incompatible with the Westminster Confession of Faith;[3] (2) continuation of the Independent Board for Presbyterian Foreign Missions, rather than forming an official denominational mission board; and (3) adoption by the General Assembly of a statement that total abstinence from all that may intoxicate is "the only true principle of temperance"—exactly the same statement first adopted by the New School General Assembly of 1840. These programs, together with McIntire's claim to represent "American Presbyterianism" (a former New School phrase), his avid (anti-Communist) patriotism, his zeal for revivalism and legalistic reforms, his emphasis on interdenominational cooperation, and his lack of concern for strict Presbyterian polity[4]—all indicate a continuation of the distinctly New School traditions within the fundamentalist wing of Presbyterianism.[5]

3. Dispensational premillennialism was a characteristic fundamentalist doctrine, popularized in the Scofield Reference Bible, dividing the history of God's redemptive work into several distinct dispensations—the last being the millennium. Samuel Hanson Cox and George Duffield, Sr., were among the precursors of this view in America. See Chapter 9, above.

4. See George M. Marsden, "Perspective on the Division of 1937," *The Presbyterian Guardian* 33(January 1964):5–8; 33(February 1964):21–23; 27–29; 33(March 1964):43–46; 33(April 1964):54–56 for a more detailed account.

5. Tracing direct lines of continuity would require a lengthy study, but two other illustrations will suffice to show that McIntire is not an isolated example of the affinities of the New School and fundamentalism:

(1) Jonathan Blanchard (1811–92), who in 1859 became the first president of Wheaton College in Illinois—still a leading center of fundamentalism—was a New School minister in Cincinnati from 1838 to 1845, subsequently becoming a Congregationalist. Clyde S. Kilby, *Minority of One: The Biography of Jonathan Blanchard* (Grand Rapids, Mich., 1959).

(2) The first International Prophecy Conference, held in New York in 1878, was one of the earliest manifestations of aggressive premillennial fundamentalism in America; see Kraus, *Dispensationalism* pp. 82–88. In advertising the conference, James H. Brookes, a former Old School Presbyterian from St. Louis, listed thirty-five speakers from various denominations. Sixteen of these were Presbyterians. Of the sixteen, seven had been Old School men in 1869, three had been New School, and six had been neither. ("Conference About Christ's Coming," *The Truth: Or, Testimony for Christ*, ed. James H. Brookes,

This suggestion of the resemblances between the New School and fundamentalism is not intended to imply that the New School was necessarily the primary source of fundamentalism in the Presbyterian Church.[6] But it does point out that characterization of New School Presbyterianism as proto-liberal is a vast and misleading oversimplification.[7] In fact, the lines of continuity become hopelessly blurred as the twentieth-century issues replace those of the nineteenth century. In some respects, such as the interest in German theology at Union Seminary, the New School doubtless contributed to the development of the later liberalism.

---

4 [August 1878]: 407–08.) The predominance of former Old School representatives indicates that the Old School may have been more conducive to fundamentalism than the New. There were, however, very nearly twice as many Old School ministers as former New School ministers in 1878, so the percentage is not significantly different. The presence of some New School representatives does indicate that New Schoolism was not incompatible with fundamentalism and that there are some direct lines of continuity.

6. The question of resemblances need not be confused with the question of direct lines of continuity. With regard to the latter, on the basis of extremely impressionistic evidence alone, it seems ilkely that a large majority of the former New School churches in the Eastern areas of that denomination's strength stood with the moderate, or liberal, Presbyterians in the succeeding era, while a considerable number (perhaps even a majority) of former New School churches in the regions west of Ohio would have been found to have a distinctly fundamentalist character in the early decades of the twentieth century. This suggests that New School affinities reflected the more general patterns of the areas in which its churches were established.

This impressionistic evidence is reinforced by the present study of theology in the New School era. By far, the most productive theological centers in the New School Church were the Eastern cities of New York and Philadelphia, while there was very little comparable formal theological discussion in the western areas where the denomination had much of its strength. This suggests that an anti-intellectualist strain may have prevailed in the western areas. Furthermore, the strength of the premillennialist party appears to have been in the Midwest, cf. note 5, above.

7. This usual interpretation is reflected, for example, in Richard B. Morris, ed., *Encyclopedia of American History* (New York, 1953), p. 552, which refers to the division of 1837–38 as "Presbyterian schism between Old School) Orthodox Calvinists) and New School (Western liberals)."

But in other respects, such as its Biblicism, the New School stood far closer to subsequent fundamentalism. George Duffield, Sr., for instance, though a leading exponent of the disputed New School views, was at the same time a stanch champion of Biblical literalism and premillennialism and could scarcely fit a proto-liberal characterization. Moreover, the major distinctive features of the New School theology, as developed by Nathaniel Taylor, contributed very little to American theological liberalism. The two systems grew out of opposed philosophical principles, and any direct continuity is most unlikely for the simple reason that the New Haven theology was nearly extinct by 1869.

Perhaps the greatest difference between the New School evangelical movement and fundamentalism was that the nineteenth-century movement was largely successful, while the twentieth-century movement was not. The New School was not characterized by an almost total repudiation of the cultural and scientific advances of the age. Rather, it met those challenges without losing its own respectability. The New School thus advanced toward the center of American cultural and religious life, while fundamentalism was forced to retreat to the hinterlands. This, of course, is a crucial difference and makes a characterization of the New School as proto-fundamentalist as misleading as proto-liberal. The New School was in many respects a constructive and progressive religious and intellectual movement with marked success in shaping American culture at large.[8]

8. For a detailed discussion of the relation of the New School to later movements see George M. Marsden, "The New School Heritage and Presbyterian Fundamentalism," *Westminster Theological Journal* 33 (May 1970).

Appendix 1
Historiography of the Causes of the Division of 1837-38: Doctrine or Slavery?

The historiographical debate over the Old School–New School Schism has focused on the question of whether doctrine or slavery was the primary cause.

Most interpreters have acknowledged that real theological differences were the decisive issue in the controversy. Earl M. Pope, in the most thorough recent study of the division, concludes that "the deep tensions which agitated the Presbyterian Church and finally brought about its division were those related to subscription and doctrine" (see his "New England Calvinism and the Disruption of the Presbyterian Church," Ph.D. diss., Brown University, 1962, p. 411). This conclusion is in substantial accord with those of several students of more specific aspects of the controversy, including Robert Hastings Nichols in *Presbyterianism in New York State* (Philadelphia, 1963); Earl R. MacCormac in "Missions and the Presbyterian Schism of 1837," *Church History* 32 (March 1963): 43; C. I. Foster in *An Errand of Mercy: The United Front, 1790–1837* (Chapel Hill, N.C., 1960), pp. 254ff.; Elwyn A. Smith, "The Role of the South in the Presbyterian Schism of 1837–38," *Church History* 29 (March 1960): 60, and Ernest Trice Thompson, *Presbyterians in the South* (Richmond, Va., 1963), 1: 296–97. The extent of this consensus is reflected in recent surveys, which agree that doctrine was the main issue in the disputes. See, for example, Clifton E. Olmstead, *History of Religion in the United States* (Englewood Cliffs, N.J., 1960), pp. 311–14; and Winthrop S. Hudson, *American Protestantism* (Chicago, 1961), pp. 105–06.

Yet there has always been a distinguished class of historians who have denied that there were real theological differences sufficient to account for the division. Philip Schaff told his German audience in the 1850s that the division of 1837 "was occasioned as much by personal collisions and local interests as by any real differences in doctrine" (see *America; A Sketch of Its Political, Social, and Religious Character*, ed. Perry Miller, Cambridge, Mass., 1961, p. 119). Robert Ellis Thompson, author of the volume on Presbyterianism in the American Church History series, stated, "Theologically the division of 1837 grew out of panic and alarm, rather than any more solid reason" (see *A History of the Presbyterian Churches in the United States*, New York, 1895, p. 124). And more recently, L. C. Rudolph, in his study of Presbyterianism in Indiana, concluded that the theological differences "hardly look so incompatible as to require the division of a great church" (see *Hoosier Zion: A Study of Presbyterians in Indiana to 1850*, New Haven, Conn., 1963, pp. 147–48).

In recent historiography the suggestion that slavery was the decisive cause of the division has excited the most lively debate. C. Bruce Staiger, expanding on the interpretations of William Warren Sweet and Gilbert H. Barnes, has presented the most able defense of this position in "Abolition and the Presbyterian Schism, 1837–38," *Mississippi Valley Historical Review* 36 (December 1949): 391–414. According to Staiger, "it is safe to say that if it had not been for the developments concerning slavery in the Assemblies of 1835 and 1836, the break would never have occurred." Elwyn A. Smith, on the other hand, "The Role of the South," p. 60, has disputed Staiger's interpretations, arguing that "radical Old School men anticipated division before the abolitionist crusade was fairly launched and the commitments of the leaders of both Schools to their respective positions were beyond reconciliation by 1831." The South played a vital role in the division, says Smith, by ensuring an Old School victory in 1837; but, "the South apart, an eventual break-up of Presbyterianism was certain." Smith's conclusion is supported by Ernest Trice Thompson's *Presbyterians in the South*. Thompson notes that, although the Southerners were already more inclined toward the Old School, they were not aroused to the dangers of New Schoolism until the abolition issue was introduced. At the Old School pre-Assembly convention of 1837, they agreed to full support for the Old School policies in return for Old School silence on the slavery issue, thus giving the Old School party sufficient strength to force the division on its own terms. The present study, Chapter 4, generally supports Thompson's analysis.

Appendix 2
The Auburn Declaration

Doctrinal Section: "Errors" alleged by the Old School
Contrasted to "True Doctrines" of the New School [1]

FIRST ERROR. "That God would have prevented the existence of sin in our world, but was not able, without destroying the moral agency of man; or, that for aught that appears in the Bible to the contrary, sin is incidental to any wise moral system."

TRUE DOCTRINE. God permitted the introduction of sin, not because he was unable to prevent it, consistently with the moral freedom of his creatures, but for wise and benevolent reasons which he has not revealed.

SECOND ERROR. "That election to eternal life is founded on a foresight of faith and obedience."

TRUE DOCTRINE. Election to eternal life is not founded on a foresight of faith and obedience, but is a sovereign act of God's mercy, whereby, according to the counsel of his own will, he has chosen some to salvation; "yet so as thereby neither is violence offered to the will of the creatures, nor is the liberty or contingency of second causes taken away, but rather established;" nor does this gracious purpose ever take effect independently of faith and a holy life.

THIRD ERROR. "That we have no more to do with the first sin of Adam than with the sins of any other parent."

TRUE DOCTRINE. By a divine constitution, Adam was so the head and representative of the race, that, as a consequence of his transgression, all mankind become morally corrupt, and liable to death, temporal and eternal.

FOURTH ERROR. "That infants come into the world as free from moral defilement as was Adam when he was created."

1. From *Minutes of the Auburn Convention, Held August 17, 1837, to Deliberate Upon the Doings of the Last General Assembly, etc.* (Auburn. N.Y., 1837).

TRUE DOCTRINE. Adam was created in the image of God, endowed with knowledge, righteousness, and true holiness. Infants come into the world, not only destitute of these, but with a nature inclined to evil and only evil.

FIFTH ERROR. "That infants sustain the same relation to the moral government of God, in this world, as brute animals, and that their sufferings and death are to be accounted for on the same principles as those of brutes, and not by any means to be considered as penal."

TRUE DOCTRINE. Brute animals sustain no such relation to the moral government of God as does the human family. Infants are a part of the human family; and their sufferings and death are to be accounted for on the ground of their being involved in the general moral ruin of the race induced by the apostacy.

SIXTH ERROR. "That there is no other original sin than the fact, that all the posterity of Adam, though by nature innocent, will always begin to sin when they begin to exercise moral agency; that original sin does not include a sinful bias of the human mind, and a just exposure to penal suffering; and that there is no evidence in Scripture, that infants, in order to salvation, do need redemption by the blood of Christ, and regeneration by the Holy Ghost."

TRUE DOCTRINE. Original sin is a natural bias to evil, resulting from the first apostacy, leading invariably and certainly to actual transgression. And all infants, as well as adults, in order to be saved, need redemption by the blood of Christ, and regeneration by the Holy Ghost.

SEVENTH ERROR. "That the doctrine of imputation, whether of the guilt of Adam's sin, or of the righteousness of Christ, has no foundation in the Word of God, and is both unjust and absurd."

TRUE DOCTRINE. The sin of Adam is not imputed to his posterity in the sense of a literal transfer of personal qualities, acts, and demerit; but by reason of the sin of Adam, in his peculiar relation, the race are treated as if they had sinned. Nor is the righteousness of Christ imputed to his people in the sense of a literal transfer of personal qualities, acts, and merit; but by reason of his righteousness, in his peculiar relation, they are treated as if they were righteous.

EIGHTH ERROR. "That the sufferings and death of Christ were not truly vicarious and penal, but symbolical, governmental, and instructive only."

TRUE DOCTRINE. The sufferings and death of Christ were not symbolical, governmental, and instructive only, but were truly vicarious, i.e. a substitute for the punishment due to transgressors. And while Christ did not suffer the literal penalty of the law, involving remorse of conscience and the pains of hell, he did offer a sacrifice, which infinite wisdom saw to be a full equivalent. And by virtue of this atonement, overtures of mercy are sincerely made to the race, and salvation secured to all who believe.

NINTH ERROR. "That the impenitent sinner is by nature, and independently of the renewing influence or almighty energy of the Holy Spirit, in full possession of all the ability necessary to a full compliance with all the commands of God."

TRUE DOCTRINE. While sinners have all the faculties necessary to a perfect moral agency and a just accountability, such is their love of sin and opposition to God and his law, that, independently of the renewing influence or almighty energy of the Holy Spirit, they never will comply with the commands of God.

TENTH ERROR. "That Christ does not intercede for the elect until after their regeneration."

TRUE DOCTRINE. The intercession of Christ for the elect is previous as well as subsequent to their regeneration, as appears from the following Scripture, viz. "I pray not for the world, but for them which thou hast given me, for they are thine. Neither pray I for these alone, but for them also which shall believe on me through their word."

ELEVENTH ERROR. "That saving faith is not an effect of the operations of the Holy Spirit, but a mere rational belief of the truth or assent to the word of God."

TRUE DOCTRINE. Saving faith is an intelligent and cordial assent to the testimony of God concerning his Son, implying reliance on Christ alone for pardon and eternal life; and in all cases it is an effect of the special operations of the Holy Spirit.

TWELFTH ERROR. "That regeneration is the act of the sinner himself, and that it consists in change of his governing purpose, which he himself must produce, and which is the result, not of any direct influence of the Holy Spirit on the heart, but chiefly of a persuasive exhibition of the truth, analogous to the influence which one man exerts over the mind of another; or that regeneration is not an instantaneous act, but a progressive work."

TRUE DOCTRINE. Regeneration is a radical change of heart, produced by the special operations of the Holy Spirit, "determining the sinner to that which is good," and is in all cases instantaneous.

THIRTEENTH ERROR. "That God has done all that *he can do* for the salvation of all men, and that man himself must do the rest."

TRUE DOCTRINE. While repentance for sin and faith in Christ are indispensable to salvation, all who are saved are indebted from first to last to the grace and Spirit of God. And the reason that God does not save all, is not that he wants the *power* to do it, but that in his wisdom he does not see fit to exert that power further than he actually does.

FOURTEENTH ERROR. "That God cannot exert such influence on the minds of men, as shall make it certain that they will choose and act in a particular manner, without impairing their moral agency."

TRUE DOCTRINE. While the liberty of the will is not impaired, nor the established connexion betwixt means and end broken by any action of God on the mind, he can influence it according to his pleasure, and does effectually determine it to good in all cases of true conversion.

FIFTEENTH ERROR. "That the righteousness of Christ is not the sole ground of the sinner's acceptance with God; and that in no sense does the righteousness of Christ become ours."

TRUE DOCTRINE. All believers are justified, not on the ground of personal merit; but solely on the ground of the obedience and death, or, in other words, the righteousness of Christ. And while that righteousness does not become theirs, in the sense of a literal transfer of personal qualities and merit; yet, from respect to it, God can and does treat them as if they were righteous.

SIXTEENTH ERROR. "That the reason why some differ from others in regard to their reception of the Gospel is, that they make themselves to differ."

TRUE DOCTRINE. While all such as reject the Gospel of Christ do it, not by coercion but freely—and all who embrace it do it, not by coercion but freely—the reason why some differ from others is, that God has made them to differ.

Selected Bibliography
of Primary Sources

Books

BOOKS BY NEW SCHOOL PRESBYTERIANS

(These include major works of the professors in New School theological seminars and of the Moderators of the New School General Assembly, and other selected works.)

Adams, William. *Conversations of Jesus Christ with Representative Men.* New York, 1868.

———, *In the World, Not of the World: Thoughts on Christian Casuistry.* New York, 1866.

———, *Thanksgiving: Memories of the Day; Helps to the Habit.* New York, 1867.

———, *The Three Gardens, Eden, Gethsemane, and Paradise: Or, Man's Ruin, Redemption, and Restoration.* New York, 1856.

The Alleged Doctrinal Differences of the Old and New School Examined by an Old Disciple. Auburn, N.Y., 1855.

Barnes, Albert. *The Atonement in Its Relation to Law and Moral Government.* Philadelphia, 1859.

———, *How Shall Men Be Just with God?* Philadelphia, 1854.

———, *Inquiries and Suggestions in Regard to the Foundation of Faith in the Word of God.* Philadelphia, 1859.

———, *An Inquiry into the Scriptural Views of Slavery.* Philadelphia, 1846.

———, *Life at Threescore and Ten.* New York, 1871.

———, *Notes Explanatory and Practical, on the Epistle to the Romans.* Philadelphia, 1835.

———, *Practical Sermons: Designed for Vacant Congregations and Families.* Philadelphia, 1845.

————, *Sermons on Revivals.* New York, 1841.

Beecher, Edward. *Narrative of Riots at Alton: In Connection with the Death of Rev. Elijah P. Lovejoy.* Alton, Ill., 1838.

Beecher, Lyman. *Autobiography, Correspondence, etc., of Lyman Beecher.* Edited by Charles Beecher. 2 vols. New York, 1864–65.

————, *A Plea for the West.* Cincinnati, Ohio, 1835.

————, *Works.* 3 vols. Boston, 1852–53.

Beman, Nathan S. S. *Four Sermons on the Doctrine of the Atonement.* Troy, New York, 1825.

————, ed. *Social Psalmist: Or, Hymns, Selected for the Private Use and Social Meetings of Evangelical Christians.* New York, 1843.

Brainerd, Thomas. *The Life of John Brainerd, the Brother of David Brainerd and His Successor as Missionary to the Indians of New Jersey.* Philadelphia, 1865.

Bryant, Alfred. *Millenarian Views: With Reasons for Receiving Them.* New York, 1852.

Church Psalmist: Or, Psalms and Hymns, Designed for the Public, Social, and Private use of Evangelical Christians, with Supplement. Philadelphia, n.d.

Cox, Samuel Hanson. *Interviews: Memorial and Useful from Diary and Memory Reproduced.* New York, 1853.

————, *Missionary Remains: Or, Sketches of the Lives of Evarts, Cornelius, and Wisner.* New York, 1835.

————, *Quakerism Not Christianity: Or, Reasons for Renouncing the Doctrines of the Friends.* New York, 1833.

Duffield, George, Sr. *The Bible Rule of Temperance: Total Abstinence from All Intoxicating Drink.* New York, 1868.

————, *Dissertations on the Prophecies Relative to the Second Coming of Jesus Christ.* New York, 1842.

————, *Millenarianism Defended: A Reply to Prof. Stuart's "Strictures of the Rev. G. Duffield's Recent Work on the Second Coming of Christ."* New York, 1843.

————, *Spiritual Life: Or, Regeneration.* Carlisle, Penn., 1832.

Fisher, Samuel Ware. *Occasional Sermons and Addresses.* New York, 1866.

Gillett, E. H. *History of the Presbyterian Church in the United States of America.* 2 vols. Philadelphia, 1864.

Hall, Edwin. *Digest of Studies and Lectures in Theology.* Auburn, N.Y., 1866.

————, *An Exposition of the Law of Baptism as It Regards the Mode and the Subjects*. New York, 1846.

Hickok, Laurens Perseus. *Empirical Psychology: Or, the Human Mind as Given in Consciousness*. Schenectady, N.Y., 1854.

————, *Rational Cosmology: Or, the Eternal Principles and the Necessary Laws of the Universe*. New York, 1858.

————, *A System of Moral Science*. Schenectady, N.Y., 1853.

A History of the Division of the Presbyterian Church in the United States of America, by a Committee of the Synod of New York and New Jersey, New York, 1852.

Hitchcock, Roswell Dwight. *The Person of Christ*. Philadelphia, n.d.

Hotchkin, James H. *A History of the Purchase and Settlement of Western New York and of the Rise, Progress, and Present State of the Presbyterian Church in that Section*. New York, 1848.

Huntington, Ezra Abel. *Notes on the Epistle to the Hebrews*. Auburn, N.Y., 1866.

Kennedy, William S. *The Plan of Union: Or, a History of the Presbyterian and Congregational Churches of the Western Reserve with Biographical Sketches of the Early Missionaries*. Hudson, Ohio, 1856.

Lansing, Dirck C. *Sermons on Important Subjects of Christian Doctrine and Duty*. Auburn, N.Y., 1825.

Nelson, Henry Addison. *Seeing Jesus*. Philadelphia, 1869.

Parker, Joel. *Courtship and Marriage: Moral Principles Illustrated in Their Application to Courtship and Marriage*. Philadelphia, 1845.

————, *Lectures on Universalism*. New York, 1841.

[Peters, Absalom.] *A Plea for Voluntary Societies*, by a Member of the Assembly. New York, 1837.

Richards, James. *Lectures on Mental Philosophy and Theology, with a Sketch of His Life by Samuel H. Gridley*. New York, 1846.

Riley, Henry A. *The Restoration: Or, the Hope of the Early Church Realized*. Philadelphia, 1866.

Robinson, Edward. *Biblical Researches in Palestine, Mount Sinai and Arabia Petrea: A Journal of Travels in the Year 1838*. 3 vols. Boston, 1841.

Skinner, Thomas Harvey. *Aids to Preaching and Hearing*. New York, 1839.

————, *Discussions in Theology*. New York, 1868.

————, *Hints, Designed to Aid Christians in Their Efforts to Convert Men to God*. Hartford, Conn. 1848.

Smith, Henry Boynton. *Apologetics: A Course of Lectures.* Edited by William S. Karr. New York, 1822.

————, *History of the Church of Christ in Chronological Tables: A Synchronistic View of the Events, Characteristics and Culture of Each Period, Including the History of Polity, Worship, Literature and Doctrines: Together with Two Supplementary Tables upon the Church in America; and an Appendix, Containing the Series of Councils, Popes, Patriarchs and other Bishops, and a Full Index.* New York, 1859.

————, *Introduction to Christian Theology.* Edited by William S. Karr. New York, 1883.

————, *Systems of Christian Theology.* Edited by William S. Karr. New York, 1884.

Smith, Mrs. Henry Boynton, ed. *Henry Boynton Smith: His Life and Work.* New York, 1881.

Tappan, Henry Philip. *The Doctrine of the Will, Applied to Moral Agency and Responsibility.* New York, 1841.

————, *The Doctrine of the Will, Determined by an Appeal to Consciousness.* New York, 1840.

————, *A Review of Edwards's "Inquiry into the Freedom of the Will."* New York, 1839.

Williston, Seth. *Millennial Discourses: Or, a Series of Sermons Designed to Prove That There Will Be a Millennium of Peace and Holiness; Also to Suggest Means for Hastening Its Introduction.* Utica, N.Y., 1849.

OTHER BOOKS

Alexander, Archibald. *Evidences of the Authenticity, Inspiration, and Canonical Authority of the Holy Scriptures.* Philadelphia, 1836.

Baird, Robert. *Religion in America: Or, an Account of the Origin, Progress, Relation to the State, and Present Condition of the Evangelical Churches in the United States.* New York, 1844.

Baird, Samuel J. *A History of the New School.* Philadelphia, 1868.

Brown, Issac V. *A Historical Vindication of the Abrogation of the Plan of Union by the Presbyterian Church in the United States of America.* Philadelphia, 1855.

Cheeseman, Lewis. *Differences between the Old and New School Presbyterians.* Rochester, N.Y., 1848.

Crocker, Zebulon. *The Catastrophe of the Presbyterian Church, in 1837.* New Haven, Conn., 1838.

Finney, Charles G. *Lectures on Revivals of Religion*. New York, 1835.
Hodge, Archibald Alexander. *The Life of Charles Hodge, D.D., LL.D.* New York, 1880.
Hodge, Charles. *Systematic Theology*. 3 vols. New York, 1871–75.
Hodgson, Francis. *An Examination of the System of New Divinity: Or, New School Theology*. New York, 1839.
Hopkins, Samuel. *The Works of Samuel Hopkins*. 3 vols. Boston, 1852.
Junkin, George. *The Vindication*. Philadelphia, 1836.
Lathrop, D. W., ed. *The Case of the General Assembly of the Presbyterian Church in the United States of America before the Supreme Court of the Commonwealth of Pennsylvania*. Philadelphia, 1839.
Miller, Samuel, Sr. *Letters to Presbyterians*. Philadelphia, 1833.
Miller, Samuel, Jr. *The Life of Samuel Miller*. Philadelphia, 1869.
The New York Pulpit in the Revival of 1858: A Memorial Volume of Sermons. New York, 1858.
Presbyterian Reunion: A Memorial Volume, 1837–1871. New York, 1870.
Rice, N. L. *The Old and New Schools*. Cincinnati, Ohio, 1853.
Schaff, Philip. *America: A Sketch of Its Political, Social, and Religious Character*. Edited by Perry Miller. Cambridge, Mass., 1961.
The Spruce Street Lectures, by Several Clergymen, Delivered During the Years 1831–2. Philadelphia, 1841.
Stansbury, Arthur J. *Trial and Acquittal of Lyman Beecher before the Presbytery of Cincinnati, on Charges Preferred by Joshua L. Wilson*. Cincinnati, Ohio, 1835.
————, *Trial of the Rev. Albert Barnes before the Synod of Philadelphia, in Session at York, October, 1835*. New York, 1836.
Taylor, Nathaniel W. *Lectures on the Moral Government of God*, 2 vols. New York, 1859.
Wayland, Francis. *The Elements of Moral Science*. Edited by Joseph L. Blau. Cambridge, Mass., 1963.
Wood, James. *Old and New Theology*. Philadelphia, n.d.
Woods, Leonard. *History of Andover Theological Seminary*. Boston, 1885.

Periodicals

THEOLOGICAL JOURNALS

American Biblical Repository. [Title varies.] Edward Robinson, 1831–34; Bela Bates Edwards, 1835–37; Absalom Peters, 1838–42; John

Holmes Agnew, 1842–46; Walter H. Bidwell, 1846–47; James
M. Sherwood, 1848–50. New York. First Series, 1831–38. Second
Series, 1839–44. Third Series, 1845–50.
American Presbyterian and Theological Review. Edited by Henry B.
Smith and J. M. Sherwood. Second Series. New York, 1863–68.
(Published as *American Presbyterian Review.* Third Series. New York,
1869–71.)
American Theological Review. Edited by Henry B. Smith. First Series.
New York, 1859–62.
Biblical Repertory and Princeton Review. [Title varies.] Edited by Charles
Hodge et al. Princeton, N.J., 1825–71.
Bibliotheca Sacra. Edited by Edward Robinson. New York and London,
1843.
Bibliotheca Sacra. [Title varies.] Edited by Edwards A. Park et al. And-
over, Mass., 1844–.
Danville Quarterly Review. [Title varies.] Danville, Kentucky, 1861–64.
Literalist. Philadelphia, 1840–42.
New Englander. New Haven, Connecticut, 1843–85.
Presbyterian Quarterly Review. Edited by Benjamin J. Wallace et al.
Philadelphia, 1852–62.
Quarterly Christian Spectator. [Title varies.] New Haven, Connecticut,
1819–38.

OTHER PERIODICALS AND NEWSPAPERS

There are an exceedingly large number of popular religious magazines
and newspapers published during this period. Gaylord P. Albaugh,
"American Presbyterian Periodicals and Newspapers, 1752–1830, with
Library Locations," *Journal of the Presbyterian Historical Society,* XLI,
nos. 3 and 4, XLII, nos. 1 and 2 (September 1963 to June 1964), lists
over two hundred such publications in the immediately preceding period;
and presumably a similar number could be compiled for the period of
this study. While these publications apparently contain little in the line
of formal theological discussion that is not also covered in the major
theological journals, they do occasionally contain articles that supplement
the present study. The most important of these publications are

American Presbyterian. (New School.) Philadelphia, 1849–?, 1856–70.
Christian Advocate. (Old School.) Philadelphia, 1823–34.
National Preacher and Village Pulpit. [Title varies, often published as
American National Preacher.] (Interdenominational.) New York and
Philadelphia, 1826–66.

New York Evangelist. [Title varies.] (New School denominational paper, 1852–69.) New York, 1830–1902.
New York Observer. (Old School.) New York, 1823–1912.
Presbyterian. [Title varies.] (Old School.) Philadelphia, 1831–

Pamphlets

A Brief View of Presbyterian History and Doctrine. Philadelphia, n.d.
Duffield, George, Sr. *The Principles of Presbyterian Discipline Unfolded and Illustrated in a Protest and Appeal of Rev. George Duffield, Entered During the Process in the Presbytery of Carlisle.* Carlisle, Penn., 1835.
Duffield, George, Jr. *The Pastor and Inquirer: Or, What It Is to Repent and Believe the Gospel.* Philadelphia, n.d.
Gilbert, Eliphalet W. *The Preseverance of the Saints.* Philadelphia, n.d.
Hatfield, Edwin F. *The Presbyterian System: Its Reasonableness and Excellency.* Philadelphia, n.d.
Miller, Samuel. *A Letter of the Rev. Samuel Miller, D.D., Addressed to the Members of the Presbyterian Church in the United States on the Present Crisis in Their Religious and Theological Concerns.* Hartford, Conn., 1853.
Presbyterianism Explained. Philadelphia, n.d.
Proceedings of the Synod of New York and New Jersey at Their Late Session, in Reference to the Publications of the American Tract Society. New York, 1845.
Richards, James. *The Extent of the Atonement.* Philadelphia, n.d.
Stowe, Calvin E. *A Letter to R. D. Mussey, M.D., on the Utter Groundlessness of All Millennial Arithmetic.* Cincinnati, Ohio, 1843.

Sermons and Addresses

Adams, William. *Thanksgiving Sermon.* "Preached November 27, 1862." New York, 1863.
Barnes, Albert. *The Conditions of Peace.* "A Thanksgiving Discourse Delivered in the First Presbyterian Church, Philadelphia, November 27, 1862." Philadelphia, 1863.
———, *The Love of Country.* "A Sermon Delivered in the First Presbyterian Church, Philadelphia, April 28, 1861." Philadelphia, 1861.
———, *The Way of Salvation.* "A Sermon Delivered at Morristown, N.J., February 8, 1829." Philadelphia, 1830.

Beman, Nathan S. S. *Thanksgiving in the Times of Civil War.* "A Discourse Delivered in the First Presbyterian Church, Troy, N.Y., November 28th, 1861." Troy, N.Y., 1861.

Brainerd, Thomas. *Patriotism Aiding Piety.* "A Sermon Preached in the Third Presbyterian Church, Philadelphia, April 30, 1864, the Day for Humiliation, Fasting and Prayer." Philadelphia, 1864.

Cox, Samuel Hanson. *The Bright and the Blessed Destination of the World.* "A Discourse before the American Commissioners for Foreign Missions." New York, 1849.

Duffield, George, Sr. *American Presbyterianism.* "A Sermon Delivered November 11, 1853." Philadelphia, 1854.

————, *Our National Sins to Be Repented of, and the Grounds of Hope for the Preservation of Our Federal Constitution and Union.* "A Discourse Delivered Friday, January 4, 1861, on the Day of Fasting, Humiliation and Prayer." Detroit, 1861.

————, *Secession: Its Cause and Cure.* "A Thanksgiving Discourse Delivered in the First Presbyterian Church of Detroit, November 28, 1860." Detroit, 1861.

Duffield, George, Jr. *The Great Rebellion Thus Far a Failure.* "A Thanksgiving Sermon Preached in the Presbyterian Church, Adrian, Michigan, November 28th, 1861." Adrian, Mich., 1861.

————, *The God of Our Fathers.* "An Historical Sermon Preached in the Coates' Street Presbyterian Church, Philadelphia, on Fast Day, January 4, 1861." Philadelphia, 1861.

————, *Courage in a Good Cause: Or, the Lawful and Courageous Use of the Sword.* "A Sermon Delivered April 21, 1861." Philadelphia, 1861.

Hickok, Laurens P. *The Idea of Humanity in Its Progress to Its Consummation.* "An Address Delivered before the Philomathian Society in Middlebury College, July 29, 1847." New York, 1847.

Skinner, Thomas H., Jr. *Comfort in Tribulation.* "An Address Delivered in the Reformed Dutch Church, Stapleton, Long Island, September 26th, 1861, a Day Kept as a National Fast." New York, 1861.

Smith, Henry Boynton. *The Inspiration of the Holy Scriptures.* "A Sermon Delivered before the Synod of New York and New Jersey in the First Presbyterian Church, Newark, New Jersey, October 17, 1855." New York, 1855.

————, *The Problem of the Philosophy of History.* "Address Delivered at Yale College, July 1853." Published in *Presbyterian Quarterly Review* 3 (1854): 1–28.

Taylor, Nathaniel W. *Concio ad Clerum.* "A Sermon Delivered in the Chapel of Yale College, September 10, 1828." New Haven, Conn., 1842.

Minutes and Related Records

The Constitution of the Presbyterian Church, in the United States of America: Containing the Confession of Faith, the Catechisms and the Directory for the Worship of God; Together with the Plan of Government and Discipline, as Ratified by the General Assembly, at Their Sessions in May, 1821; and Amended in 1833. Philadelphia, 1834.

Index of Presbyterian Ministers: Containing the Names of All the Ministers of the Presbyterian Church in the United States of America from A.D. 1706 to A.D. 1881. Compiled by Willis J. Beecher. Philadelphia, 1883.

Minutes of the Fiftieth Anniversary of the Synod of Albany, Convened in Schaghticoke, September 20th, 1853. Albany, N.Y., 1853.

Minutes of the General Assembly of the Presbyterian Church in the United States of America. Philadelphia, 1789–1837.

Minutes of the General Assembly of the Presbyterian Church in the United States of America. New School. New York, 1838–69.

Minutes of the General Assembly of the Presbyterian Church in the United States of America. Old School. Philadelphia, 1838–69.

A Digest of the Acts and Deliverances of the General Assembly of the Presbyterian Church in the United States of America. Compiled by William E. Moore. Philadelphia, 1861.

Proceedings of the General Convention of Congregational Ministers and Delegates in the United States, Held at Albany, New York, 1852. New York, 1852.

Report of the Proceedings of the General Assembly of the Presbyterian Church in the United States of America. Philadelphia, 1868.

Index

Abolition, 28, 88–103, 135, 251.
  See also Antislavery; Slavery
Abstinence, 23–27, 100, 238. See also
  Temperance
"Act and Testimony," 60, 68
Adam, 252–53; sin of, 33, 36, 41,
  44, 49, 53, 55, 58, 85, 121, 134,
  177, 178 n. 36
Adams, John, 7
Adams, William, 162, 209
Adopting Act of 1729, 39, 68
Albany: Synod of, 66; Convention of
  Congregationalists, 125, 128–30,
  134
Alexander, Archibald, 42, 92, 232
Allen, Ethan, 8–9
Allen Street Presbyterian Church, 108
American Anti-Slavery Society, 15,
  95, 238
American Bible Society, 15, 17–18, 73
American Biblical Repository, 105–
  07, 109–10, 113–14, 116 n. 22,
  122, 126
American Board of Commissioners
  for Foreign Missions, 14–15, 20,
  72, 195–96
American Colonization Society, 15,
  92, 95, 99
American Education Society, 15, 30,
  63 n. 16, 72, 74
American Home Missionary Society,

  15, 17, 26, 56, 63 n. 16, 72–73,
  125, 130
Americanism, 199–211. See also
  Nationalism
American Peace Society, 15
American Presbyterian and Theologi-
  cal Review, 180, 208, 219
American Seamen's Friend Society, 15
American Sunday-School Union, 15,
  19, 73
American Temperance Society, 15
American Temperance Union, 27
American Theological Review, 178–
  79, 186, 193–94, 206
American Tract Society, 16, 73, 120,
  121 n. 32, 126
Amherst College, 157, 161–62
"Amillennialism," 190 n. 24
Ancient Church, 58, 113
Andover Theological Seminary, 14,
  26, 43–44, 46, 107, 110 n. 10, 119,
  131, 153, 157, 159
Antichrist, 9, 16, 26
Anti-Communism, 246 n. 2, 247
Antidisestablishmentarianism, 12
Anti-intellectualism, 4–5, 234, 245,
  248 n. 6
Antinomianism, 215
Antislavery, 35, 87, 94, 119, 186,
  188, 238. See also Abolition;
  Declaration of 1818; Slavery

"Anxious bench," 77–78
Apostles' Creed, 114
"Apostolic, Protestant Confession,"
    114
Arian heresy, 41
Aristotelian philosophy, 152
Arminian heresy, 41, 79, 135, 216
Atonement, 38–39, 41, 45, 51–53,
    120, 135, 168, 182, 211, 218;
    tract on, 137–39; in Auburn
    Declaration, 253
Atwater, Lyman, 217–19, 225–27
Auburn, N.Y., 81, 117
Auburn Convention, 64, 79, 84–85,
    116
Auburn Declaration, 64, 82 n. 70,
    84–85, 135, 139–40, 214, 218,
    223; appended, 252–55
Auburn Theological Seminary, 43–
    45, 107, 109, 153–54, 180, 195,
    224, 226
Augustine, 58, 140, 229
Awakening, religious, 13, 15, 22,
    186. See also Great Awakening;
    "Second Great Awakening"

"Babylon the great," 187
Backus, Dr. John, 224
Baconian philosophy, 152
Baird, Samuel, 57, 76, 215, 227
Balch, Hezekiah, 40–41
Bancroft, George, 106, 172–73,
    237 n. 10
Bangor Seminary, 159
Bangs, Nathan, 19
Baptism: infant, 20, 137; by immer-
    sion, 114
Baptists, xi, 4–5, 19, 73, 127, 183
Barnes, Albert, 27–28, 52–55, 61,
    95–98, 135, 193, 223, 228;
    writings of, 61, 85, 110–13, 133,
    139, 142 n. 1, 146–50; antislavery
    spokesman, 96 n. 12, 101–02,
    188–89; and Civil War, 200–01

Barnes, Gilbert, 20, 251
Beecher, Edward, 57, 118
Beecher, Henry Ward, 119, 149
Beecher, Lyman, 9, 12–13, 18, 28,
    46–47, 117 n. 26, 133, 135, 186,
    232; embodiment of New School
    Presbyterianism, 20–23; and
    moralism, 23–25, 27; and intel-
    lectual reform, 29–30; president
    of Lane Seminary, 30, 119; charges
    brought against, 56–57; and
    schism, 65; attitude of, toward
    confessionalism, 67–69; and the
    "new measures," 77; abolitionism
    of, 94–96; anti-Catholicism of,
    115–16 n. 22
Bellamy, Joseph, 34–35, 38, 179,
    232
Beman, Nathan S. S., 54, 59, 77, 95,
    133, 135, 197, 200, 203–04, 223
Benevolence, 35–38, 51, 105–06,
    176
"Benevolent empire," 92–93, 120.
    See also Evangelical united front
Berlin, University of, 160
Bible, 21, 110; principle of total
    abstinence lacking in, 26; and the
    Sunday-school movement, 30; and
    the Westminster Confession, 68;
    slavery and, 96, 100–02; Albert
    Barnes' comments regarding, 111–
    12, 189; in New School theology,
    113–14, 127, 134, 142–50, 249;
    and Disciples of Christ, 113; and
    New School tracts, 138–41; in
    thought of Henry B. Smith, 169–71
Bible Presbyterian Synod, 246
Biblical Repository. See American
    Biblical Repository
Biblical studies, 43, 105, 110, 170,
    179, 192–93; German, 150, 169,
    193
Bibliotheca Sacra, 110, 162, 218
Birney, James, G., 238

Blacks. *See* Abolition; Antislavery; Slavery

Blanchard, Jonathan, 247 n. 5

Boston, 47, 93

Bourne, Reverend James, 91

Bowdoin College, 119, 158–59, 161

Boyle, James, 80–81

Brainerd, Thomas, 201–02

Breckinridge, Robert J., 85, 92, 98, 215

British evangelicals, 14, 23. *See also* Evangelical Alliance

Broad Church, 40, 114–15

Brookes, James H., 190 n. 24, 247

Brooklyn, 107, 119

Brown, Isaac, 132

Brown University, 102, 232

Bryan, William Jennings, 245

Bryant, Alfred, 194–95

Bushnell, Horace, 1, 152, 156, 162, 166

Butler, Bishop, 242

Byron, 106

Calvin, John, xi n. 4, 41, 46, 138, 229

Calvinism, xi, 2, 6, 38, 41–42, 46–47, 219, 229, 235; in thought of Jonathan Edwards, 32; doctrine of, 33–34, 164; "old," 42–43; in thought of Nathaniel Taylor, 49, 52; in New School Presbyterianism, 127, 134–36, 138–41, 151, 154, 223–24; American, 166, 178

Cambridge, Massachusetts, 236

Campbell, Alexander, 113–14

Cane Ridge, revival at, 13

Carlisle, Pa., 52, 208; Presbytery of, 55–56

Cayuga, Presbytery of, 80

Center Church on New Haven Green, 46, 218

Cheeseman, Lewis, 132–33

Cheever, George B., 107–08, 115, 115–16 n. 22, 118–19

Christ, 26; death of, 38–39; and revivalism, 78, 182–84; Gospel of, 90; and slavery, 102; Kingdom of, 105, 182–98; in thought of Henry B. Smith, 158–59, 167–69; in premillennialism, 190–91; in Auburn Declaration, 253–54. *See also* Atonement

Christianity, xii, 4, 8, 22, 164 and passim

Christian movement, 14, 113

Christian Spectator, 18

Church of the Puritans, 119

Cincinnati, 30, 56, 66–69, 94

Civil War, 90, 117, 141, 155, 181, 183, 199–213, 240; era, 185, 238

Cleveland, Reverend John P., 65

Coleridge, Samuel Taylor, 106, 152–53

Colleges, 4–5, 16, 29–30

Colonization, 92–94, 96. *See also* American Colonization Society

Colton, Calvin, 12 n. 9, 17

"Committee of Correspondence," 62

Committee on Church Extension, 130

"Committee on the State of the Country, The," 209

Common sense, 47, 112, 152, 154, 167, 177, 200, 234, 238 n. 15, 242

Common Sense philosophy, 47–48, 102, 107–08, 233, 235, 238, 241–44

Communism, 26–27

Confessionalism, 67–69, 116 n. 24, 124, 216

Confessionalist parties, 115

Confessional Lutherans, 73

Confession of Faith. *See* Westminster Confession of Faith

Congregational consociations and associations, 11, 24, 116, 118

Congregationalism, x, 5, 20, 131,
    157, 161
Congregationalists, xi, 1–2, 8–10, 14,
    46, 118, 125, 128, 155; relations
    with Presbyterians, 10–12, 19–20,
    61–63, 71, 107, 116–20, 122, 125–
    30, 134, 137, 178, 226 (see also
    Plan of Union); as college presi-
    dents, 30; Albany Convention of,
    128–29
Congregationalists of the Midwest,
    125
Connecticut, 7, 9–10, 12–14, 24, 46,
    118, 179
Connecticut Yankees, 10
Constitution, 200, 204, 207
Cotton, John, 190 n. 25
Cox, Samuel, 107, 117, 135, 195–96,
    247 n. 3
Crocker, Zebulon, 75
Cross of Christ, 182–83
Cumberland Presbyterian Church, 14,
    116 n. 24, 221 n. 17

D'Alembert, 9
Dancing, 28
Daniel, book of, 192
Dartmouth College, 206
Darwin, Charles, 147 n. 11, 148,
    149 n. 14, 179
Darwinism, 243
Declaration of 1818, 90–91, 98–99,
    101
Democrats, 240
Denominationalism, xi, 18–19, 117–
    41, 155, 178, 180, 210–11, 236–
    37
Denominations, as agencies for
    reform, 87–89, 101, 236
De Tocqueville, Alexis, 4, 16, 106
Detroit, 191, 202
Disciples of Christ, 113. See also
    Christian movement
Disestablishmentarianism, 240
"Dry banquets," 28

Duffield, George (fl. during Revolu-
    tion), 203
Duffield, George, Jr., 182–84, 197,
    203
Duffield, George, Sr., 28, 52, 55–56,
    122–23, 133, 135, 154, 223, 228,
    247 n. 3; premillennialism of,
    191–94, 195 n. 42, 196–97, 249;
    comments on national sins, 202–
    03; views of, attacked, 218–19;
    literalism of, 249
Dutch Reformed Church, 5, 19, 221
    n. 17
Dwight, Timothy, 7–10, 12–15, 20,
    24, 29, 44–46, 179

Education, ministerial, 30, 43 n. 27,
    44, 69, 73, 83, 116 n. 24, 131,
    157; of slaves urged, 90; higher,
    233
Edwards, Jonathan, 13, 31, 40, 57,
    174, 177–79, 186; thought of,
    32–36, 45; followers of, 34, 176;
    tradition of, 46; debate over
    doctrine of the will of, 107–08;
    criticized, 112; works of, repub-
    lished, 120
Edwards, Jonathan, Jr., 38–39
Edwardseans, 13, 34–35, 43–44, 83,
    166–67, 233; tradition of, 178
Elementary schools, 30
Elkins, Stanley, 88, 238
Ely, Ezra Stiles, 41
Emerson, Ralph Waldo, ix, 58, 106,
    111
Emmons, Nathaniel, 159
England, 8; religious thought of,
    147, 179
Enlightenment, 3, 6, 22, 31, 38, 47,
    105, 231, 242; Scottish, 47, 233;
    American, 233
Episcopal Church, 5, 127, 183
"Errors and True Doctrines." See
    Auburn Declaration

Evangelical Alliance, 117
Evangelicalism, ix-x, 3–6, 9–10, 12–
    18, 23, 29–30, 52, 84, 86–88, 149,
    185, 246, 249; British, 14, 18, 23;
    nationalism and, 17–18, 22; and
    "Moral Governor," 35; Common
    Sense in, 47–48, 241–44; of New
    School, 67, 84; climate of opinion
    of, 104–12; in Germany, 160, 169;
    and nineteenth-century values,
    230; and natural law, 231; and
    moral law, 232–34; and the free
    individual, 235–39; and America's
    Mission, 239–41
Evangelical united front, 19–20, 30,
    58, 61, 67, 71–75, 106, 117–18,
    210, 236. See also "Benevolent
    empire"
Evolution, 147–49, 179, 243

Fichte, 153
Finn, Huck, 1
Finney, Charles G., 4, 5 n. 10, 44,
    59, 76–80, 93–95, 122–23, 130,
    133, 234
First Church in Philadelphia, 53
Flavel, John, 120–21
Foster, Charles I., 18, 20, 75, 117,
    250
France, 16
Free agency, 106–07, 167
Free individual, 235–39
Free love, 81
Free will, 1, 121–22, 255
French Revolution, 7, 196
Fundamentalism, ix, 245–49

Gabriel, Ralph, 231, 235, 239, 241
Garrison, William Lloyd, 93
General Assembly. See New School
    General Assembly; Presbyterian
    General Assemblies (Old and
    New); Presbyterian General
    Assembly

General Association of Connecticut,
    11
General Association of New York,
    63, 129–30
"General atonement," 38 n. 15. See
    also Atonement
Genesee, Synod of, 63
Genesis, 143–45
Geneva, Synod of, 63, 65, 81
Geology, 143–45, 147, 242
German Reformed Church, 5, 73;
    Seminary of, 152
German thought, 108–09, 150–51,
    153–54, 160–61, 168–70, 248
Germany, 108, 160, 171
Gettysburg, Pennsylvania, 114
Gieseler, Johann Karl Ludwig, A
    Text-book of Church History, 175
Gilded Age, 240–41
God, 8, 13, 26, 31, 36; government
    of, 18, 21–23, 34–35, 51; in
    Calvinism, 33; Jonathan Edwards'
    view of, 34; in thought of Na-
    thaniel Taylor, 50–51; in Presby-
    terian controversies, 58, 136; law
    of, 90, 231; in Westminster Con-
    fession, 100; in thought of Henry
    B. Smith, 164–66, 180; Union
    ordained by, 206–07; America
    chosen by, 210; in Auburn Decla-
    ration, 252–55
Goodwin, D. R., 179
Governmental Theory of the Atone-
    ment, 38, 41
Grace, 1, 38–39, 106–07, 121, 123,
    176
Gray, Asa, 149
Great Awakening, 3–4, 6, 12–13, 32,
    40, 77, 140–41
Green, Ashbel, 54–55, 57
Greene, John C., ix–x
Greenville College, 40
Grotius, Hugo, 38

Hagenbach, Karl Rudolf, *A Textbook of the History of Doctrines,* 175
Hall, Edwin, 226
Halle, University of, 160
Haroutunian, Joseph, 242
Hartford, 162
Hartford Seminary, 46
Harvard, 149
Hatfield, Edwin R., 208
Hawthorne, 106
Hegel, 106, 151, 153, 160
Hengstenberg, Ernst Wilhelm, 160
Hickok, Laurens P., 108–09, 152–54, 233–34
High Church, 111, 115, 237; Presbyterians, 73–74; Lutheran confessionalism, 114; Episcopalians, 115
Historiography: American, ix; regarding schism, 250–51
History of the Church of Christ in Chronological Tables, 174–75
History of the New School, 215, 227
Hitchcock, Roswell D., 199–200
Hodge, Charles, 69,73–74, 83, 131 n. 12, 149, 156, 170, 177, 215–17; comments of, on slavery, 100; opposed to Church reunion, 219–23, 227
Hofstadter, Richard, 5, 110
Holmes, Oliver Wendell, 236
Holy Communion, 26–27
Holy Spirit, 46, 50–51, 53–56, 78, 106, 171, 185; in thought of Jonathan Edwards, 32–34; and regeneration, 37–38, 50, 82, 84–85, 109; author of Bible, 149–50; according to Auburn Declaration, 253–54
Hopkins, Mark, 241
Hopkins, Samuel, 34–38, 40–41, 45,

50, 92, 179, 186, 232; tradition of, 49, 75
Hopkinsianism, 34, 38, 40–46, 50–53, 57–58, 69, 83, 166–67
Hudson, Winthrop S., 4, 243, 250
Hume, 48
Hymns, 182–84, 197–98

Illinois, 10, 61; Presbytery of, 57; Synod of, 66
Illinois College, 57, 118
Illuminati, 7, 8
Independent Board for Presbyterian Foreign Missions, 247
Indiana, 10, 56; Synod of, 66
Indianapolis Presbytery, 56
Indians, 202, 251
International Prophecy Conference, 247
Islam, 104, 195
Israel, 201–02, 204, 206
Israelites, 21–22

Jackson, President, 58–59
James, Henry (the elder), 152
Jefferson, Thomas, 9
Jeffersonianism, 235
Jerusalem, 190
Jews, 191, 195–96
Journals. *See* Publications, religious
Judgment, 185, 190 n. 24

Kant, 153; tradition of, 108
Kentucky, 13, 77, 92, 132
Kingdom of Christ, 182–98
Kingdom of God, 241
Kirby, William, 57
Know-Nothingism, 240

Lane Theological Seminary, 30, 67, 69, 94, 115, 119, 180, 224, 226
Lansing, Dirck Cornelius, 45
La Rue Perrine, Matthew, 45
Lewis, Taylor, 144–45, 153

Lexington, Virginia, Presbytery of, 91, 188
Liberalism (theological), 245–46, 248–49
Lincoln, Abraham, 205
Locke, 152
Loetscher, Lefferts A., *The Broadening Church: A Study of Theological Issues in the Presbyterian Church since 1869,* 246 n. 1
London Missionary Society, 14
Longfellow, 158
Lord's Prayer, 124 n. 41
Low Church, 115, 236–37, 246; Episcopalians, 19, 183
Lutheran Church, 5; Seminary of, 114

MacCormac, Earl R., 250
McCosh, James, 241
Machen, J. Gresham, 245–46
McIntire, Carl, 246–47
McLane, James W., 115
McLoughlin, William G., x
Mahan, Asa, 95
Mahometan government, 104, 195
Maine, 158–59
Marat, 7
Massachusetts, 10, 43, 118, 161
Mather, Cotton, 190 n. 25
Mead, Sidney E., 5, 199
Melville, 106
Mercersburg movement, 73
Mercersburg, Pa., 152
Methodism, English, 3
Methodist Pietism, 239
Methodists, xi, 4, 19, 24, 73, 80, 116, 127, 183
Mexicans, 202
Michigan, 10, 130, 195; Synod of, 66; University of, 107
Michigan City, 125
Middle class, xi–xii, 2, 240–41
Midwest, 4, 248 n. 6

Millenarian movement. *See* Premillennialism.
Millennialism, 239, 246. *See also* Postmillennialism; Premillennialism
Miller, Perry, x, 3, 5, 239–40, 251
Miller, Samuel, 42, 78–79, 83, 92
Miller, William, 191
Mission, America's, 200, 239–41
Missionary movement, 14–15, 18, 193–96
Missionary Society of Connecticut, 14
Missions, 3, 13, 125, 128, 130
Missouri, 61
Moral government, 35, 39, 51, 176, 232, 253
Moralism, 18, 231–35, 240, 242, 244; and revivalists, 80; of antislavery agencies, 88; American, 238
Morality, 33–35, 37, 51, 188, 234; and Common Sense, 48–49, 238; in Auburn Declaration, 252–55
Moral Society of Yale College, 9
Mormons, 202 n. 12
Morris, Richard B., ed., *Encyclopedia of American History,* 248
Morristown, New Jersey, 27, 52
Moses, 206
Musgrave, George W., 228–29
Myrick, Luther, 80–81

National covenant, 21, 200–01, 203–04, 206–07
Nationalism, xii, 17–18, 22, 199–211. *See also* Mission, America's
Nature of man, 36–37, 44–45, 49, 56, 84, 107, 123, 235
Neander, Johann August Wilhelm, 160, 172
Negroes, free, 94. *See also* Abolition; Antislavery; Slavery
Nettleton, Asahel, 77
Nevin, John, 152, 156

New Divinity, 40, 76, 78, 177, 218, 226; party, 13–14, 26

New England, 20, 23, 31, 33, 38, 40, 118; religious awakening in, 9; evangelism in, 12–14; theology of, 41, 43–46, 51, 53, 57, 83, 85; seminaries in, 131; religious controversies in, 159; Transcendentalism in, 160; thought in, 161–62, 166–69, 175–76, 178, 186, 196

New Englander, 118, 130

New Englanders, 39–40, 43–45, 56, 69, 119, 125, 156

New Haven, 18, 118, 143, 218

New Haven Seminary, 131, 220. *See also* Yale, divinity school

New Haven theology, 45–46, 55–58, 76, 81, 83, 107, 166–67, 176, 217–18, 220–23, 226, 249. *See also* Taylor, Nathaniel William

New Jersey, 14, 27, 44, 52; Synod of, 66; Synod of New York and, 120–21, 132, 135, 169

New Lights, 13

New Measure revivalists, 226. *See also* Finney, Charles G.

New School: earliest use of the term, 43; use of term in New England, 166–67.

New School General Assembly, 27, 118, 123–24; first, 86; of *1840,* 100, 118, 188, 247; of *1846,* 123–24, 195; of *1847,* 123; of *1849,* 124; of *1850,* 124–25; of *1852,* 126, 129, 137; of *1855,* 129–30; of *1856,* 154; of *1861,* 204–05; of *1863,* 180; of *1864,* 202, 212; of *1866,* 209; triennial, 133

New School Presbyterianism, x–xii, 41, 44, 55, 82; rise of evangelicalism in, 7–30; controversy with Old School, 20, 54–56; 58, 60–65, 83; and moralism, 26–28; numerical strength of, 65–66; and the West-

minister Confession, 68; and the schism, 69–71, 93–103; and the united evangelical front, 71–75, 104–127, 210; and revivalism, 75–81; theology of, 82–87, 112, 116, 133, 155–58; and colonization, 92; denominationalism of, 117–41; and science, 142–50, 242–43; and philosophy, 150–55; Henry B. Smith and, 157–81; hymns of, 182–84, 197–98; and Kingdom of Christ, 184, 186; antislavery stand of, 188; and premillennialism, 193–94; and Civil War, 199–200, 210; and the national covenant, 200–01; conservatism in, 213, 235–37; and debate on reunion, 214–19, 221–24; orthodoxy of, 225–27; tolerance of, 227–28; and climate of opinion, 230–31; in the twentieth century, 245–49

"New School Presbyterian Mind, The," xii

New Side, 40, 136, 245

New Testament, 114

Newtonian model, 231

New York, 1, 43, 59, 169, 187, 209, 247; settlement of, 10–11; religion in, 13–14, 16; temperance in, 25; Synod of, 63, 66, 89, 120; Congregational Association of, 63; revivals in, 76; perfectionism in, 81; and Philadelphia, Synod of, 89–90; Western, abolitionism in, 93–95; and New Jersey, Synod of, 120–21, 132, 135, 169; denominationalism in, 129; New School Presbyterians in, 180, 195, 197; upstate, 2, 226

New York Anti-Tobacco Society, 15

New York City, 41, 108, 115, 119–20, 156, 208, 248 n. 6; Third Presbytery of, 69; Henry B. Smith in, 156–57; revivalism in, 182

New York Evangelist, 27, 126
New York University, 107
Nichols, James Hastings, 156
Nichols, Robert Hastings, 250
Noyes, John Humphrey, 81

Oberlin, 59, 94–95, 130
Oberlinism, 130, 135
Ohio, 10, 63, 66
Old School: earliest use of term, 43;
    use of term in New England, 166–
    67
Old School General Assembly, 121,
    124; of *1842,* 85; of *1867,* 216,
    225; of *1868,* 225; of *1869,* 224–
    26
Old School Presbyterianism, xi, 20,
    46, 52, 166, 176–77; and tee-
    totalism, 27; journal of, 45; con-
    troversies of, 53–58, 113, 118, 122,
    126, 132, 134, 137, 149, 155;
    defeat of, 54; and schism, 59–71;
    numerical strength of, 66 n. 23;
    and the Westminster Confession,
    68–69; and seminaries, 69; and the
    evangelical united front, 71–76;
    Board of Foreign Missions of, 74;
    and revivalism, 78–81; opposed to
    New School doctrines, 82–83, 86;
    criticized, 84; and Auburn Decla-
    ration, 85–86; and colonization,
    92; and the schism, 93–103, 116,
    251, Albert Barnes' view of, 111;
    polemical writers of, 133–35;
    Henry B. Smith's view of, 159;
    covenant theology of, 175; pre-
    millennialists in, 190; effect of
    Civil War on, 210–11; and debate
    on reunion, 214–18, 221–25, 227–
    28; tradition of, 246; and funda-
    mentalism, 247 n. 5
Old Side, 40
Old Testament, 21–22, 201–02, 206
Olmstead, Clifton E., 250

Oneida: Presbytery, 76, 80; com-
    munity, 81 n. 65; revivals, 95
Onondaga, Presbytery of, 80
Origin of Species, The, 147
Orthodox Presbyterian Church, 245
Oswego, 16

Paine, Tom, 9
Palestine, 110, 191
Paley, William, 242
Papacy, 9, 104, 187 n. 11; over-
    throw predicted, 193, 195. *See also*
    Roman Catholic Church
Park, Edwards Amasa, 131 n. 12, 156
Patton, William, 117
Paul, 58, 123, 172, 229
Pelagianism, 83, 134, 216
Pelagius, 58
Pennsylvania, 28, 52, 114, 152;
    Supreme Court of, 70
Perfectionism, 79–81, 122–23, 130,
    236, 239
Peters, Absalom, 72–73, 104–06,
    113–14, 118, 127, 156, 186
Phi Beta Kappa Society, 206
Philadelphia, 137, 192, 228, 248 n. 6;
    alleged plot to burn, 8; Albert
    Barnes in, 28, 95, 189; Presby-
    terian Synod of, 41; strict con-
    fessionalists of, 42; First Church in,
    53; Presbytery and Synod of, 54,
    61, 89; Presbyterian Assemblies in,
    60 n. 4, 64, 124; New School
    Presbyterians in, 180, 201–03;
    revivalism in, 182–83; Presbyterian
    National Union Convention in,
    221
Philosophes, 29
Philosophy: of John Witherspoon,
    48; and New School Presbyterian-
    ism, 150–55; faith and, 162–65.
    See also Common Sense philoso-
    phy; German thought

Pietism, 31–32; German, 3, 31;
    Moravian, 160; Methodist, 239
Pittsburgh, 61
Plan of Reunion, 228
Plan of Union: area of, 86; of *1801,*
    10, 41, 43, 62–63, 70–71, 98,
    118–19, 125, 128, 133–34, 213;
    Synod of Geneva, 43–44, 80
Plato, 152–53
Political party allegiances, 59 n. 3,
    240–41
Pond, Enoch, 159, 169
Pope, Earl M., 250
Porter, Noah, 241
Porter Rhetorical Society, 161
Postmillennialism, 185–90, 193, 196
Premillennialism, 190–98, 210, 248
    n. 6; dispensational, 246–47
Prentiss, George L., 206–07
Presbyterian, 57
"Presbyterian," the term, 10
Presbyterian Alliance, 10, 20
Presbyterian Church, 5, 39, 41–42,
    56–59, 63 n. 16, 76, 92, 131, 137,
    156, 245, 250; doctrines in, 81–
    82; abolition and, 88–103
Presbyterian churches in nineteenth
    century, smaller groups, 221 n. 17
Presbyterian Church of America,
    245–46
Presbyterian-Congregational Alliance,
    10, 20, 44. *See also* Plan of Union
Presbyterian constitution, 70–71,
    116, 124
Presbyterian General Assemblies (Old
    and New), 215, 222, 224–25, 228
Presbyterian General Assembly, 8, 11,
    14, 54–55; influence of, 20, and
    the temperance movement, 25; and
    Hopkinsianism, 40–42; James
    Richards in, 44; and the schism,
    59–65, 70–71, 74–75, 89–92; of
    1837, 79, 82, 97–99; of *1833–
    1835,* 95; of *1836,* 96, 98–99; and

Carl McIntire, 247. *See also* New
    School General Assembly; Presby-
    terian General Assemblies
Presbyterianism, xi–xii, 10–11, 166;
    Scotch-Irish composition of, 39;
    controversy in, 39, 58, 63–64, 68,
    178; eighteenth century, 40; in
    New England, 43; teachings of
    Albert Barnes in, 53; tracts about,
    140–41
Presbyterianism Explained, 140
Presbyterian National Union Con-
    vention, 221–22
Presbyterian Quarterly Review, 126–
    30, 132, 134, 137, 142–44, 146–
    47, 150–54, 179, 180, 192–93
Presbyterian reunion, 158, 178, 180,
    183, 211; proposals for, 212–13;
    debate on, 214–24; accomplish-
    ment of, 225; views of, 226–29
Presbyterians, 1–2, 4, 10; fears of,
    8; moderate stance of, 14; in
    evangelical union, 19; as college
    presidents, 30; young, 52; attitude
    of, toward James Richards, 45
Presbyterian schism, 59–87, 245–46,
    248 n. 7; and slavery, 93–103, 117;
    historiographical debate on, 250–
    51
Prescott, 106
Princeton, 31, 40, 42, 92; party, 57,
    69, 73, 83, 190
Princeton College, 40, 218, 241
Princeton Review, 57, 131 n. 12, 177,
    216–20, 225, 227
Princeton Theological Seminary, 42–
    44, 48, 52, 58, 78, 157, 170, 226,
    232, 245
"Protestant Crusade," 115. *See also*
    Roman Catholic Church
Protestant Half Orphan Society, 15
Protestantism, xi–xii, 2–6, 31, 58,
    111; anti-Church tendencies in, 72;
    evangelical, 87, 106, 235–36; unity

of, 128; and science, 149, 180; crusading spirit of, 182–85; anti-Germanism of, 195; and the millennium, 197–98, 208; and Americanism, 199–201, 206, 210, 239–42; New School's place in, 210; values of, 231–32; and prohibitions, 239; apologetic of, 242–44
Publications, religious, 2, 5, 118, 121 n. 32, 125–27. See also Tracts
Puritanism, 236, 239; doctrines of, 21–22, 120–21; tradition of, 23, 86, 186; and prohibition, 24
Puritans, Church of the, 119
Puseyite religion, 115

Ranke, Leopold von, 172
Rationalism, 47, 160, 232–34, 240, 246
Realism, 48
Reform, x, 4, 35, 46, 58, 119, 184, 239; theology for, 31 ff., social, 37, 101, 141, 155, 181, 185–88, 194, 207, 238; of of Presbyterian polity, 69; denominations as agencies for, 87–89, 236; moral, 230
Reformation, 31; Calvinist, 141; twentieth-century, 246
Reformed church, xi, 3, 5–6, 9, 14, 19, 58, 73, 221 n. 17; theology of, 1–2, 158, 177, 219, 223, 243
Reformed Presbyterian Church, 221 n. 17
Reformers, 25–26, 28, 88, 186, 240
Regeneration, 37–38, 50, 54–56, 78, 82, 84–85, 107, 109, 135, 218; in Auburn Declaration, 253–54
Reid, Thomas, 47
"Religion of the Heart," 5
Republicanism, 240–41
Reunion. See Plan of Reunion; Presbyterian reunion
Revelation, book of, 187, 192–93
Revivalism, 3–6, 13–16, 18, 22, 58,

67, 101, 122, 155, 181; prohibitionism and, 25–26, 239; of Albert Barnes, 27; theology for, 31 ff.; in New England 46; perils of, 75–82; on Kentucky frontier, 113, 116 n. 24; New Side, 136; and social reform, 185–86, 230, 239–40; New Measure, 226; and the American climate of opinion, 234–36; of New School, 246
Revival of 1858, 155, 182–83, 211
Revolution, American, 22, 28, 200, 203; idealism of, 89
Rian, Edwin H., The Presbyterian Conflict, 213 n. 3, 246 n. 1
Rice, Nathaniel L., 132–35
Richards, James, 44–45, 79, 81, 109, 137–39, 179
Rights, human, 101–02
Robinson, Edward, 110, 150, 156
Roman Catholic Church, 73, 113, 115, 127; Lyman Beecher's view of, 29; Albert Barnes' view of, 111
Rousseau, 9
Rudolph, L. C., 251
Rush, Dr. Benjamin, 24

Satan, kingdom of, 26
Schaff, Philip, xi, 152, 156, 251
Schelling, 153
Schleiermacher, Frederic, 106, 160, 168–69, 175
Schmucker, Samuel, 114
Schneider, Herbert W., 233
Science, and the New School, 142–50, 242–43
Scofield Reference Bible, 247
Scotch-Irish, 39–40
Scotland, 47
Scottish philosophy, 40, 99, 152, 176. See also Common Sense philosophy
Sears, Edmund H., 152
Second Coming, 185, 190 n. 24. See

also Postmillennialism; Premillennialism

"Second Great Awakening," x, 3, 6, 20, 140–41

Seventh Commandment Society, 15

Shedd, William G. T., 153, 224

Shelley, 106

Sherwood, James M., 180

Silliman, Benjamin, 143

Sin, 58, 238; in thought of Samuel Hopkins, 35–36; in thought of Jonathan Edwards, Jr., 38–39; in thought of Ezra Stiles Ely, 41; original, 43, 121, 135, 218; in thought of James Richards, 44–45; in thought of Nathaniel Taylor, 49–50; in thought of Samuel Hopkins, 50; in thought of George Duffield, 55; slavery a, 90, 95, 209; slavery not a, 100; in thought of Jonathan Edwards, 177–78; the nation's, 202; according to Auburn Declaration, 252–55

Singer, C. Gregg, *A Theological Interpretation of American History*, 246 n. 1

Sinners, 37, 45, 51, 53, 84–85; and revivalism, 77–78, 81–82, 183

Skepticism, 48

Slavery, 67, 181, 185, 212–13; American, 88; and the Presbyterian schism, 93–103; 251; discussed in New School assemblies, 119, 123, 129, 154, 188; opposed by New School, 199, 205; a sin, 201–02, 209, 238. *See also* Abolition.

Smith, Elwyn A., 250–51

Smith, Henry B., 117 n. 26, 147 n. 11, 156, 206, 234 n. 7, 243; theology of, 157–82; belief in progress, 189–90; church unity advocated by, 212–13, 216, 221–22; Hodge

criticized by, 219–21; orthodoxy of, 226; historical consciousness of, 237

Smith, James Ward, 242

Smith, Timothy L., 186

Social reform. *See* Reform.

Societies: religious, 13–14; temperance, 25; Bible and tract, 73. *See also* Evangelical united front; Voluntary societies

Society for the Encouragement of Faithful Domestic Servants in New York, 15

Socinian heresy, 41

Southern Presbyterian Church, 215, 221 n. 17

Spencer, Herbert, 149 n. 14

Spinoza, 153

Spirit. *See* Holy Spirit

"Spring Resolutions," 211

Squier, Reverend Miles P., 65

Staiger, C. Bruce, 251

"Standing Committee on Church Extension," 125

"Standing Committee on Home Missions," 125

"Stand up, stand up for Jesus," 182–84, 198

Stearns, George, 157 n. 1

Stearns, Lewis F., 170

Stewart, Dugald, 47, 108

Stowe, Calvin E., 115–16, 119, 195

Stowe, Harriet Beecher, 115

Strauss, D. F., 151, 171

Stuart, Moses, 43, 193, 195

Sturtevant, J. M., 57

Sunday-school movement, 30. *See also* American Sunday-School Union

Sweet, William Warren, 251

"Systematic Beneficence," 137

Systematic theology, 166, 175, 177, 182

Talmud, 148
Tappan, Arthur, 26, 94–95
Tappan, Henry Philip, 107–08
Taylor, Nathaniel William, 54, 56–
    58, 75, 84, 131, 143, 176, 218,
    249; theology of, 46–52; and the
    schism, 65; and "moral govern-
    ment," 232; and sin, 239. See also
    New Haven theology
Temperance, 15, 23–28, 93, 101.
    See also Abstinence
Ten Commandments, 124 n. 41
Tennessee: East, 40; Synod of, 41, 66
Tenth Presbyterian Church, 228
"Testimony and Memorial," 62, 64,
    70, 82
Theology: and the undoing of the
    evangelical movement, 30; for
    revivalism and reform, 31–58;
    popular, 182
Tholuck, Friedrich August Gottreu,
    160, 169
Thompson, Ernest Trice, 250–51
Thompson, Robert Ellis, 251
Thoreau, ix
Thornwell, James, 97
Total abstinence. See Abstinence
Tracts, New School, 137–41
Transcendentalism, 108–09, 113,
    153, 160, 236
Trinity College, 179
Troy, N.Y., 77
True Dutch Reformed Church 73
Tyler, Bennet, 46, 179
Tyng, Dudley A., 183
Tyng, Stephen H., 183

Union College, 144, 153–54
Union Theological Seminary (N.Y.),
    156–58, 162, 169, 170, 180, 190,
    200, 224, 226, 248
Unitarianism, 6, 10, 43, 47, 51, 56,
    113–14, 135, 236

United evangelicalism, waning of,
    104–27
United front. See Evangelical united
    front
United Presbyterian Church, 221 n.
    17
United Synod of the Presbyterian
    Church, 129 n. 7
Universal benevolence, 35, 37. See
    also Benevolence
University of Michigan, 107
University of the City of New York,
    107
Upham, Thomas G., 158
Utica, Synod of, 63

Vander Velde, Presbyterian Churches
    and the Federal Union, 212 n. 1,
    214 n. 5
Victorianism, 18, 22
Virginia, 91
Voltaire, 7–8, 196
Voluntary principle, 12–13
Voluntary societies, 3, 15, 18, 67,
    74–75, 104, 226, 236. See also
    Evangelical united front
Von Ranke, Leopold, 172

Waldenses, 140
Wallace, Benjamin J., 126–27, 152–
    55, 180
War of 1812, 17
Wayland, Francis, 102, 232
Weld, Theodore Dwight, 94–95
West, 67; migration to, 9–11, 30.
    See also Midwest
West Amesbury, 161
Western Reserve, Synod of, 63, 66
Westminster Assembly of 1648, 36 n.
    10
Westminster Calvinism, 224
Westminster Cathechism, 43–44, 124

Westminster Confession of Faith,
    36 n. 10, 38–42, 44, 56, 64, 84,
    86, 100, 123–24, 127, 134, 176–
    77, 247; Lyman Beecher and, 67–
    68; dissension over, 68–69; on
    imperfection of man, 80; in de-
    bates on reunion, 215–17, 219,
    221, 224
Westminster Standards, 167, 213,
    225
Westminster Theological Seminary,
    246
Wheaton College, 247 n. 5
Wheelock, James, 56
Whitefield, 229
Williams College, 14, 241
Williamstown, Massachusetts, 118
Williston, Seth, 187, 194

Wing, Conway P., 208–09
Witherspoon, John, 40, 48
Women, 77
Wood, James, 81, 132
Woods, Leonard, 43–44, 46, 107,
    159, 168, 179
Wordsworth, 106
Wright, Fanny, 19

XYZ Affair, 7–8

Yale, 7, 9, 52, 232; College, 10, 46;
    revival at, 14; as an evangelical
    center, 29; divinity school at, 46,
    131, 220; graduates of, acquitted,
    57; scientists at, 143; President
    Porter of, 241